craftinmotion

CALLIGRAPHY

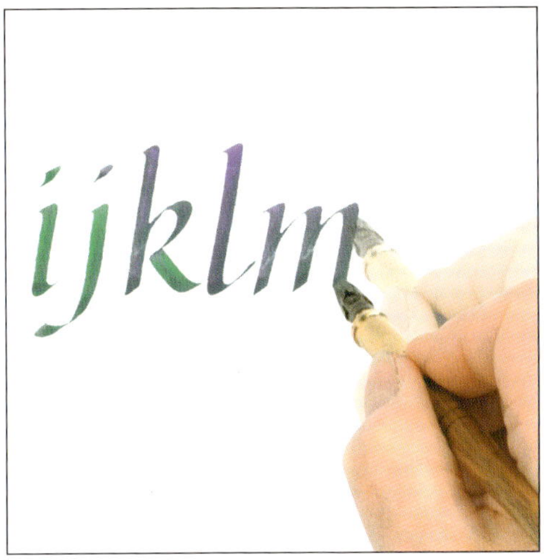

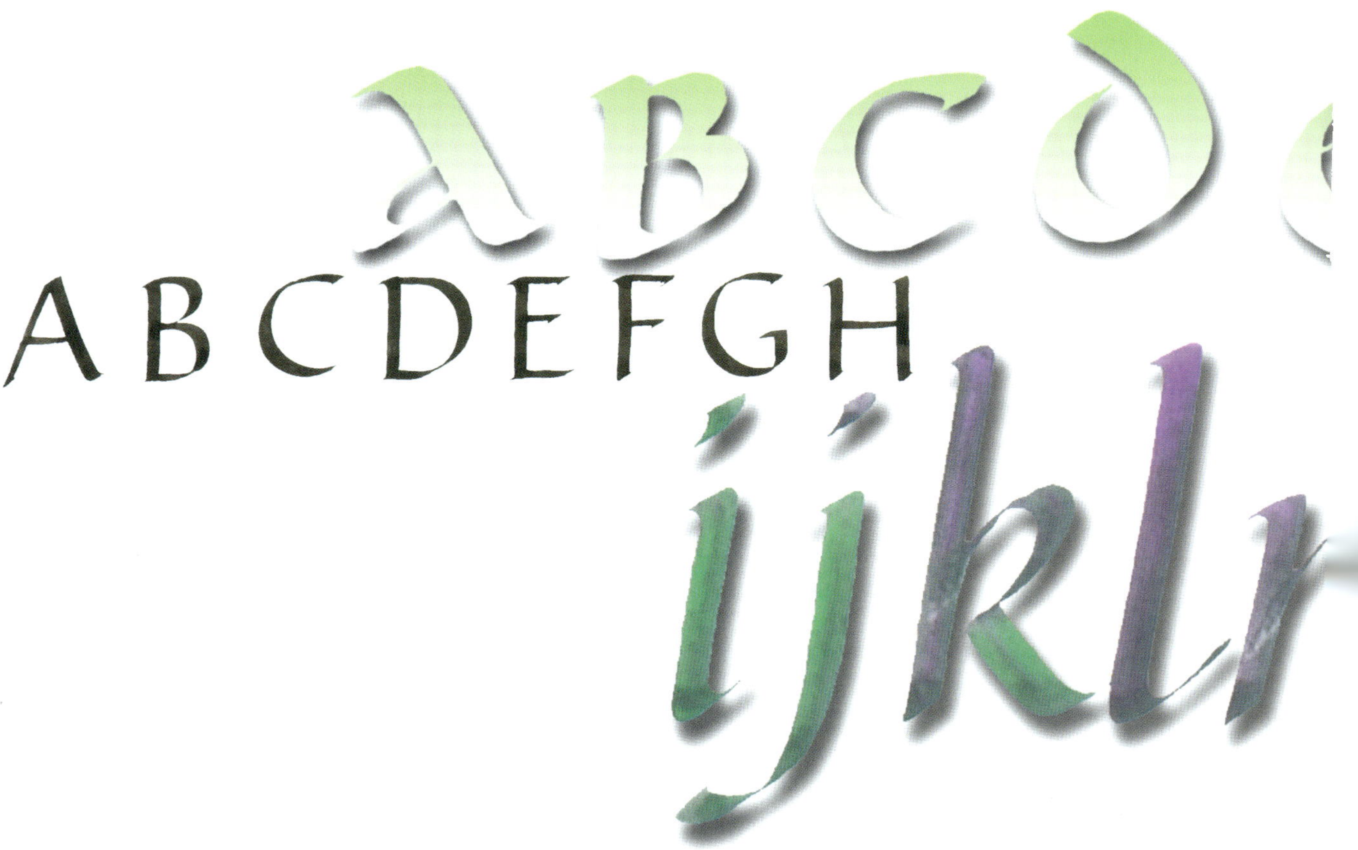
ABCDEFGH

craftinmotion

CALLIGRAPHY

techniques to get you started

Maureen Sullivan

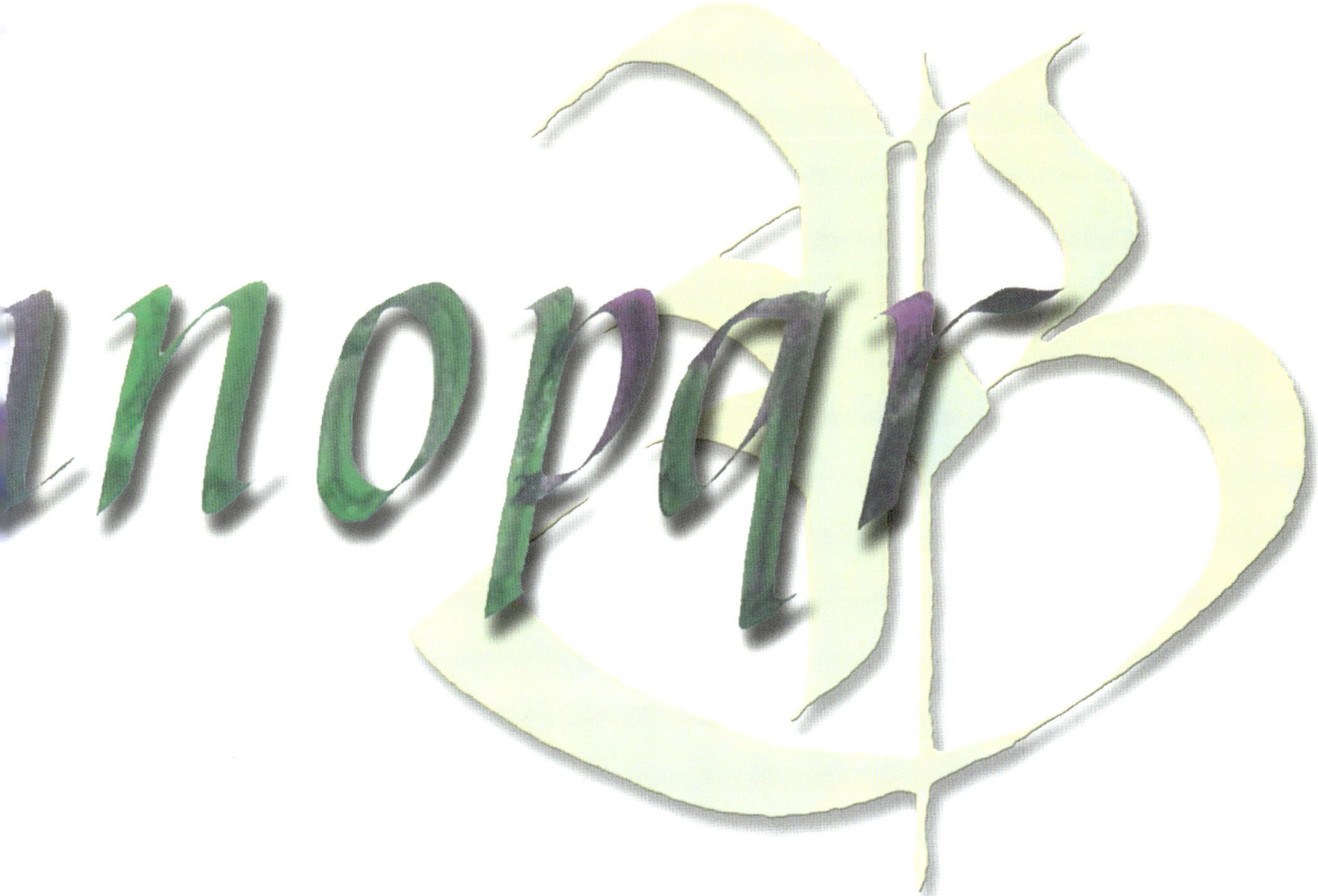

Search Press

First published in Great Britain in 2005 by
Search Press Limited
Wellwood, North Farm Road
Tunbridge Wells, Kent TN2 3DR

Created and conceived by
Axis Publishing Ltd
8c Accommodation Road
London NW11 8ED
www.axispublishing.co.uk

Creative Director: Siân Keogh
Editorial Director: Anne Yelland
Managing Editor: Conor Kilgallon
Design: Sean Keogh, Simon de Lotz
Production: Jo Ryan, Cécile Lerbière
Photography: Mike Good

ISBN 1-84448-104-2

Suppliers

If you have difficulty in obtaining any of the materials and equipment mentioned in this book, please visit the Search Press website for details of suppliers: www.searchpress.com
Alternatively, you can write to the Publishers at the address above, for a current list of stockists, which includes firms who operate a mail-order service.

Printed in China

Contents

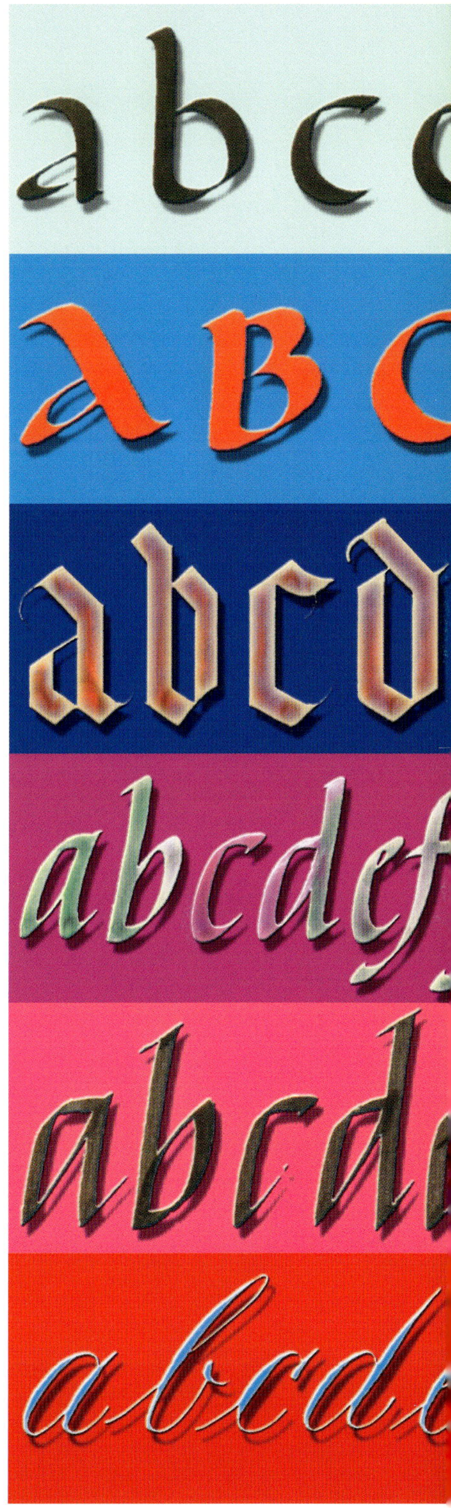

Introduction

Writing has its origins in ancient art, when the painted images found on the walls of caves gradually turned into the patterns of symbols used in Sumerian cuneiform and Egyptian hieroglyphics. Then, in around 2,000BC in Greece, these symbols became legible script, which the ancient Mediterranean civilisations then turned into an art form. The Romans, in particular, were responsible for this and as the armies of Rome spread, so too did their language and culture, which were absorbed and adapted by the local populations.

In fact, all the major cultural and religious movements from ancient times right up to the 20th century contributed to the development of calligraphy. First came Christianity, which in the first millennium was the basis for a wealth of magnificent Bibles and other religious writings. The *Lindisfarne Gospels*, the *Book of Kells* and the *Ramsey Psalter* came out of the monasteries of Britain and Ireland and were instrumental in the development of the different hands, such as uncials and Caroline minuscule.

During the medieval period, the gothic hand emerged, which matched the angular shape of the architecture of the time, and as the first printing presses

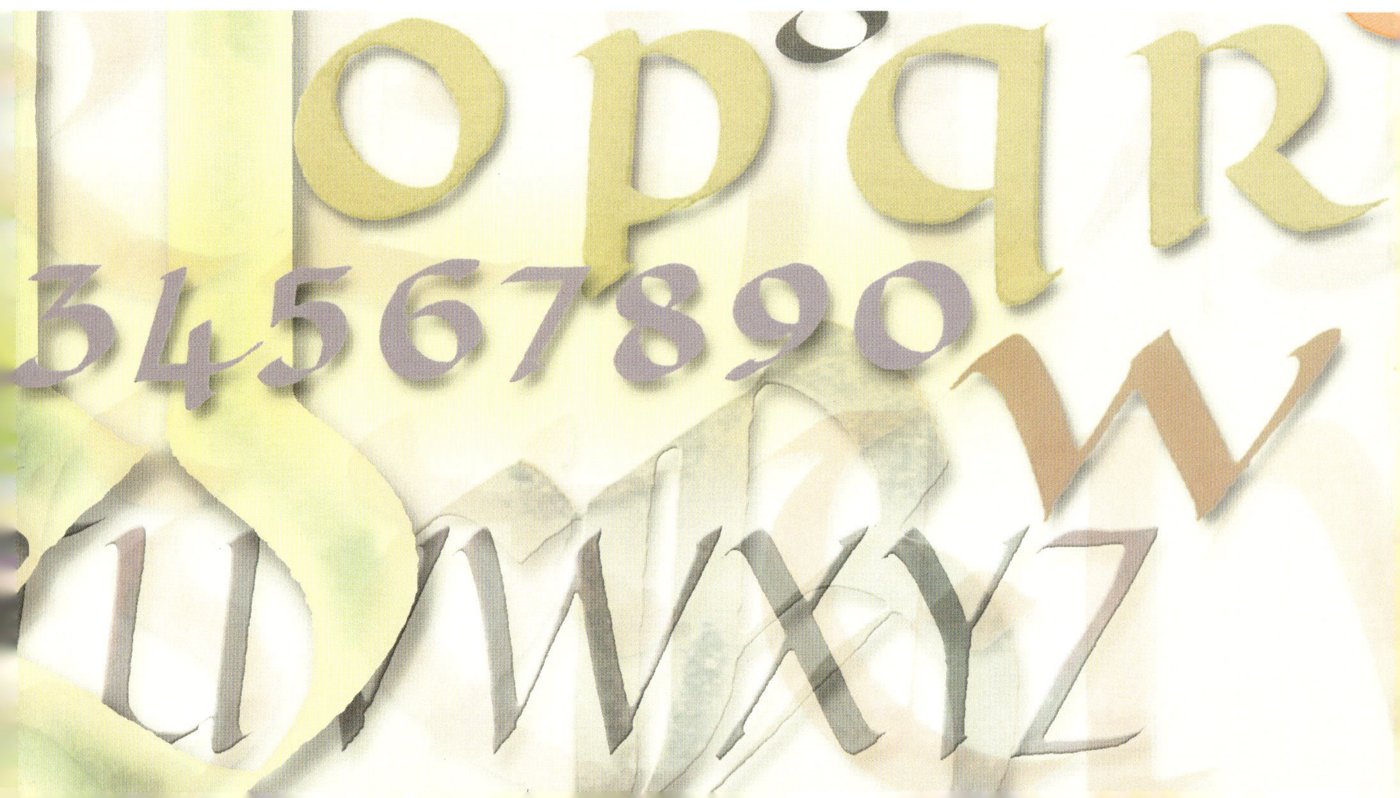

were developed by Gutenberg, so this hand was used as the basis for the first woodblock type. Later, the Renaissance saw the creation of the italic hand, which allowed letters to be written more quickly and joined together.

As technology moved on, so too did the demand for printed material. Copperplate, created by incising sheets of copper with a pointed tool, replaced woodblock type, and the quill became almost obsolete. But towards the end of the 19th century, William Morris started the Arts and Crafts movement, aimed at reviving traditional skills. This led to Edward Johnston's study of medieval manuscripts in the British Library and his rediscovery of the broad-edged pen, which brought about the revival of the craft of calligraphy. Johnston's study of the *Ramsey Psalter* was the inspiration for the development of his Foundational hand, based on a circle and a vertical straight line.

In this book you will find out how to create many of the hands mentioned above, from the 2,000-year-old Roman capitals to Edward Johnston's Foundational hand, as well as the materials and techniques you will need to successfully create the art of beautiful writing.

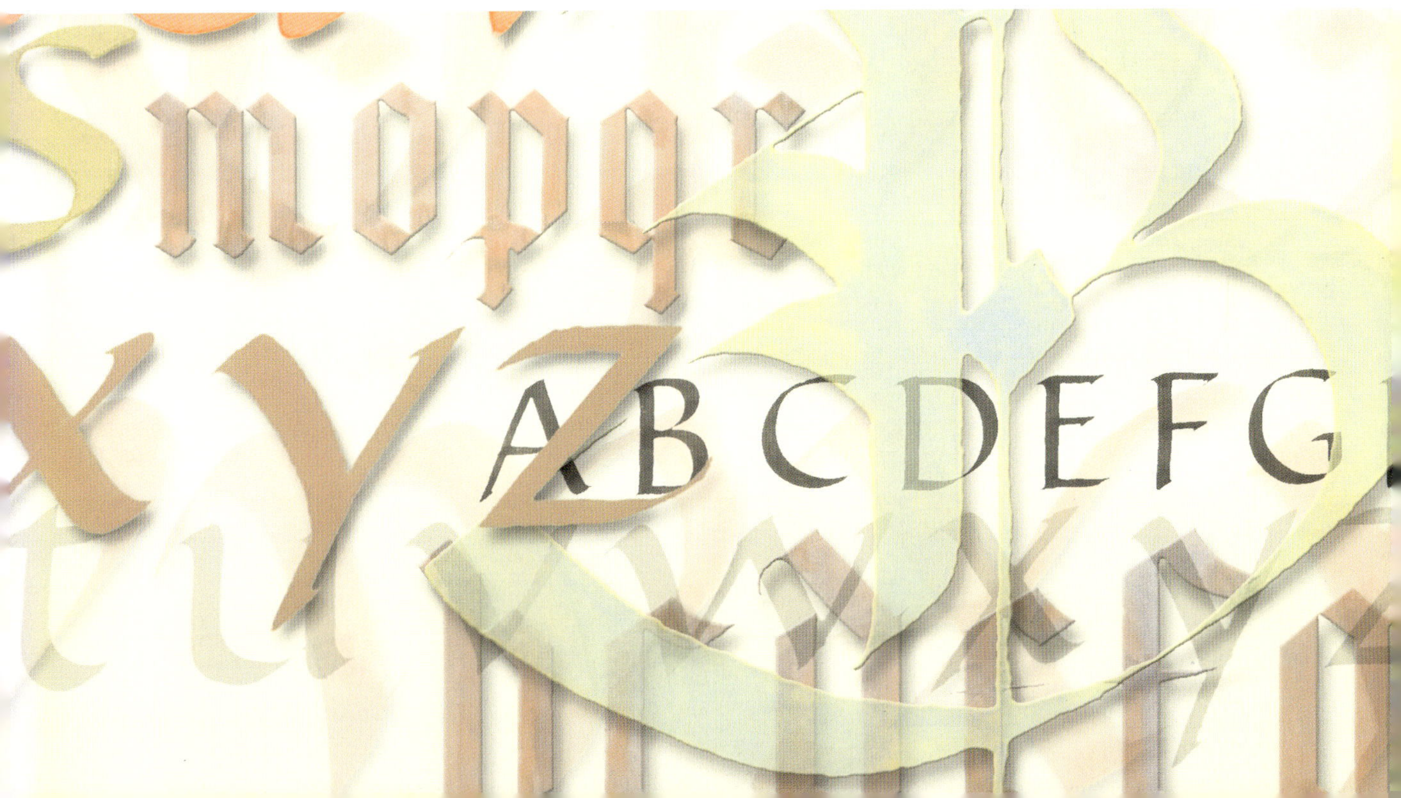

Pens and nibs

The pen is the most important tool in your calligraphy kit. Its origins stretch back over 1,500 years to the reed and quill used by the early Christian monks to produce their illuminated manuscripts. Modern pens try to replicate this style, allowing ink to flow simply over a nib.

Pens come in a number of shapes and sizes for creating a wide variety of lettering styles. The simplest, and most widely used, are called 'dip' pens and come in two parts – a penholder (the barrel) and a nib.

penholders and nibs

Try out several penholders and see which ones fit your hand the best. Whichever one you choose should feel comfortable and well-balanced. Check to see that the nib fits snugly in the end so that it doesn't move around as you write.

The nib is detachable so any number of sizes can be inserted into the same penholder, without the need for owning a large number of pens. The nibs used in calligraphy are called 'broad-edged' nibs. The standard shape is the 'square cut' nib, used mainly by right-handed people. The two other shapes are 'right oblique' nibs, also used by right-handers, and 'left oblique' nibs, which are used by left-handers. Before using nibs for the first time, wash them in soapy water to remove the coating left by the manufacturing process.

reservoirs

The final component is the reservoir. This is a wedge-shaped device that is attached to the underside of the nib, about 1/8in (3mm) from the tip. If the reservoir is too tight, it will restrict the flow of ink; too loose, and it will fall off. Fill the reservoir using an old brush, rather than dipping it into the ink bottle.

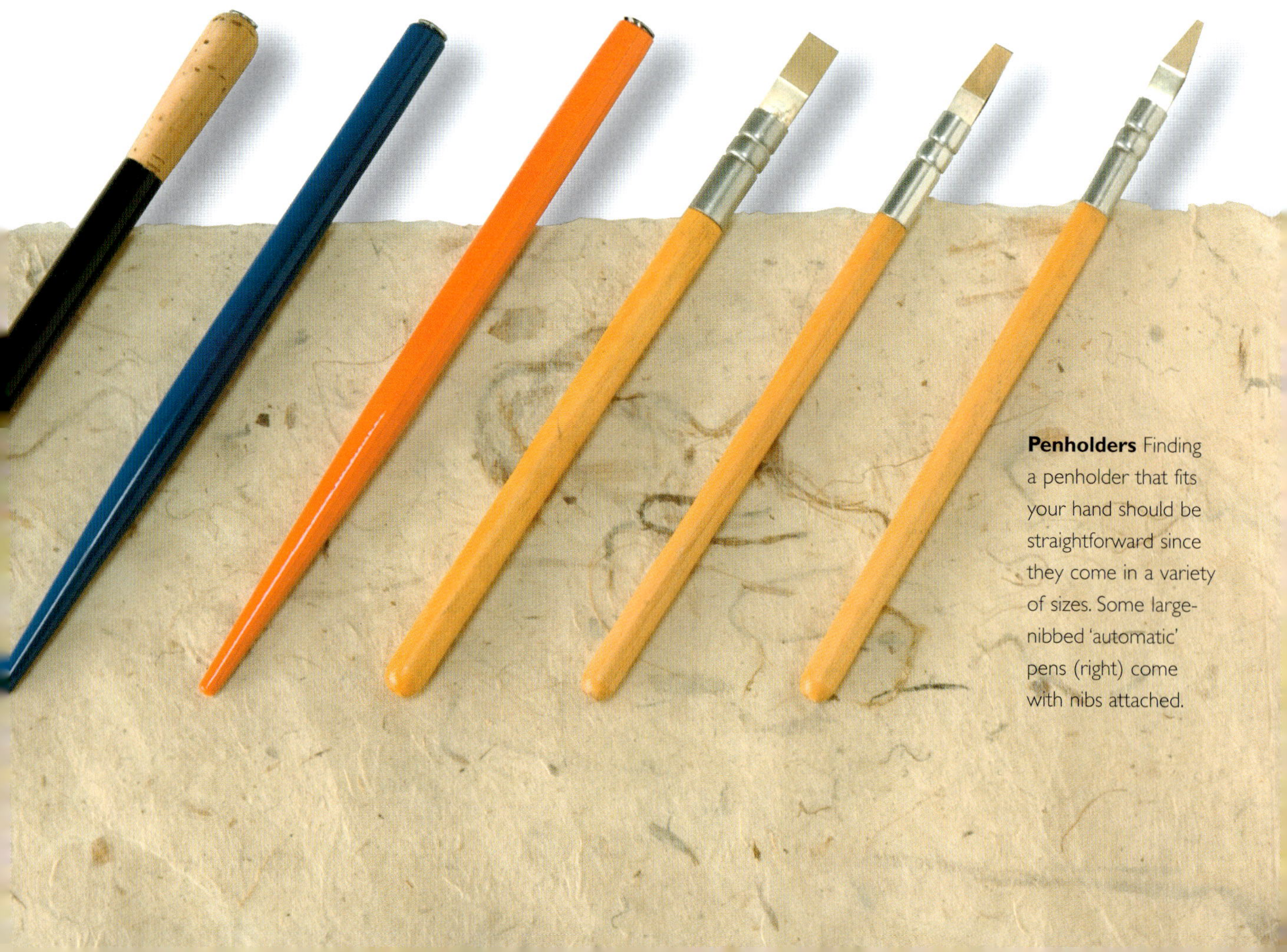

Penholders Finding a penholder that fits your hand should be straightforward since they come in a variety of sizes. Some large-nibbed 'automatic' pens (right) come with nibs attached.

Nib sizes The size of a nib is often denoted by a number but many more sizes are available for every writing need. Left-handers often use 'left oblique' nibs, which are tapered to the left (shown on the right). Right-handers use 'square cut' nibs and 'right oblique' nibs (shown below and bottom).

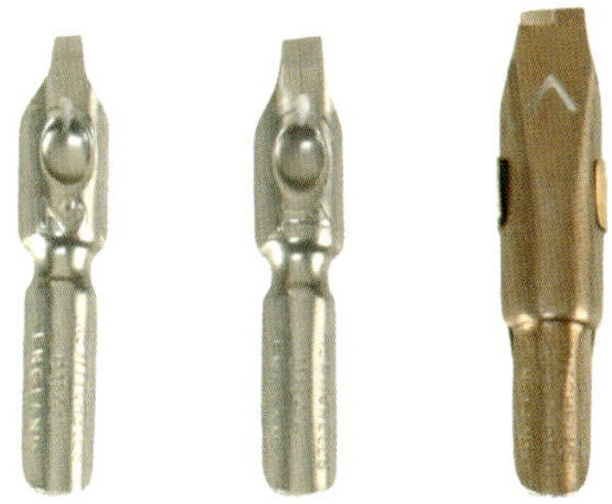

SIZE 2 SIZE 1 POSTER PEN

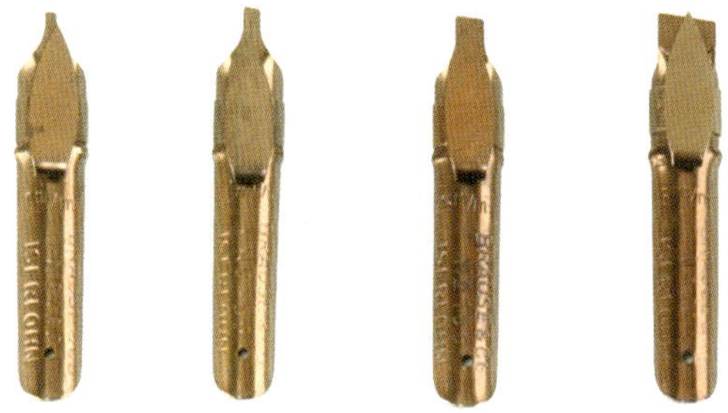

SIZE 4 SIZE 3 SIZE 1 1/2 POSTER PEN

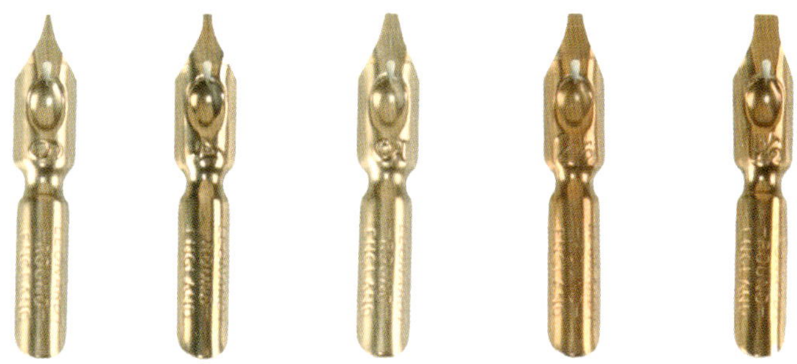

SIZE 5 SIZE 4 SIZE 3 SIZE 2 SIZE 0

KEEPING NIBS SHARP

All nibs lose their edge over time. To keep them sharp, use a sharpening stone. Keep the reservoir on the nib to hold it steady.

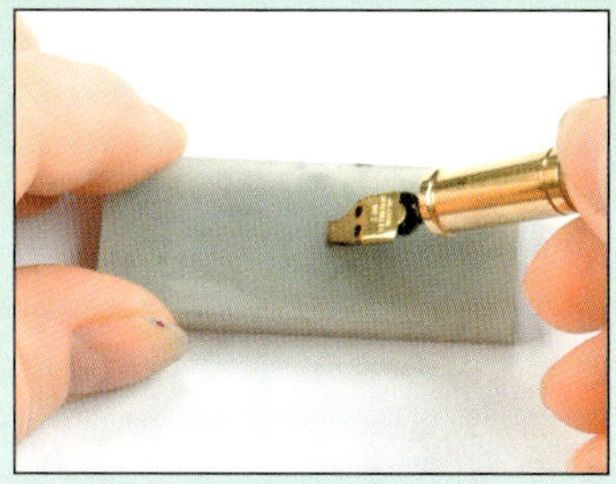

1 Stroke the edge of the nib over the stone from left to right a few times with light, even pressure.

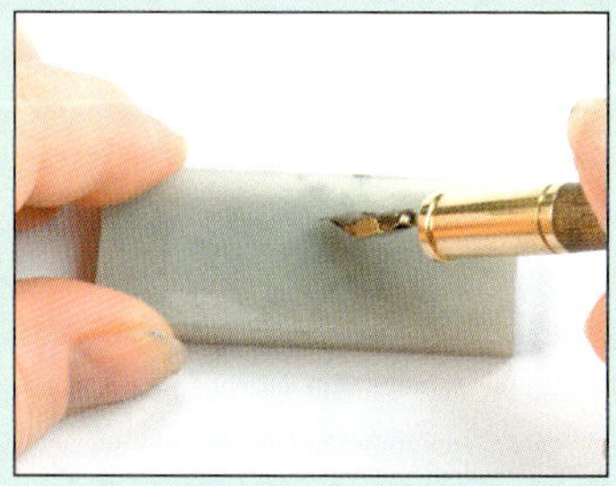

2 Use a light circular motion on the writing edge, then 'tip' the edges.

ATTACHING A RESERVOIR

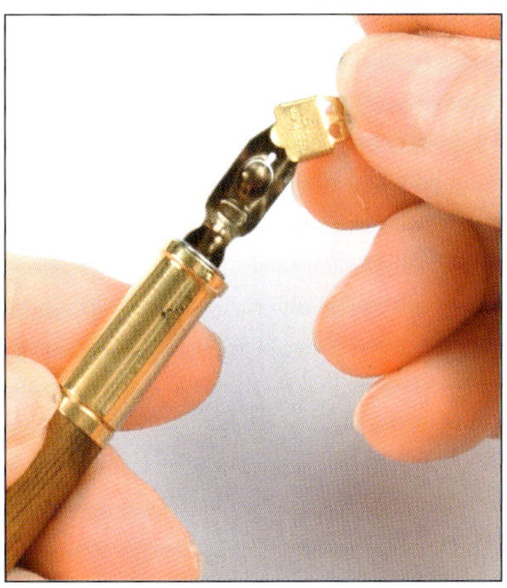

1 Most reservoirs attach to the underside of the nib and are held in place by clips.

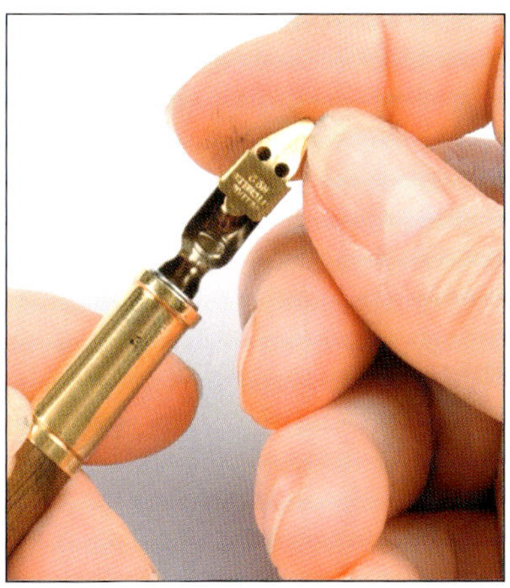

2 The reservoir should just slip on, but if it is too tight, loosen the clips very slightly with some pliers.

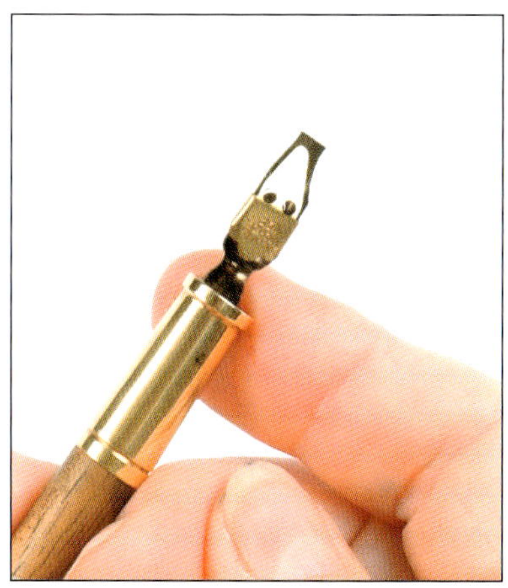

3 Check that the reservoir is about 1/8in (3mm) from the edge of the nib and is not too tight.

Inks and paints

Inks and gouache create colour on the page. Inks are the simplest and are used mostly for creating black writing. Gouache is used for creating colour and often comes in tubes. Different colours can be mixed together to create almost any colour you want.

How well your work turns out is, to a large extent, dependent on the quality of the inks and gouache you use. Always buy better quality materials rather than cheaper ones – the results really are worth it.

inks

The best types to use are black, non-waterproof ink, or Chinese ink. Avoid waterproof and acrylic inks, which are thicker and dry quickly, so are much less forgiving and are harder to work with. Also check the label to see whether the ink is fade-proof. It can be very frustrating to see your work gradually disappear as light falls on it. Avoid waterproof ink, as it contains an agent that interferes with the ink flow and clogs the nib.

The alternative is Chinese stick ink. This is the traditional way of preparing black ink, and it comes as a solid stick. You will need a slate (or inkstone) and water to grind it down and reconstitute it. This ink produces excellent results, but is usually only used by experienced calligraphers as it is much less convenient than ready-made inks. If you do use stick ink, make sure you thoroughly dry the stick afterwards, otherwise it will crack and splinter.

gouache and watercolours

Although coloured inks are available, gouache and watercolours are best for creating colour on the page. Gouache usually comes in tubes and is opaque, making it ideal for writing on coloured backgrounds where you do not want the colours to show through. A wide variety of colours can be created from just six paints, such as red, blue, green, yellow, black and white. When mixed with a little water, quality gouache will flow easily through the nib.

Watercolours are another favourite among calligraphers and are perfect for background washes, or for writing letters that are more transparent and allow the background to show through.

As for the inks, look for quality, fade-proof materials. The label will usually indicate this.

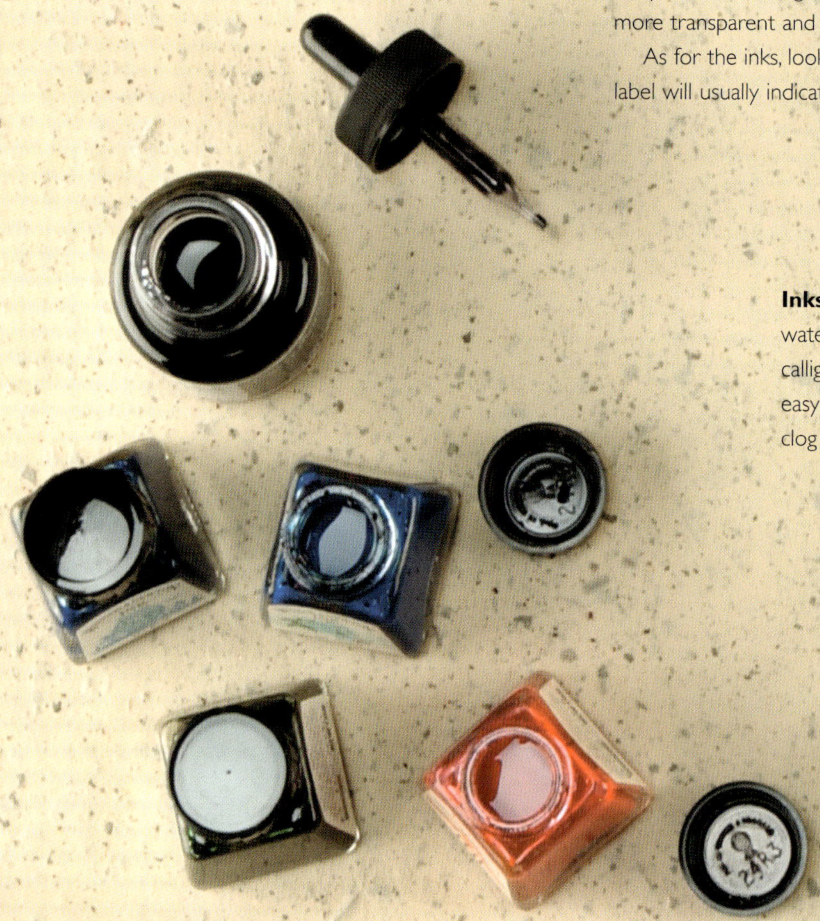

Inks Choose non-waterproof inks for calligraphy – they are easy to use and won't clog the nib.

Gouache Although inks are available in different colours, gouache is the preferred method of applying colour to the page. Gouache typically comes in tubes and, when mixed with a few drops of water, will flow through the nib easily. Colours can also be mixed to produce a wide variety of others.

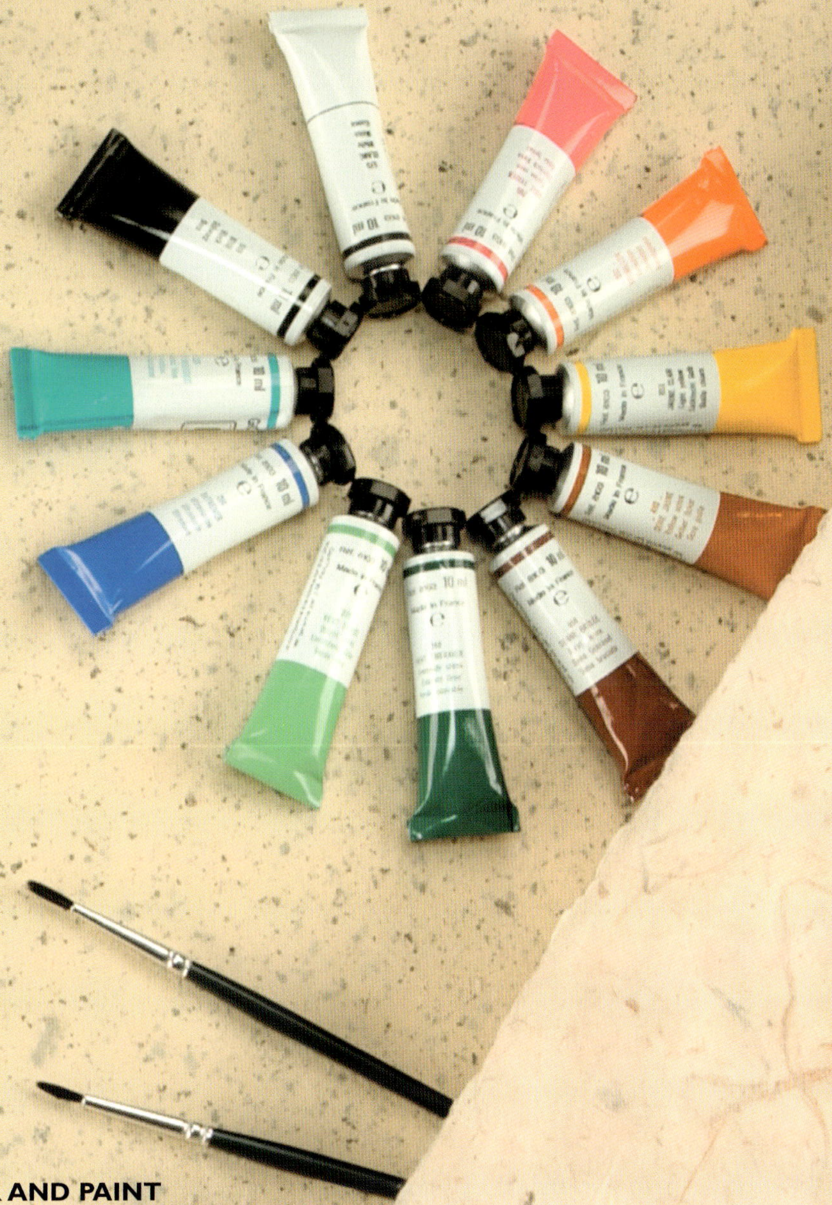

Brushes In calligraphy, brushes are used for mixing paints and for loading the pen, as well as for painting. An inexpensive synthetic brush, no. 2 size, is good for loading nibs. Use better quality sable brushes for painting.

LOADING NIBS WITH INK AND PAINT

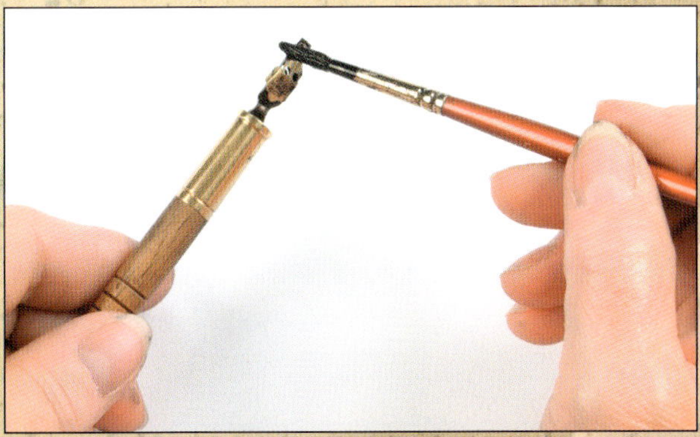

Loading a small nib Ink is placed onto the nib using a brush, rather than by dipping the pen in the bottle. Fill the brush with a small amount of ink and dab it on the underside of nib, where it is held by the reservoir.

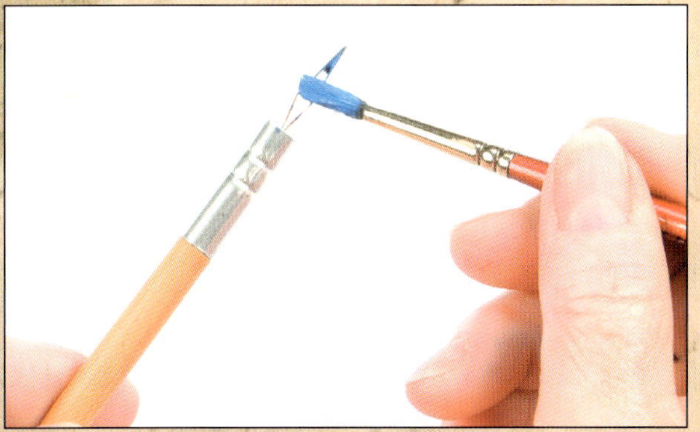

Loading a large nib Larger nibs, such as poster pens and automatic pens, are loaded with a brush in the same way as the smaller nib. Fill each side of the nib with a different colour to produce a line written in two colours.

Papers

The type of paper you use will have a great impact on the results you can achieve. Each type of paper has been developed for its ability to hold a range of inks and paints and to produce a range of artistic effects.

Use paper that has a smooth, but not shiny, surface. This will enable your nib to move across the page easily without catching in the fibres and creating small spatters of ink. A smooth surface is also ideal for practising your letterforms. Once you are happy with your work, you can move onto heavier, more textured papers. 'Layout' paper (sometimes called 'layout bond' paper) is economical practice paper and is semi-transparent, making it ideal for experimenting with layouts, since it is thin enough to trace from one sheet to another.

Typically, layout paper comes in pads available from any art shop, with sheets weighing around 80gsm. Paper that is heavier than this starts to becomes opaque.

heavy weight papers

While layout paper is excellent, its light weight makes it more suited to practising calligraphy than producing finished artwork. For completed pieces, use heavy weight paper, which comes in a great variety of weights and textures, depending on what you are trying to achieve, the type of nib you are using and the inks and colours you are applying.

The first of these papers is 'drawing' (or 'cartridge') paper. This produces good results and is reasonably priced, but be careful to check that you buy one with a smooth surface.

Watercolour papers come in a variety of surface textures. The smoothest is 'hot-pressed' paper which is ideal for fine

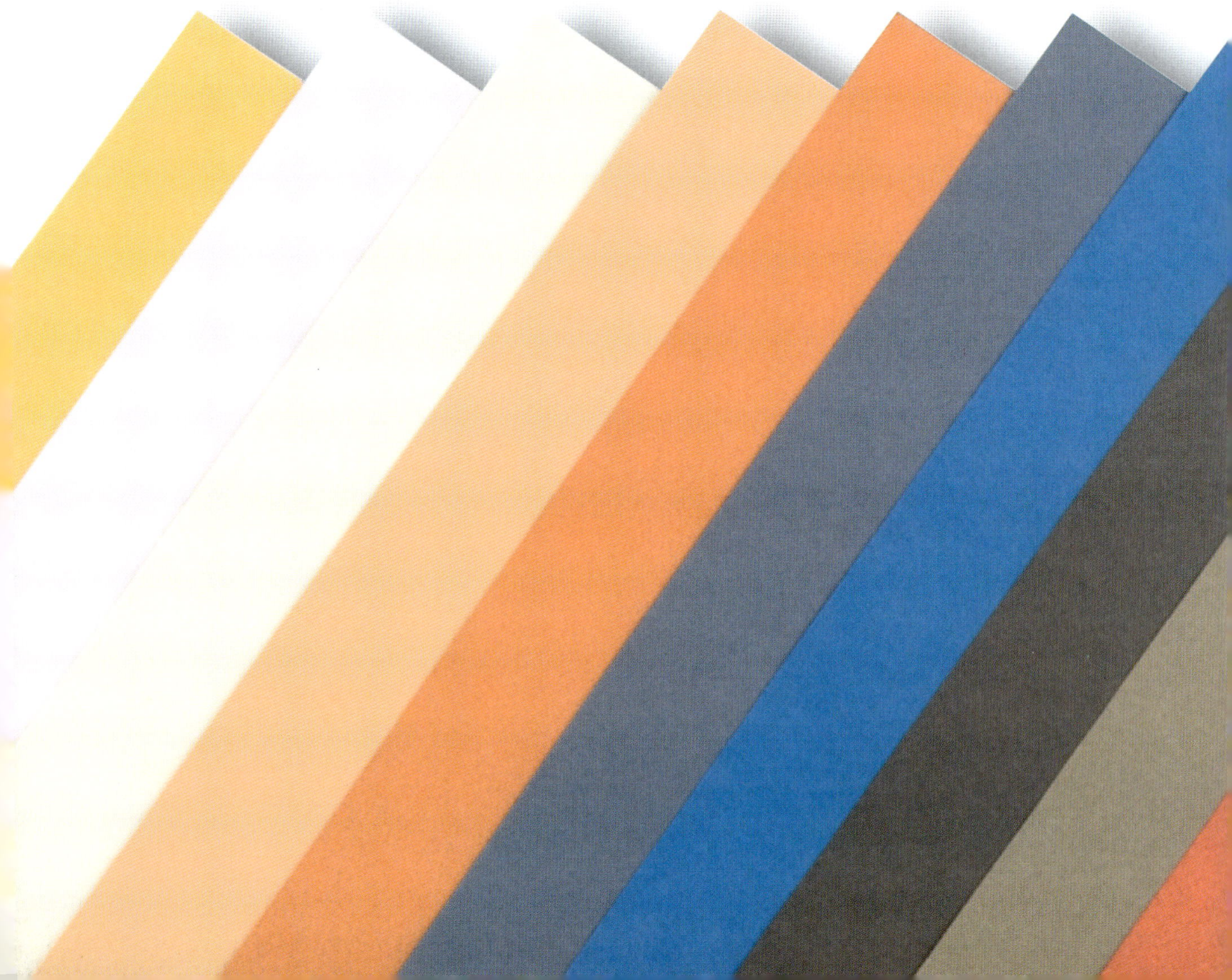

writing. 'Cold-pressed' paper has a slightly textured finish and is also called 'NOT' paper. 'Rough' paper is the most heavily textured, but bear in mind that the more textured the surface, the larger the nib you need – it is very difficult to achieve fine writing on very rough paper.

Watercolour paper is not the only textured paper. You will also find smooth (wove), lined (laid) and toothy finishes on a variety of other papers.

choosing the right paper

It sounds obvious to say, but be careful to choose a paper that suits the type of calligraphy you are trying to create. A letter can be written on some good quality, smooth stationer's paper, but a certificate or a piece of art to mount on a wall needs to be made from something more substantial. Also bear in mind any background colour you want to add to your work. If a watercolour wash is applied, you will need a thick paper that does not wrinkle when it dries. A 300gsm paper will work well here. This also holds true when using ink. If lots of ink is applied to a paper that is too thin, 'bleeding' occurs, where the ink blots into the surrounding paper resulting in thick, fuzzy strokes. The key is to experiment and see which combinations of inks, paints and papers work well together.

Alternatively, try some of the many coloured papers that are available. These come in a variety of weights and textures to suit almost all needs, and mean that you do not have to colour your own backgrounds.

Papers Choosing the right paper weight and surface texture is key to getting the results you want from your calligraphy. Papers also come in a wide range of colours so you can experiment with different background effects.

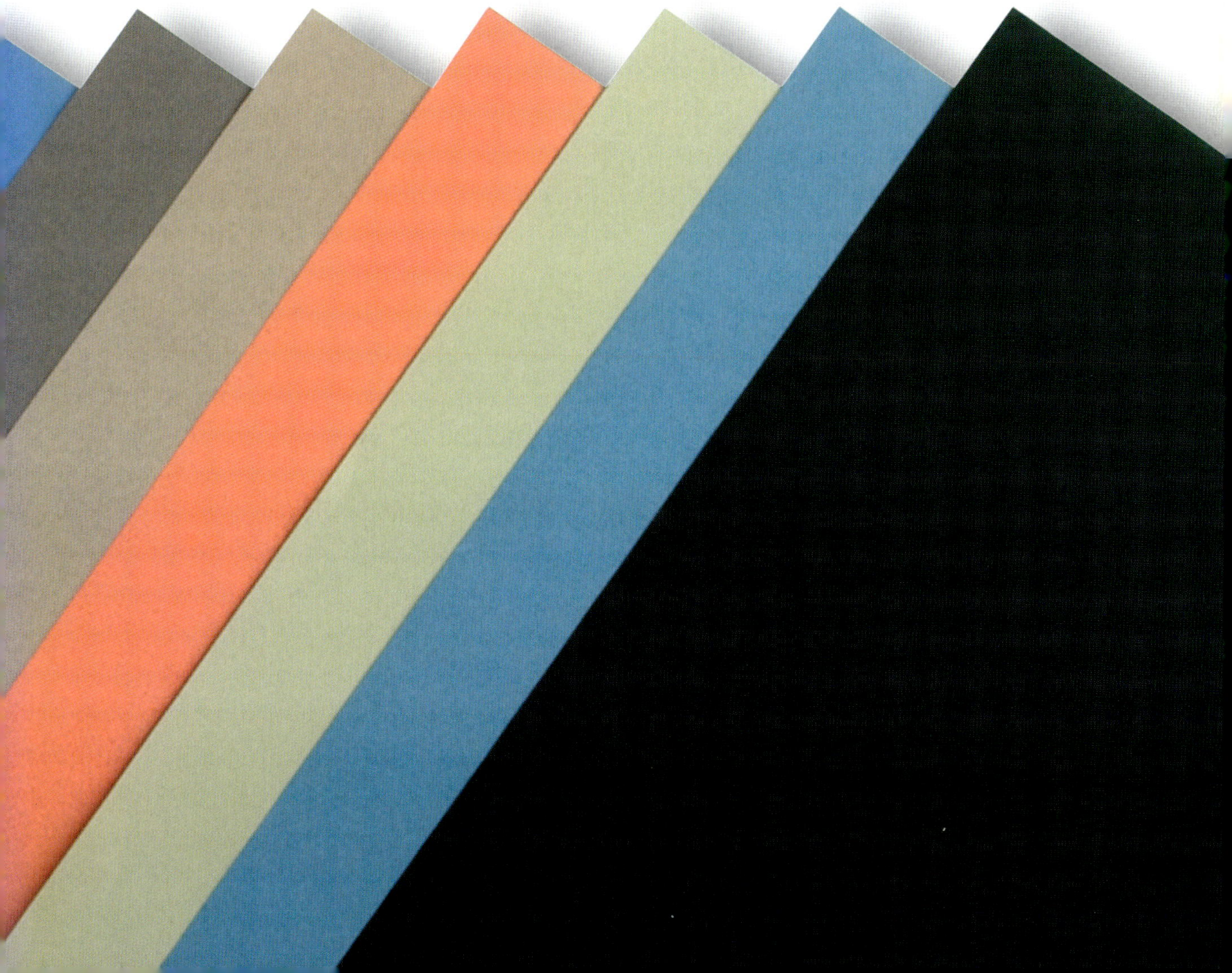

Basic techniques

The basic techniques in calligraphy are very different to those of ordinary writing. You need to learn how to handle a broad-edged nib, how to create consistent letterforms and how to put it all together to create your piece of art.

Learning how to create calligraphy means that you have to reconsider your writing techniques. Whereas a ballpoint pen has a pointed nib, the nibs used in calligraphy are flat and wide. This gives you much more to think about when writing.

holding the pen

The first thing to learn is how to hold the pen. Grip the penholder firmly but comfortably, and make sure it feels right in your hand before you put pen to paper. The main point is that you cannot just pull the pen across the page without thinking as you would with a ballpoint. Your fingers, hand, wrist and arm all have to move to slide the nib across the page. Practise moving your arm and hand across the page, keeping the pen nib at a consistent angle. Also practise pulling the pen down in straight lines and making curved strokes. Your movements need to be slower and more deliberate than normal.

controlling the nib

The next issue is the amount of pressure to put on the nib. A standard ballpoint is very forgiving – you can write with as much or as little pressure as you want and the ink still comes out to produce legible script. The nib of a calligraphy pen needs to be handled more carefully and the writing edge placed very gently on the page.

As you move the nib over the paper, place light, but even, pressure over the whole of the width of the nib. Practise this a few times without any ink in the reservoir. If you press too hard, you will see the slit in the nib open up, which will stop the smooth flow of ink onto the paper. Pressing too hard also tires your fingers and hand, which will quickly start to feel cramped and uncomfortable.

Also, if you press too hard on one side, the nib will start to bend and distort, with one side ending up higher than the

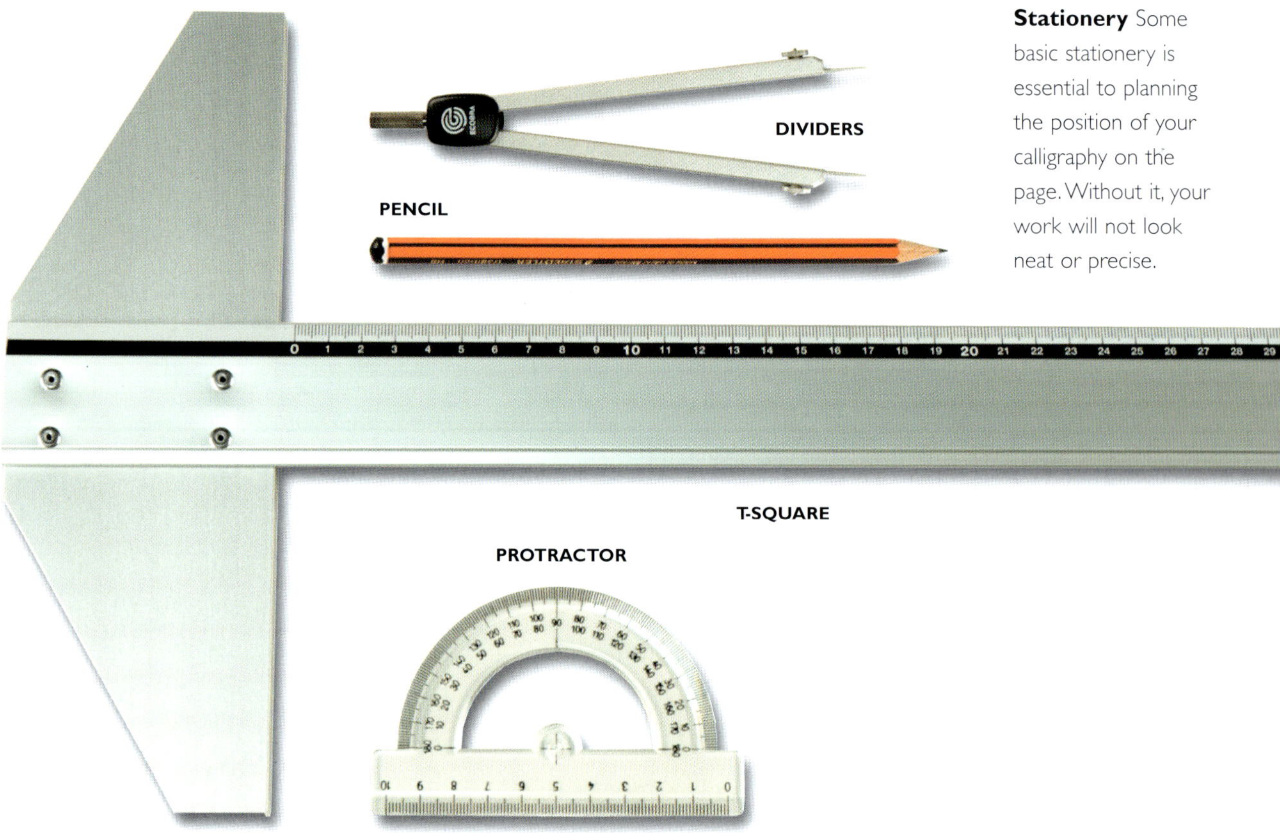

Stationery Some basic stationery is essential to planning the position of your calligraphy on the page. Without it, your work will not look neat or precise.

ESTABLISHING NIB WIDTHS

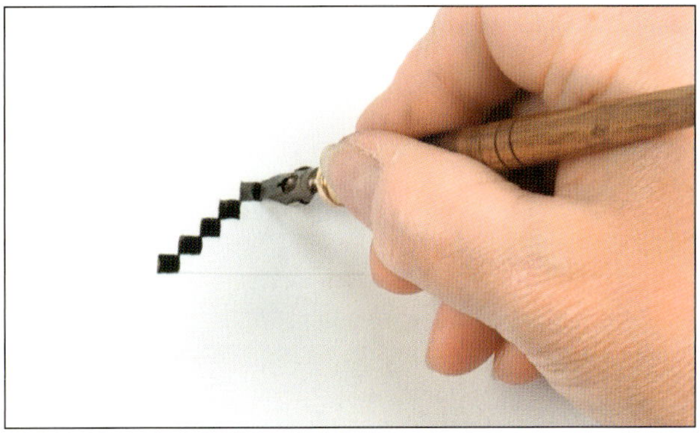

The height of the letters is known as the 'x-height' and is measured in nib widths. Draw a line across the page, then build a 'staircase' of nib widths with the pen at 90 degrees.

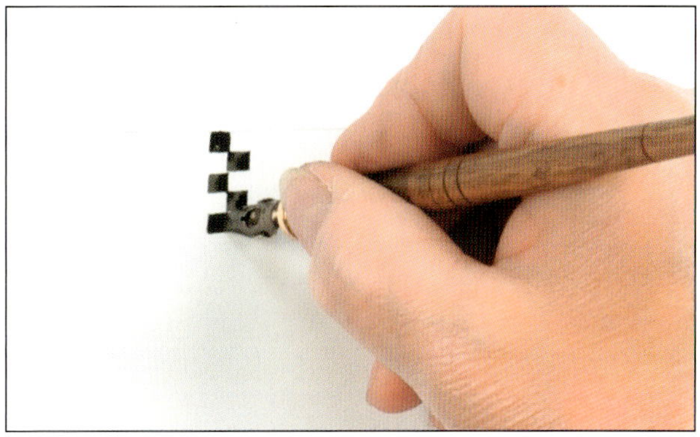

Alternatively, draw a line across the page, then form a 'ladder' of nib widths leading down from it. The bottom edge of the final nib width is the marker for the baseline.

RULING THE PAPER

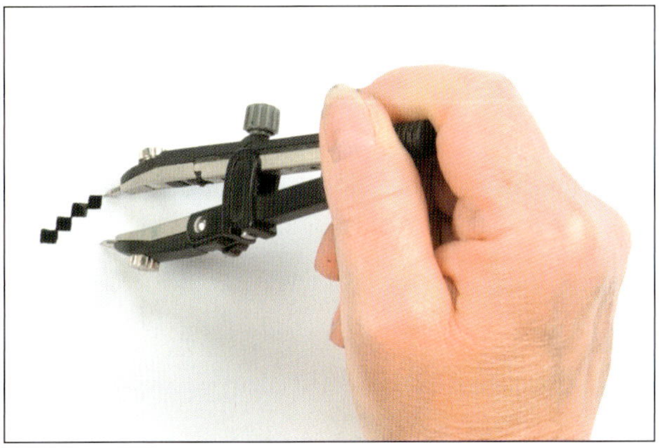

1 Create the tram lines that mark the top and bottom of each letter. Use a divider to measure the x-height, placing one point on the line and the other at the top of the staircase.

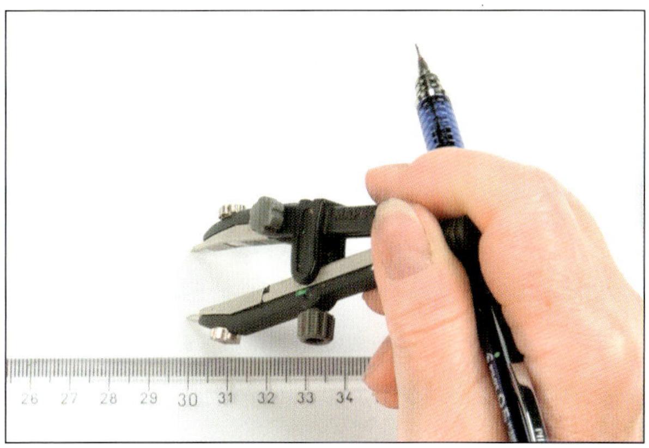

2 Move the divider to the end of the line and place one point on it. Gently press the other point into the paper to mark where the top line will come.

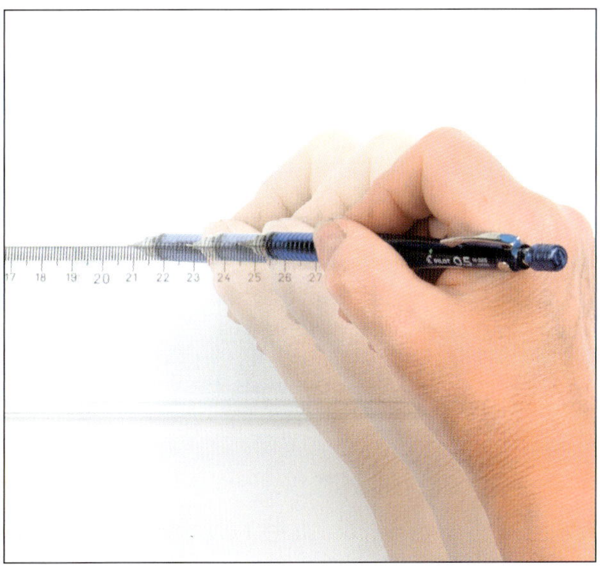

3 Join the top of the staircase to the point you have pressed into the paper. Your tramlines should be a consistent width apart along their length.

KEEPING TO THE RULES

1 Follow the information given at the start of each hand to find out the nib-width heights.

2 Using the same nib-width method, add an extra line above and below the tramlines to mark the height and depth of the ascenders and descenders.

3 The tramlines mark the top and bottom of the body of the lower case letter 'x', the 'x-height'.

Basic techniques continued

other. This results in uneven pen strokes. The problem is compounded if you are writing on paper with a rough texture. Instead, try to imagine that the nib is gliding across the page on a thin film of ink, in much the same way that an iceskater glides across the ice on a film of water. Aim to get your strokes as graceful and as fluid as you can.

pen angles

The next stage is to practise holding the nib at the right angle. To start, imagine a horizontal line across the page. A common nib angle is at 45 degrees to this line, and many hands are written in this way. However, there are others, written at varying angles, such as 15 and 30 degrees. Maintaining a consistent nib angle is essential to producing good work and this is a recurring theme throughout the hands. As you write, you will see that the vertical lines are thick and the diagonals become thinner. This is what gives the letterforms such beauty – there is a perfect balance and distribution between thick and thin strokes. The importance of consistency quickly becomes clear, too.

So try to keep a constant check on the way you are working as you write. Bear in mind that your fingers, hand and arm are all involved in creating the letterforms; that your nib pressure needs to be even as you write; and that your pen angle needs to be consistent from letter to letter. This is a lot to remember to start, so do not be put off if you can't get it all right straight away. Calligraphy requires practice and patience, which is what makes it so rewarding.

LEFT- OR RIGHT-HANDED?

Whichever hand you use makes no difference to the quality of the work you can produce. However, since the nib has to be held at the same angle for both hands, there are differences in the way a left-hander has to hold the pen compared to a right-hander.

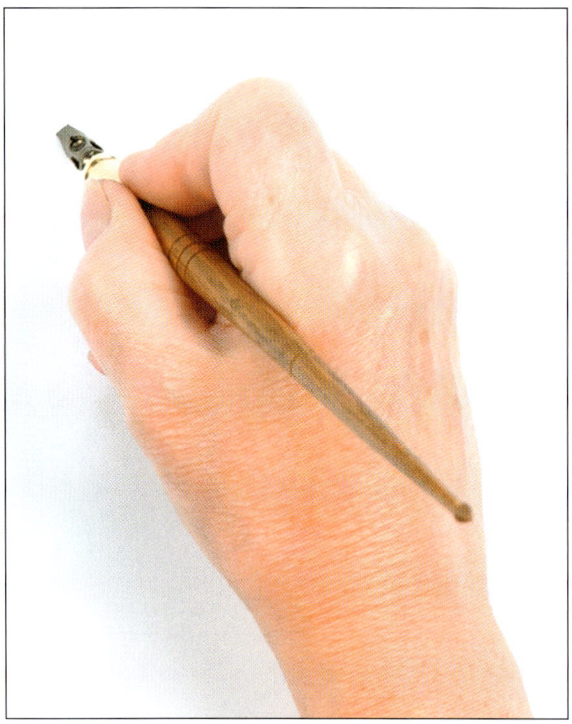

Right-hander If you are right-handed, hold the pen between your thumb and first finger, keeping the nib at a diagonal angle. Calligraphy requires a precise and skilful touch, so maintain a light, but comfortable, pressure on the penholder.

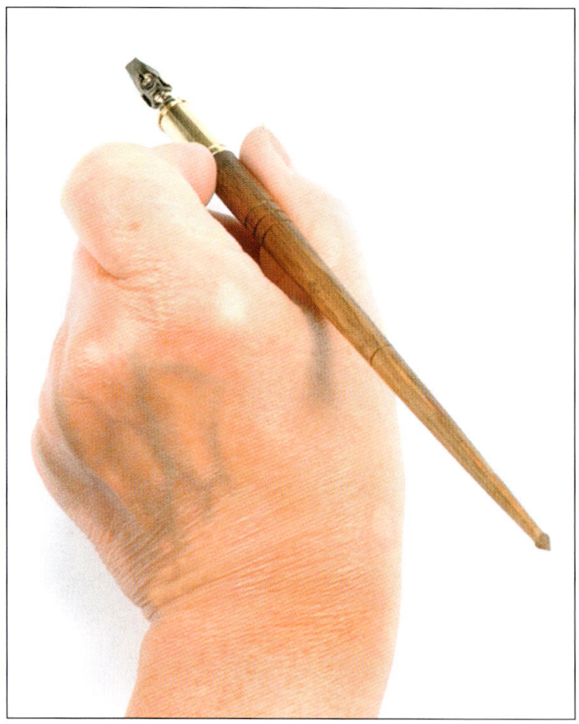

Left-hander If you are left-handed, point your hand to the left, keeping the pen at a diagonal angle. Turn the page slightly to help you with this. Also keep your elbow close to the side of your body to help maintain the right position for your hand.

PEN ANGLES

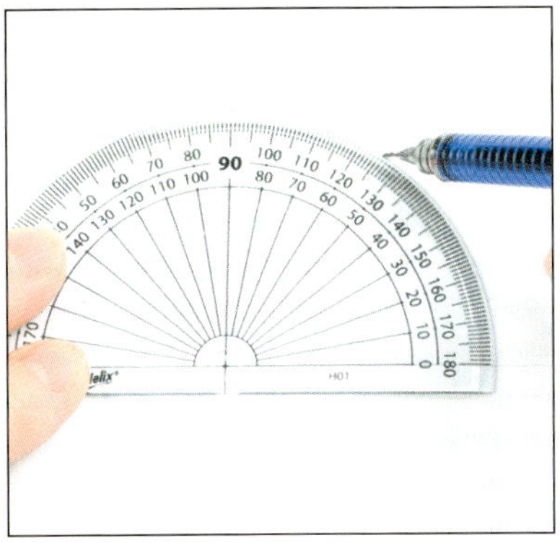

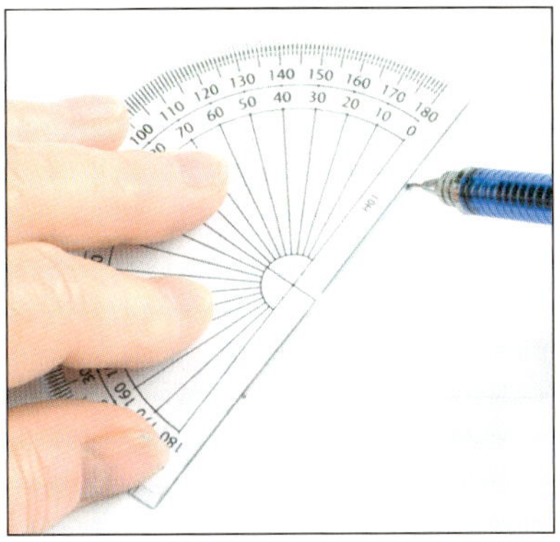

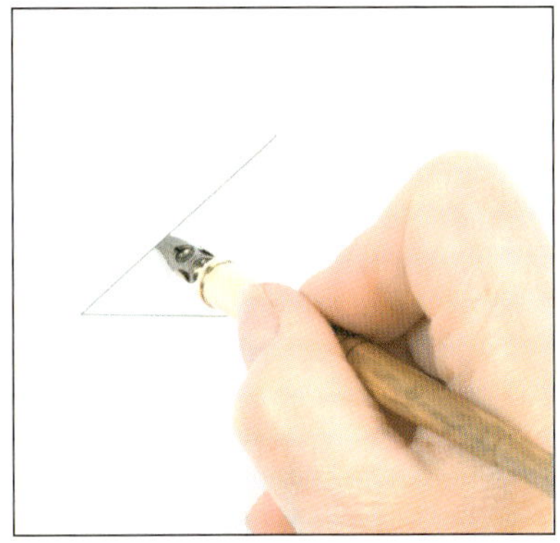

1 Maintaining a consistent pen angle is important in producing good-quality work. Place a protractor on the baseline and mark off the required angle.

2 Use the edge of the protractor (or a ruler) to draw a line from the mark to the baseline.

3 You now have the correct angle at which to place your nib on the page.

BASIC STROKES

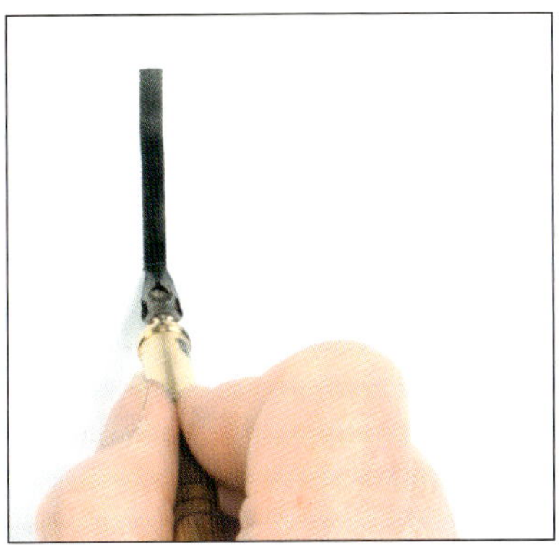

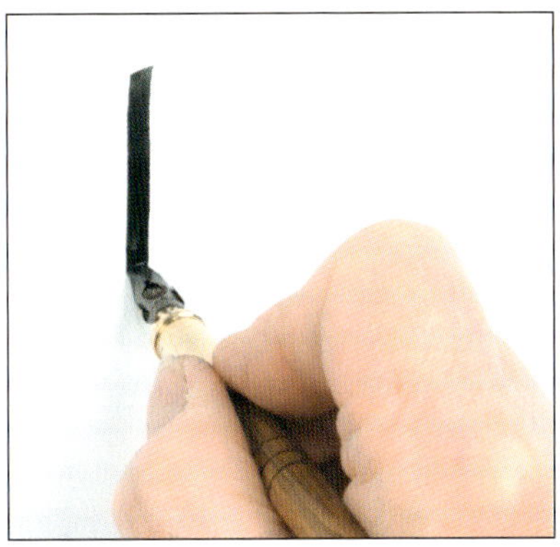

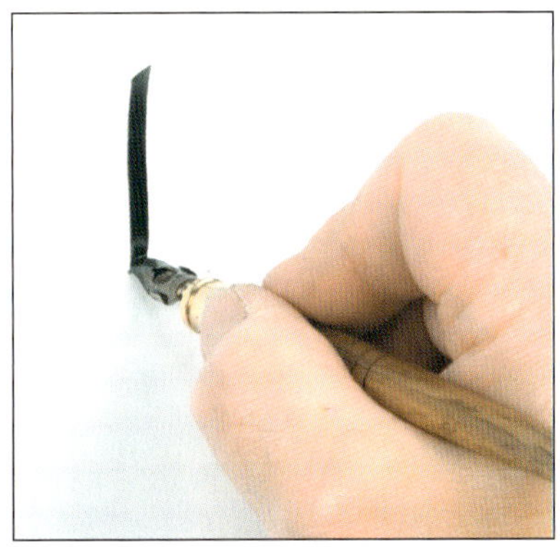

Practise pulling the pen down with a nib angle of zero degrees. This produces the thickest line possible.

Now try the same exercise with a nib angle of 15 degrees. The line starts to get thinner.

Then pull the pen down with a nib angle of 45 degrees.

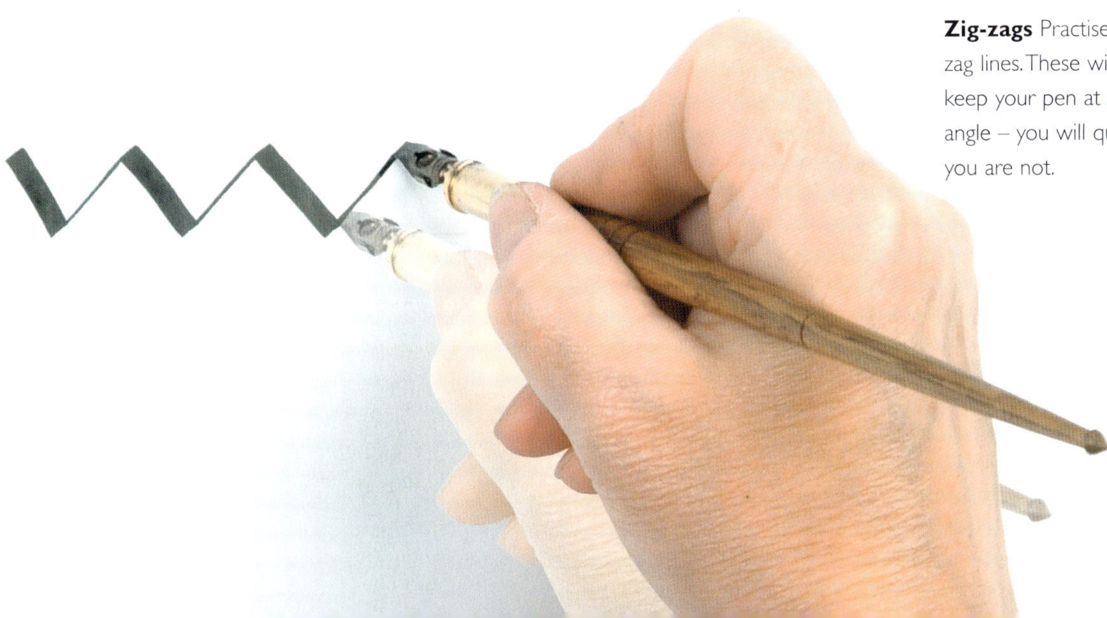

Zig-zags Practise some zig-zag lines. These will help you keep your pen at a consistent angle – you will quickly see if you are not.

Basic techniques *continued*

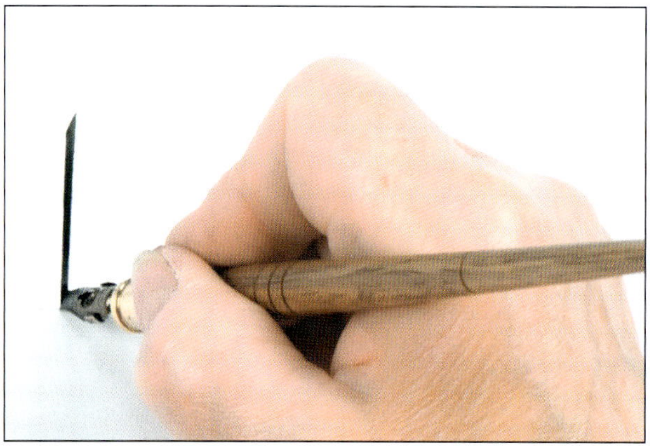

Try the same experiment with the pen at 60 degrees. As the angle becomes sharper, so the line gets thinner.

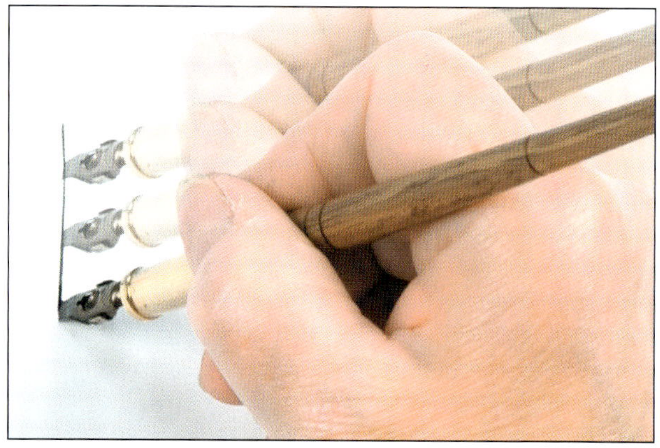

Finally, try a line with an angle of 90 degrees, so the pen is at right angles to the baseline. This is the thinnest line possible, and is used to create decorative hairlines on some hands.

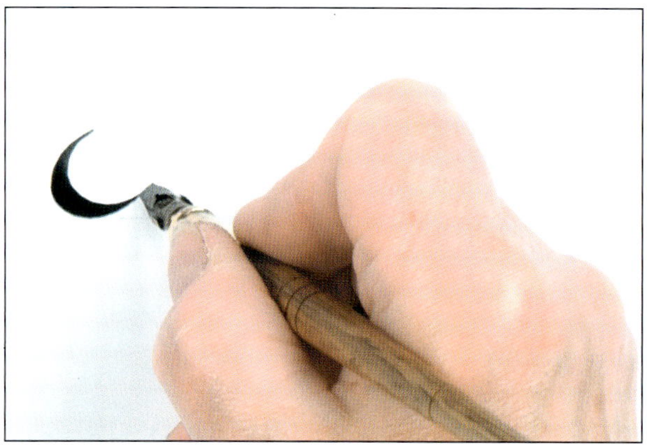

Next, practise some curves with a 30-degree pen angle, such as the first half of the letter 'o', shown here.

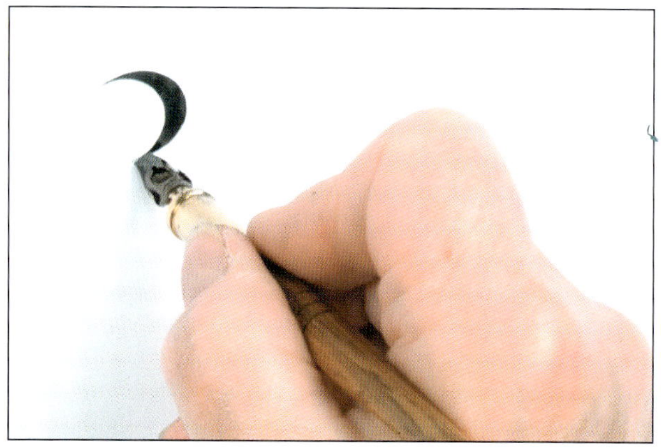

Similarly, practise the same stroke in the opposite direction. See how the letter starts with a thin line that gets thicker, then thinner, all in one movement.

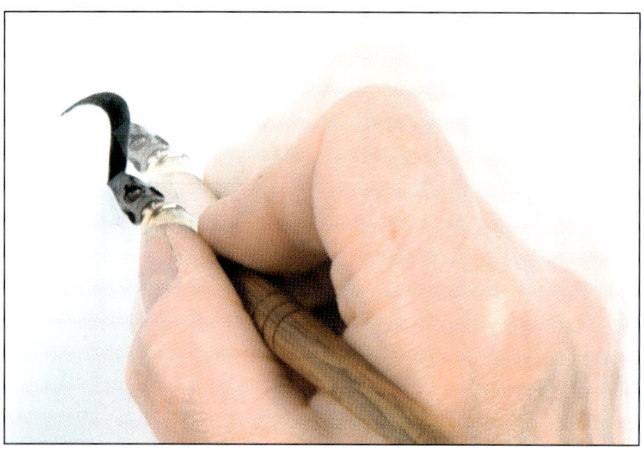

Try linking a curve to a vertical line, such as the arch and downstroke from the letter 'n'. The thin line gradually becomes thicker as it curves around.

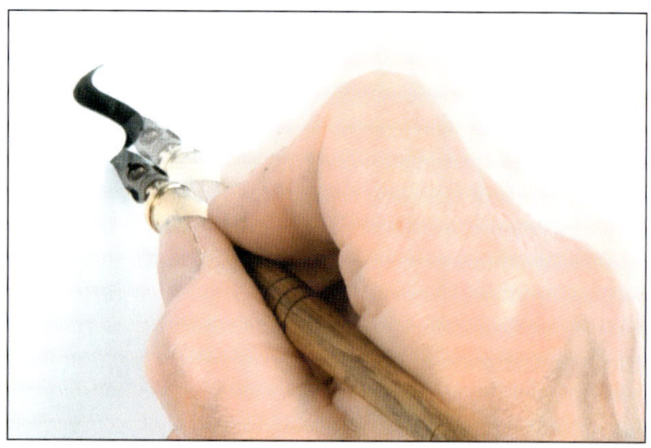

Finally, try creating the two curves that make up the letter 's'. Because the pen angle is consistent, the thin lines at the top and bottom are parallel, creating a precise letterform.

guidelines and basic strokes

Before you start writing, you need to be sure that your letterforms will look straight on the page. To do this, draw ruled guidelines (tramlines) across the page, like those found in an exercise book. The distance between the lines is the height of the body of the letter, and is called the 'x-height'. The x-height is measured in nib widths, and is predetermined for all the hands. Strokes that rise above the x-height, such as the vertical upstroke of the letter 'd', are called ascenders, and strokes below the x-height, such as 'g', are called descenders. The heights of the ascenders and descenders are also predetermined and are measured in nib widths. This information, along with nib angles and all the other technical aspects for each letter are given next to the alphabets at the start of each hand.

Then you can begin to put together the basic strokes that form letters. The key to good calligraphy is that each letter should be crisp. Load your pen with a brush and start the letter (each letter is broken down into its component strokes in 'The Hands' chapter). Make a small sideways movement to start. This encourages the ink to flow into the slit in the nib and smoothly flow onto the paper. Make this movement on a piece of scrap paper, or use it to form the 'serif', the small hook or line that starts the letter.

Start with some vertical downstrokes at a variety of angles to see how the line widths differ for each angle, then draw some zig-zags to see how consistent pen angles produce both thick and thin lines. Practise some curves to see how the thickness of the lines change as the pen moves in a circular motion. The letter 'o', which is the basis for all the letters in each hand, demonstrates this well. Also practice taking your pen off the page and replacing it at the top of a previous stroke to see how to make clean, smooth joins between the strokes.

NAMING THE PARTS OF LETTERS

The component parts of each letter are named to make them easy to describe, and you will come across them in the course of this book. However, these names are not standardized – you may find the same parts described differently elsewhere.

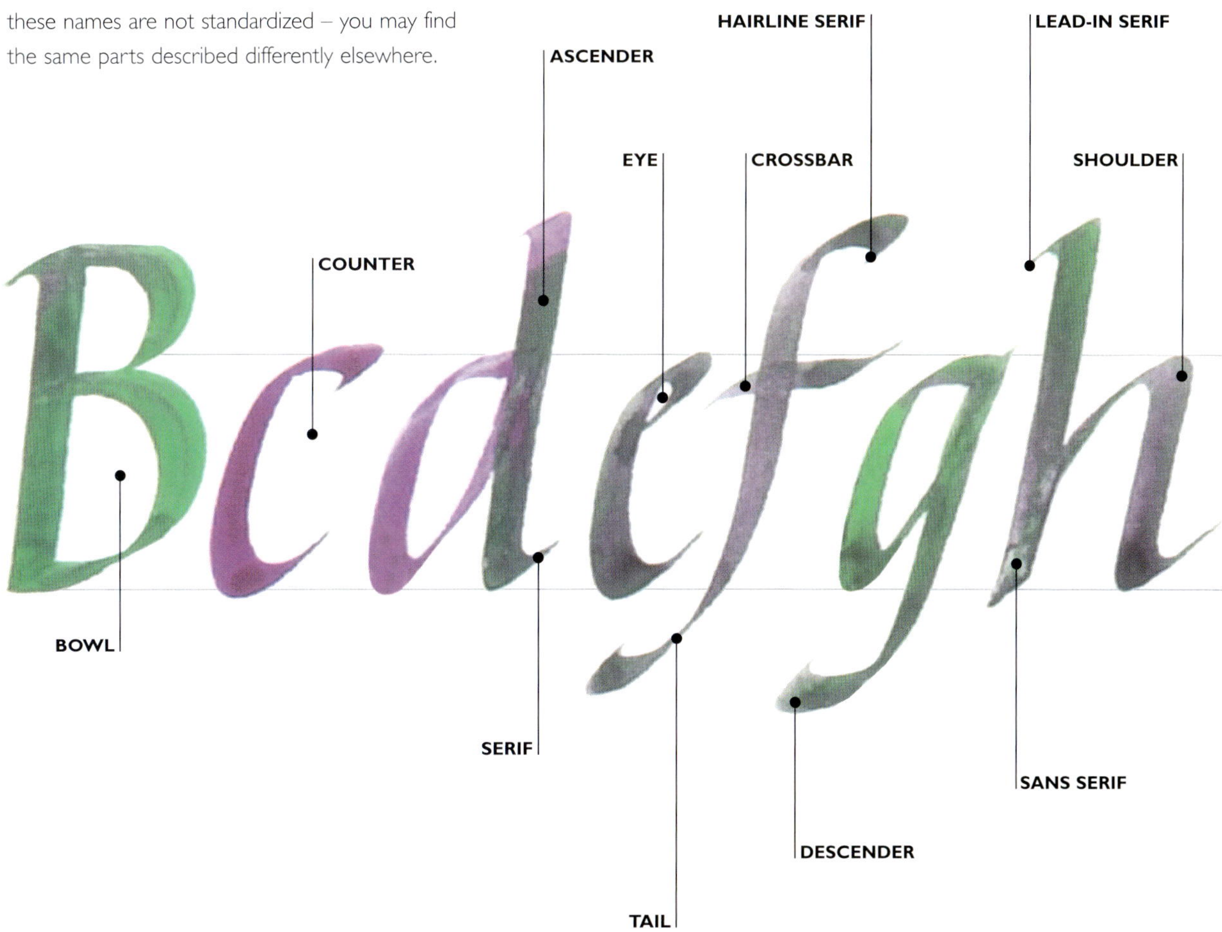

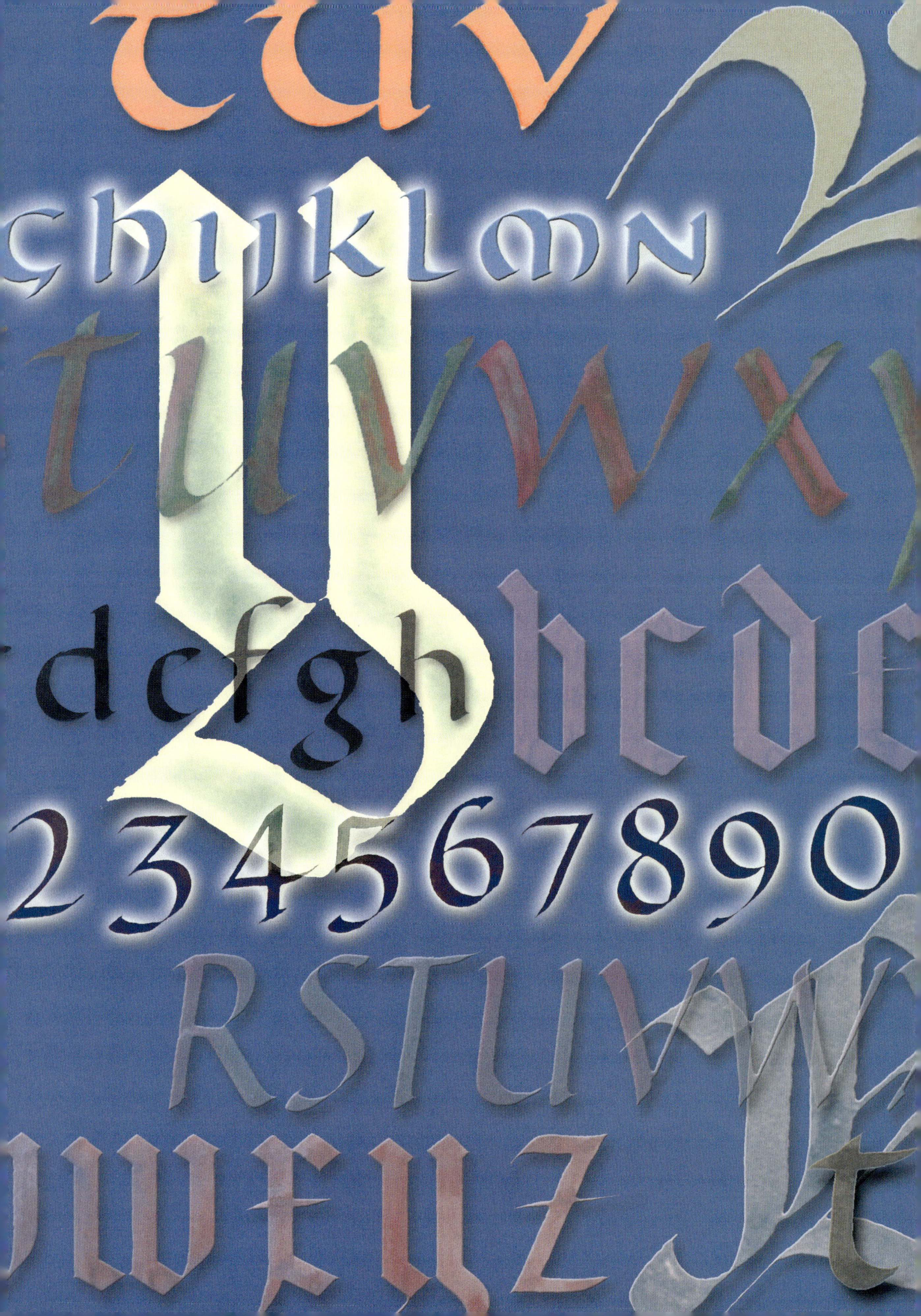
tuv
234567890
RSTUV

The hands

The different writing styles are called 'hands', and in this chapter you will learn how to create six of the best.

Each hand is divided into several sections. First, a full alphabet is provided for your reference, along with essential technical information, such as nib angles and nib widths. Since many letters share the same characteristics, each hand is then split into 'groups' of letters. The main letters from each group are illustrated in detail, along with stroke reminders to show how to create the rest. The final section in each hand demonstrates how to put the letters together in a line, showing a selection of letters all correctly spaced.

Foundational

Formulated by Edward Johnston, the Foundational hand is based on a circle and a vertical straight line. Johnston based his hand on a script from the 10th century *Ramsey Psalter*.

LOWER CASE

X-HEIGHT
4 nib widths

PEN ANGLE
30 degrees; 45 degrees for thick strokes of v, w, x and y

LETTER SLOPE
Upright

FORM
Circular o

ASCENDERS
2½–3 nib widths

DESCENDERS
2½–3 nib widths

SERIF STYLE
Circular

SPACING
Equal area of spacing between letters

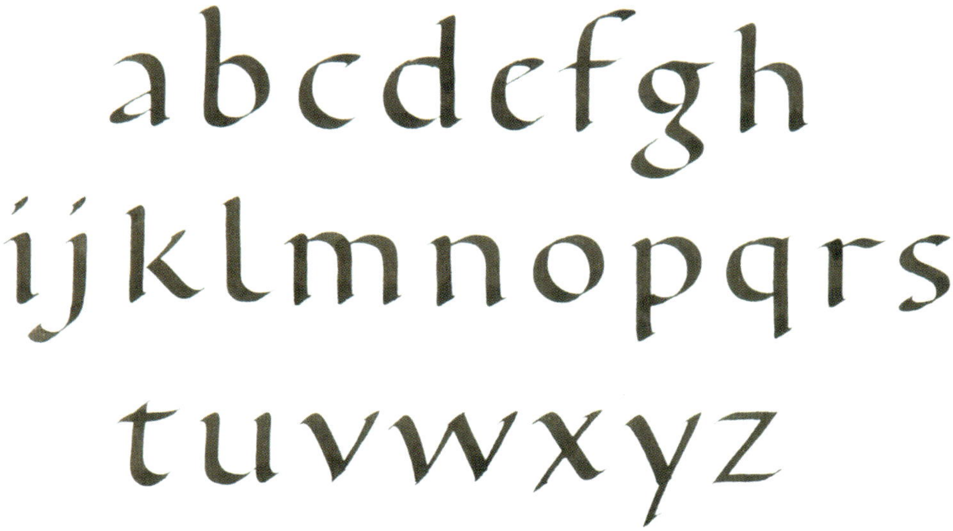

CAPITALS

X-HEIGHT
7 nib widths

PEN ANGLE
30 degrees; 45 degrees for thick strokes of A, V, W, X, Y; 60 degrees for first stroke of M and first and last stroke of N; 0 degrees for Z diagonal

LETTER SLOPE
Upright

FORM
Circular O

SERIF STYLE
Circular

SPACING
Letters: Visually equal areas, approx. ⅔-width of N counter. Words: Slightly less than O width

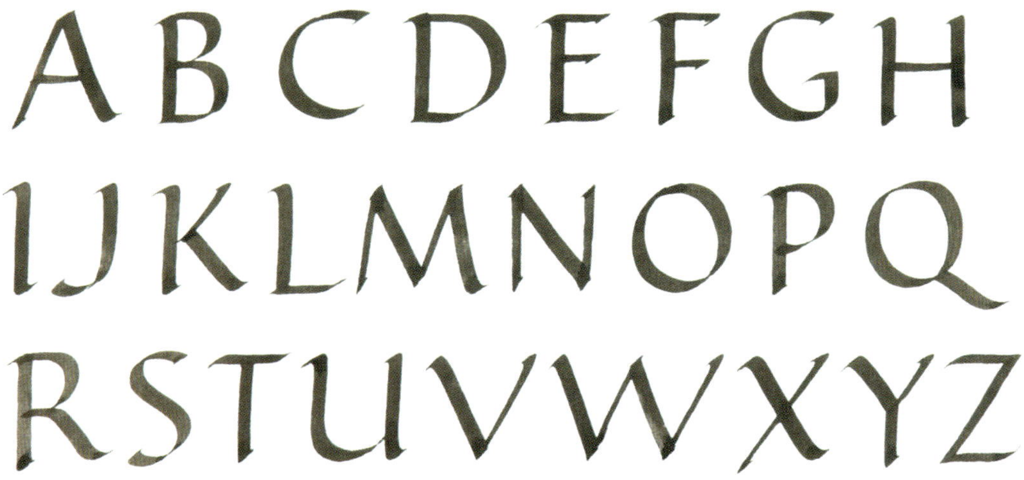

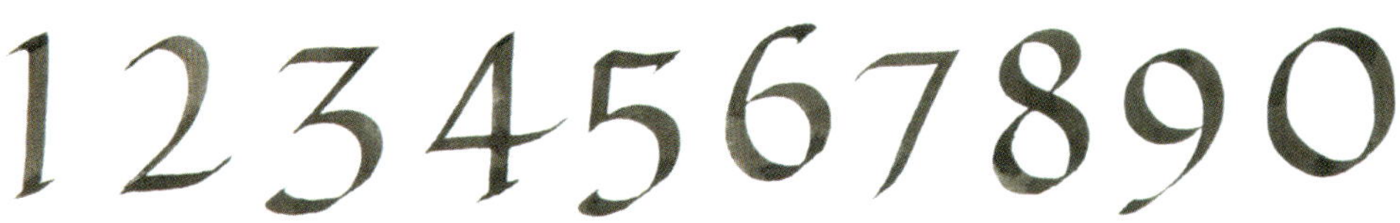

circular letters – o, e and p

The letter 'o' is circular in the Foundational hand. This circular shape therefore also forms the basis for the letters 'b', 'c', 'd', 'e', 'g', 'p', and 'q'.

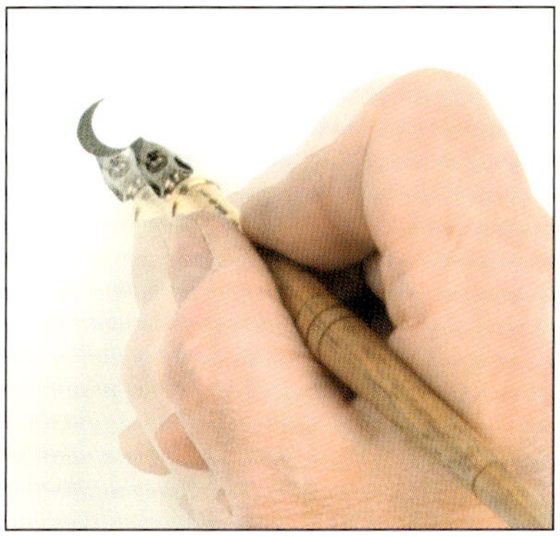

1 Start the letter with the pen nib at 30 degrees. Pull the pen round smoothly for the first half of the stroke.

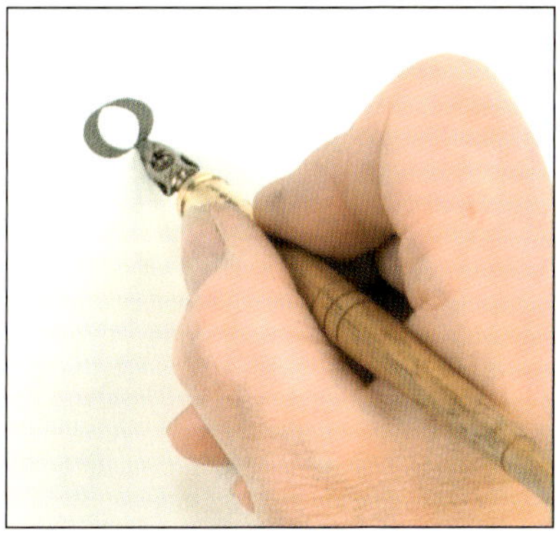

2 Complete the letter with a mirror image stroke. The final letter should be circular with smooth joins.

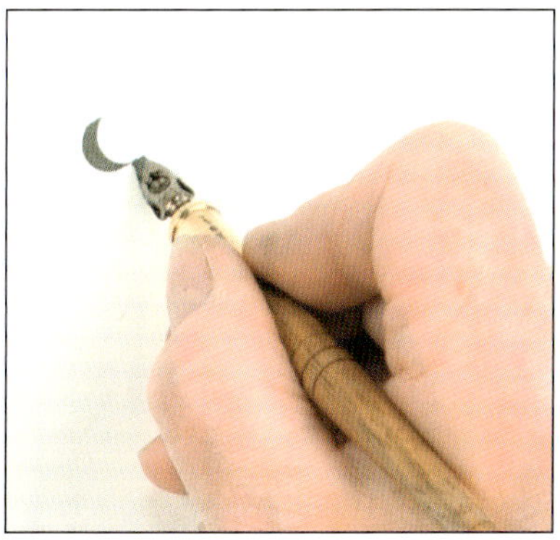

1 The first stroke is like the 'o', but in this case, slightly straighten the back of the letter so it does not appear to be falling over.

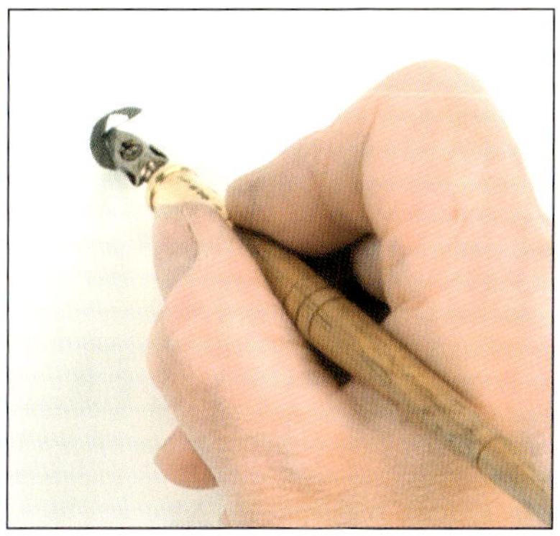

2 Take your pen off the paper and complete the top of the letter. The top joins just above half way.

Stroke reminder

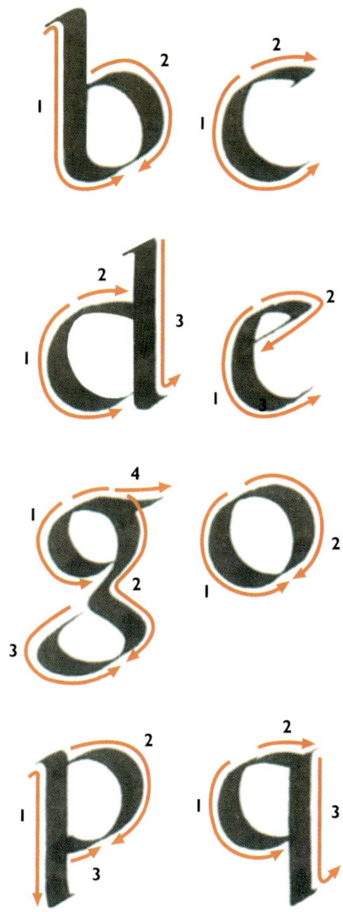

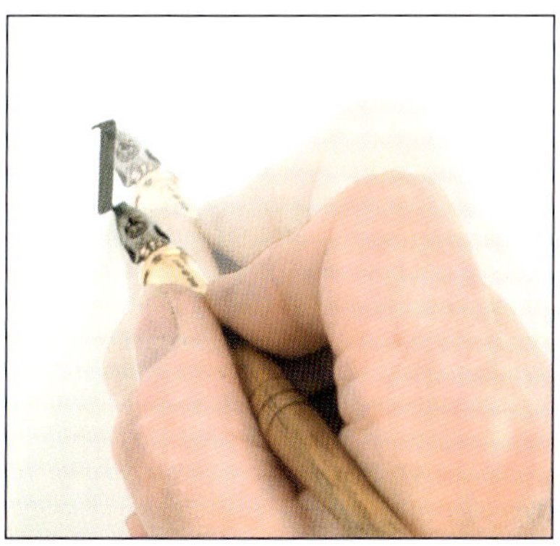

1 Start the vertical downstroke with a serif.

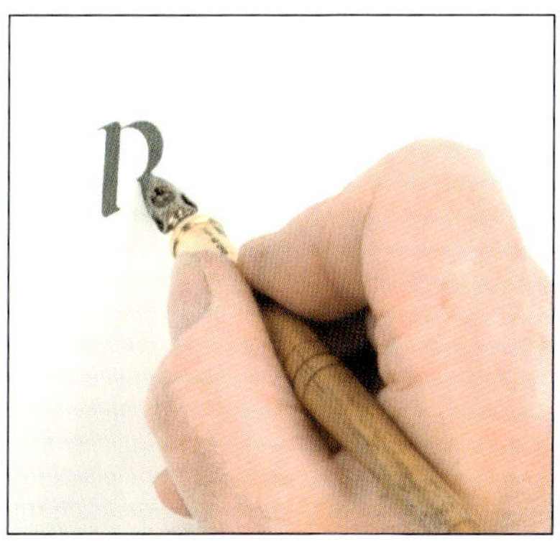

2 Keep the pen top flat and pull it around smoothly to form the bowl, reflecting the curve of the 'o'.

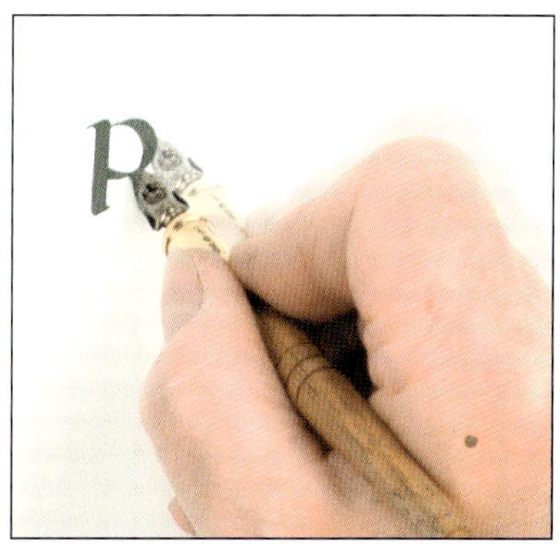

3 The bottom of the bowl is a flattened curve and begins halfway down the stem.

diagonal letters – k, v and x

The diagonal letters are 'k', 'v', 'w', 'x', 'y' and 'z'. Remember that the pen angle changes for the thick strokes of the letters 'v', 'w', 'x' and 'y' and all the strokes of 'z'.

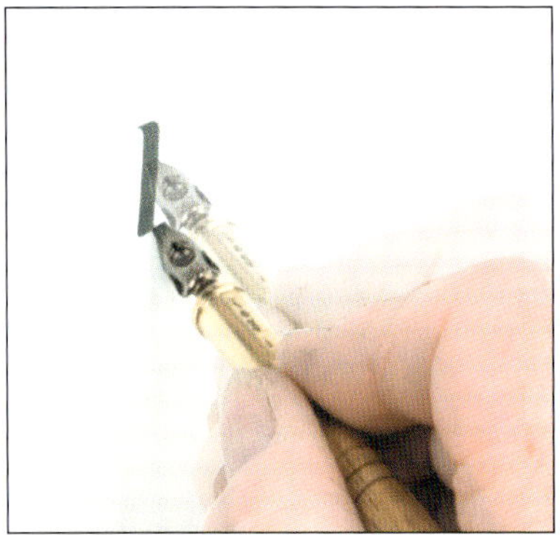

1 Begin three nib widths above the x-height and start with a serif. Then pull the pen down vertically.

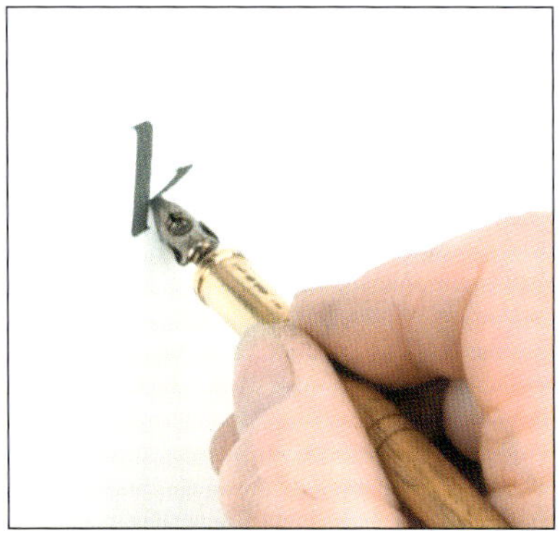

2 Just touch the first downstroke with the nib. Create the diagonals at 90 degrees to each other.

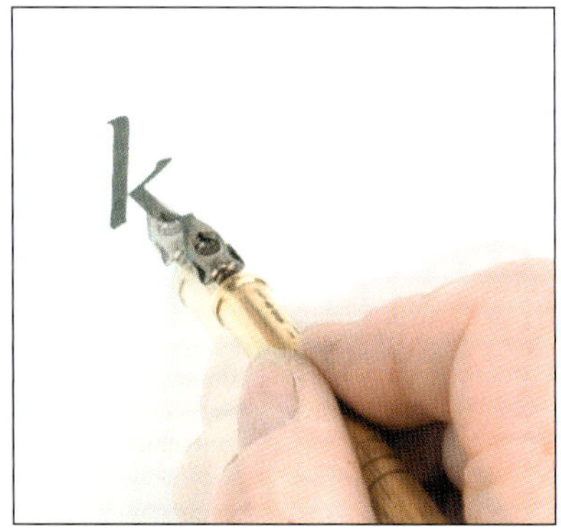

3 Make the diagonal strokes straight. Only the serifs on entry and exit are curved.

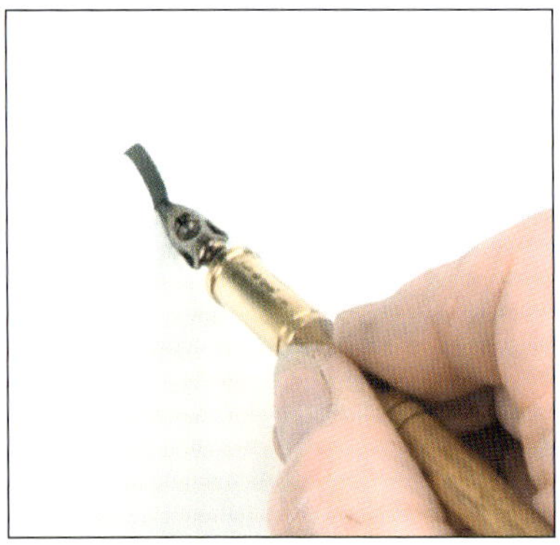

1 Steepen the pen angle to 45 degrees to make the first stroke. It is important to keep the strokes symmetrically upright.

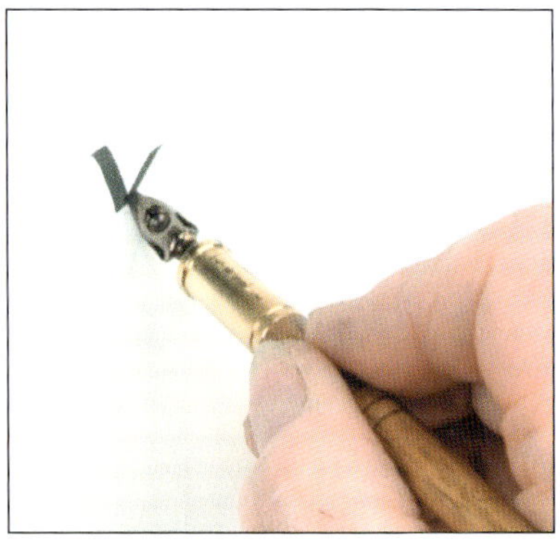

2 Make the second stroke less steep. The strokes should look upright to the eye.

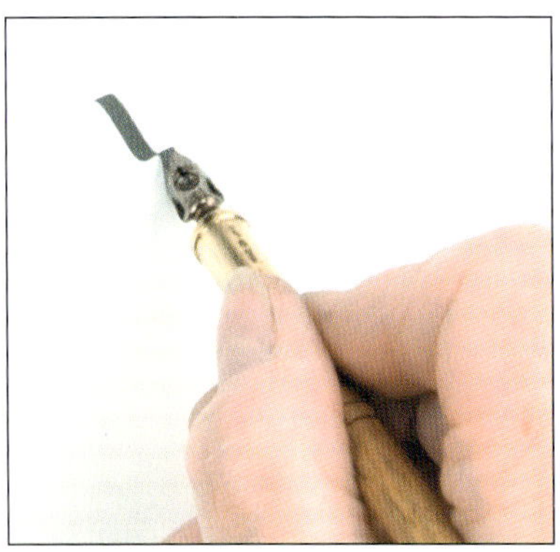

1 As with the letter 'v', steepen the pen angle to 45 degrees for the first thick stroke.

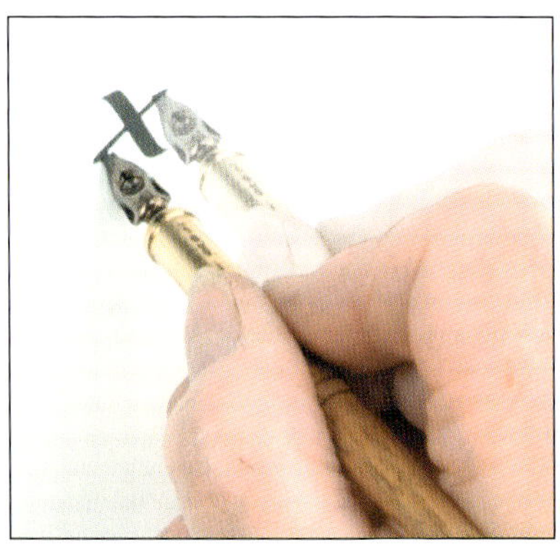

2 The second, slightly flatter, stroke should cross the first stroke just above the halfway point.

Stroke reminder

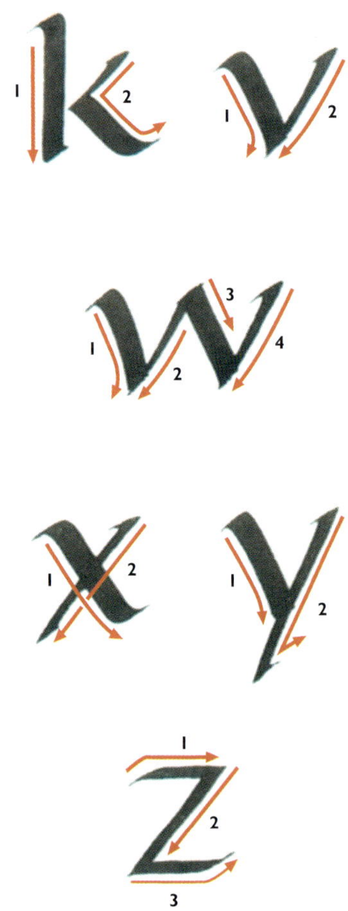

ungrouped letters – f, s and j

The ungrouped letters in the Foundational hand are 'f', 'j' and 's'. However, they all have related curves.

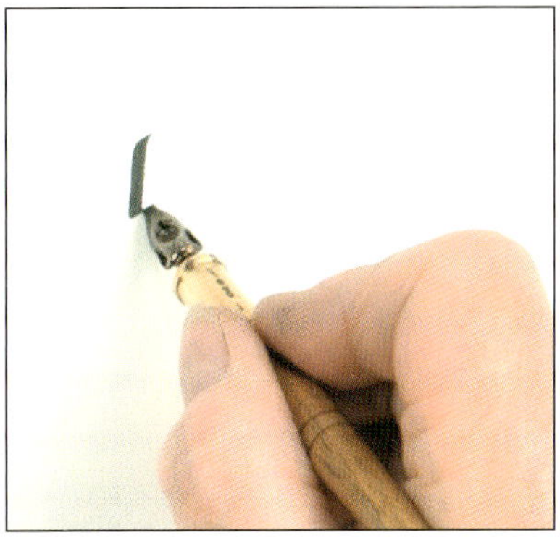

1 Pull the pen down from three nib widths above x-height to the baseline, ending with a small serif.

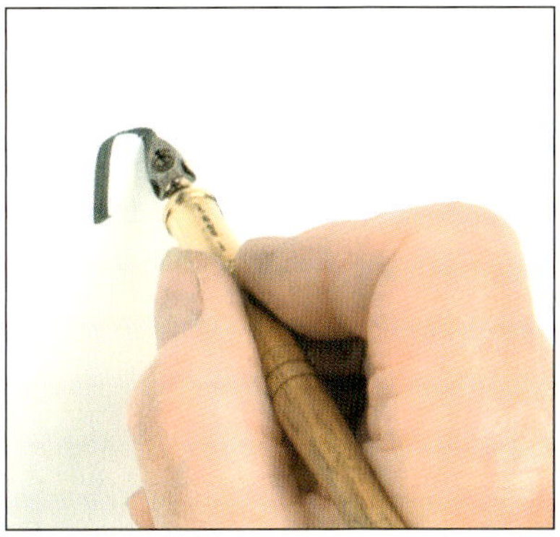

2 Working from the top of the first stroke, form the slightly flattened top of the letter.

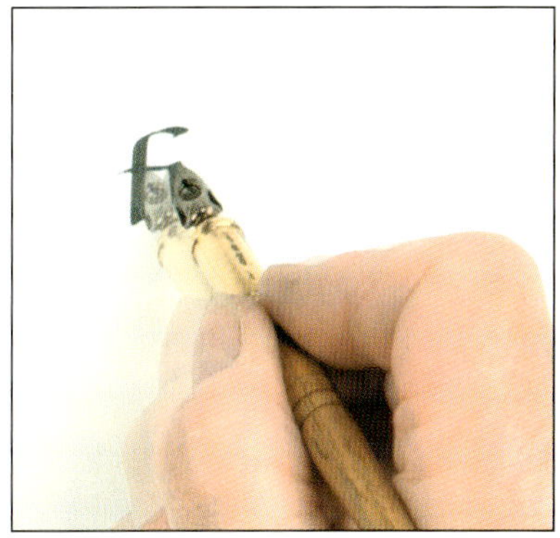

3 To complete the letter, place the top of the crossbar on the line.

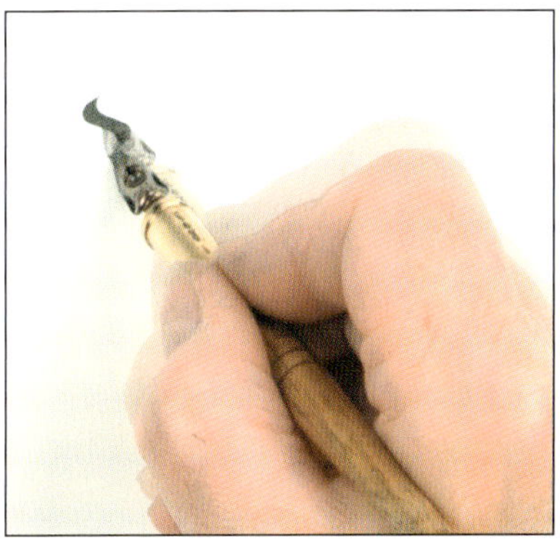

1 The first stroke of the letter 's' is fairly horizontal.

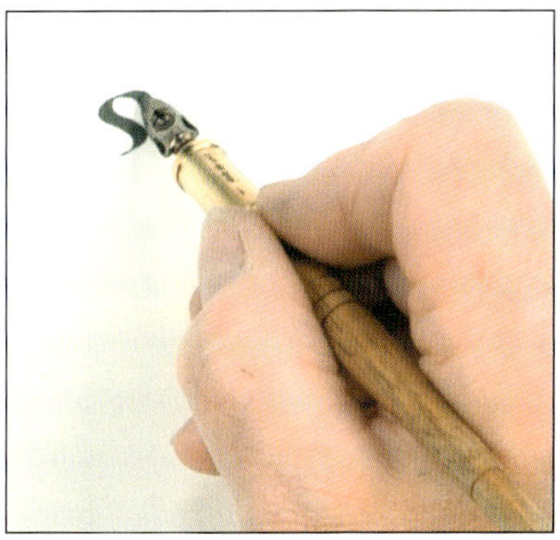

2 Both top and bottom counter curves are flattened. In addition, the top bowl is slightly smaller than the bottom one.

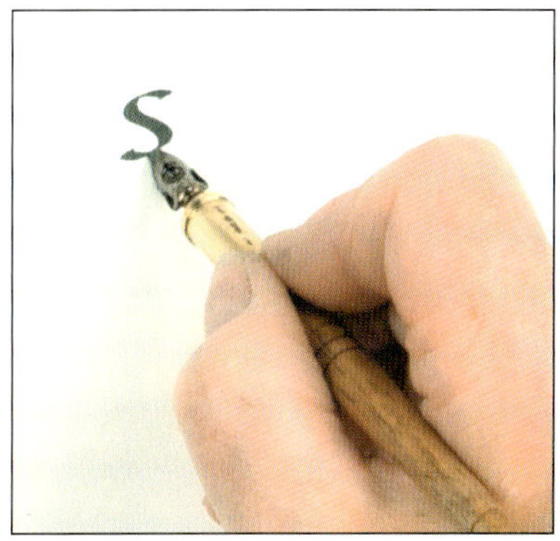

3 The letter should align vertically at the front.

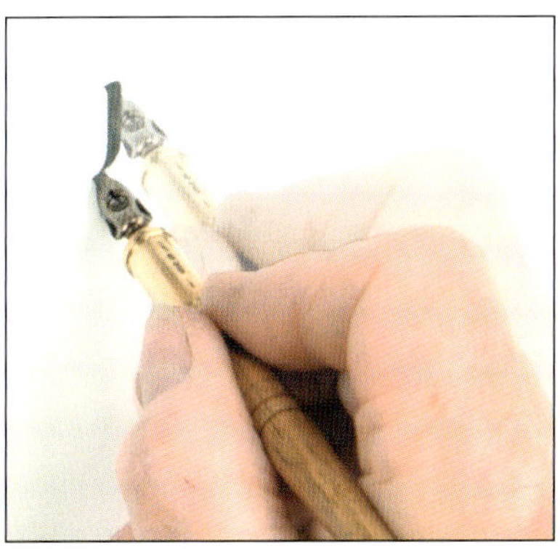

1 Pull the pen straight down until the ascending stroke finishes $2^1/_2$–3 nib widths below the baseline.

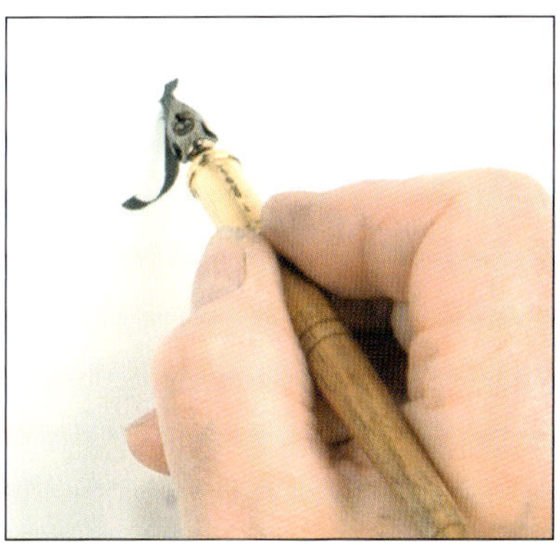

2 Join the curved tail smoothly to the bottom of the downstroke. Add a dot, which relates to the serifs.

Stroke reminder

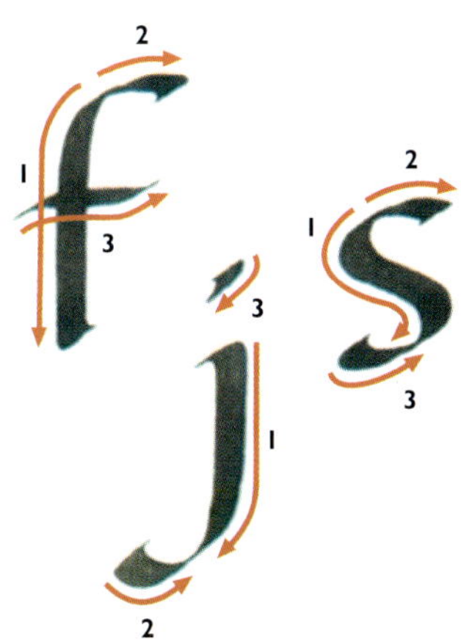

clockwise arches – m, a and h

The letters in this group are 'a', 'h', 'm', 'n' and 'r'. The letter 'i' is also included. The strong branching arches that form the tops of the letters are emphasized in this hand.

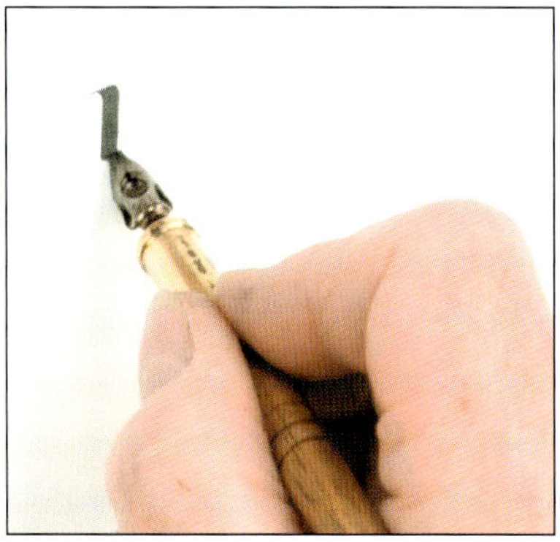

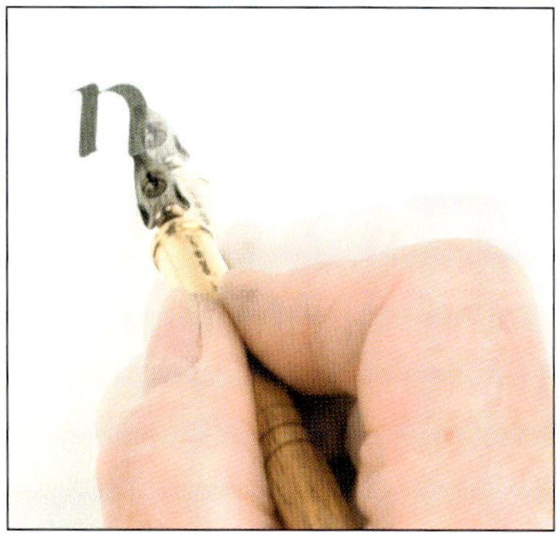

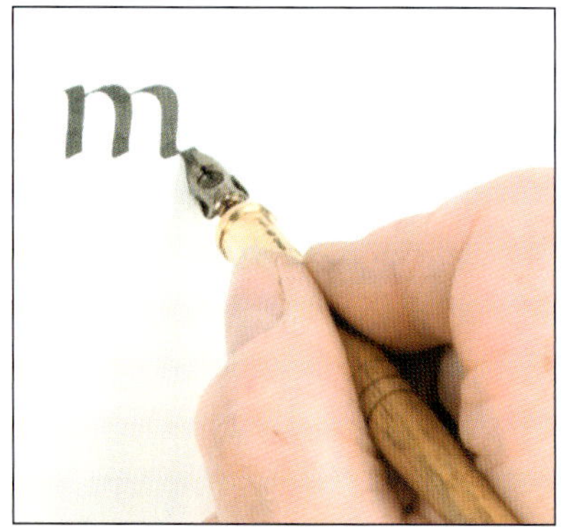

1 The first stroke starts with a lead-in serif. The bottom serif ends the downstroke and is smaller.

2 Start within the downstroke (the stem) and make a strong circular arch, as in the letter 'a'.

3 Repeat for the second arch. Each half of the letter should be of equal width. Finish with a slightly larger serif than you started with.

Stroke reminder

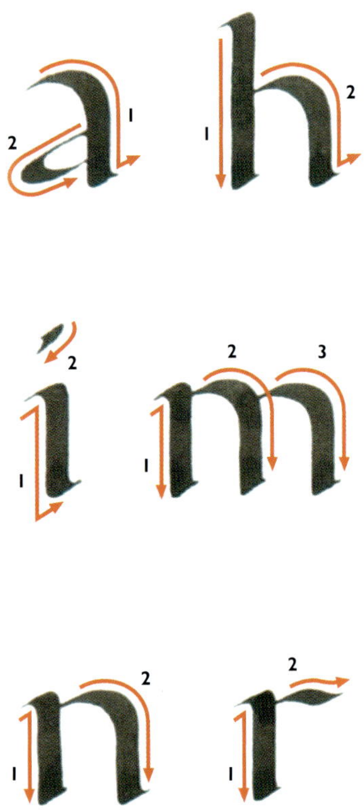

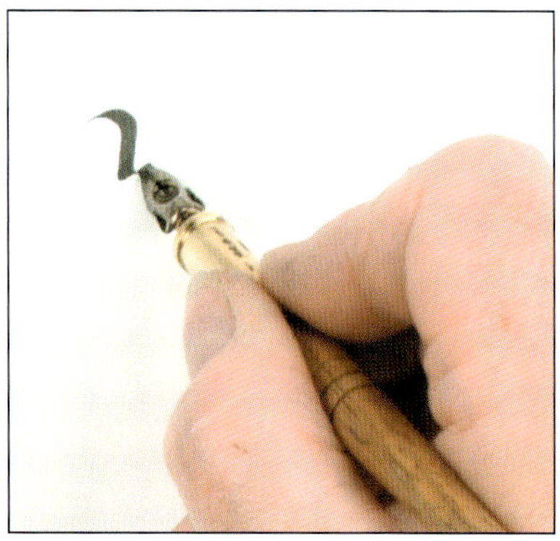

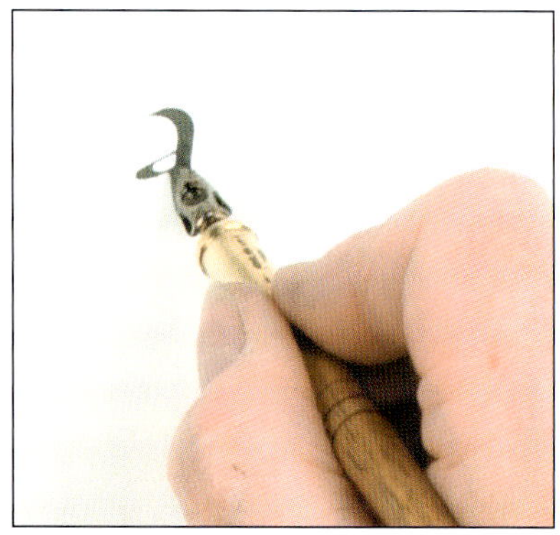

1 The top curve of the 'a' relates to the 'o' – a circular arch with a vertical downstroke and serif.

2 Start the bowl below half way. Bring the pen down to the baseline, reflecting the curve of the 'o'.

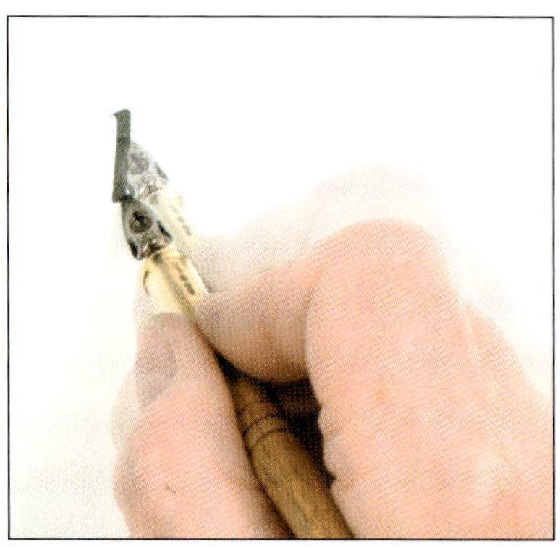

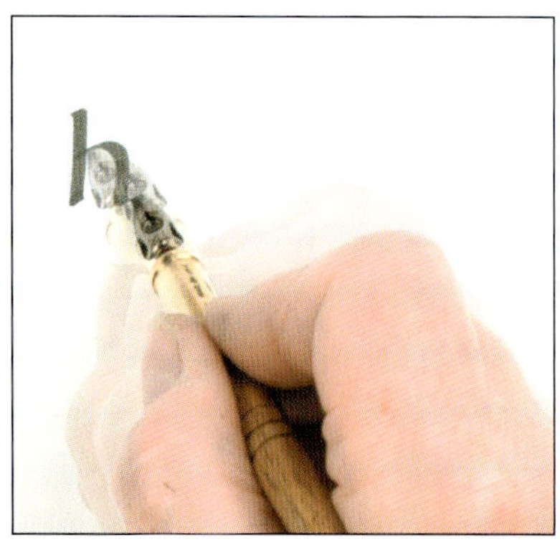

1 The ascender starts with a serif and is three nib widths above x-height. Pull the pen down to the baseline.

2 The arch of the 'h' reflects the same shape as the 'o'. Pull the pen down and add a small serif to finish the letter.

anti-clockwise arches – l, t and u

There are only three letters in this group – 'l', 't' and 'u'. In this case, the base of the arch follows the curve and proportion of the 'o'.

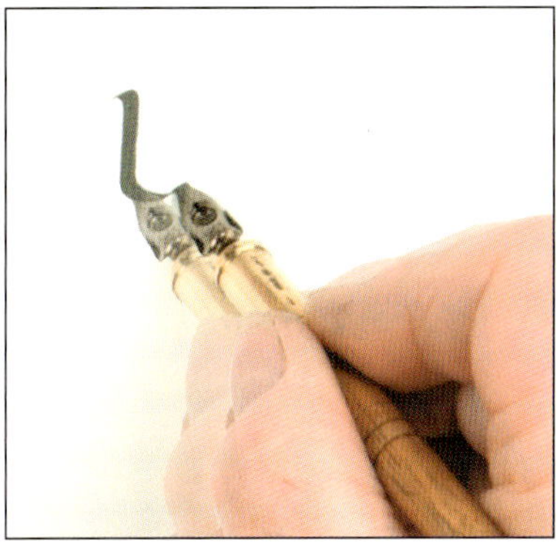

1 Start the ascending stroke with a serif. Pull the pen down vertically and finish with a curved base.

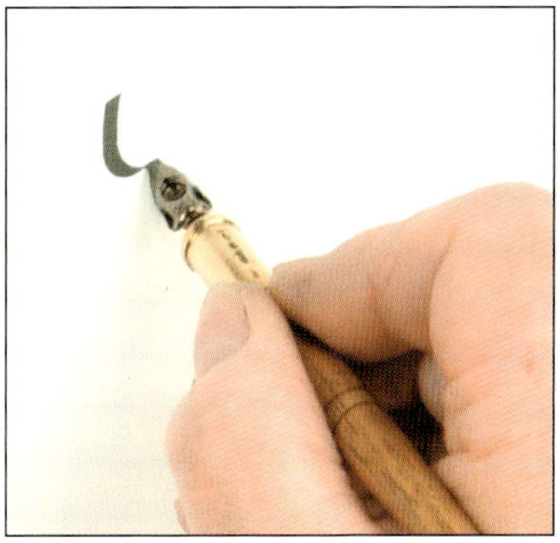

1 Start the stroke slightly above the top line, and with no serif. Pull the pen down and around to create a circular bowl.

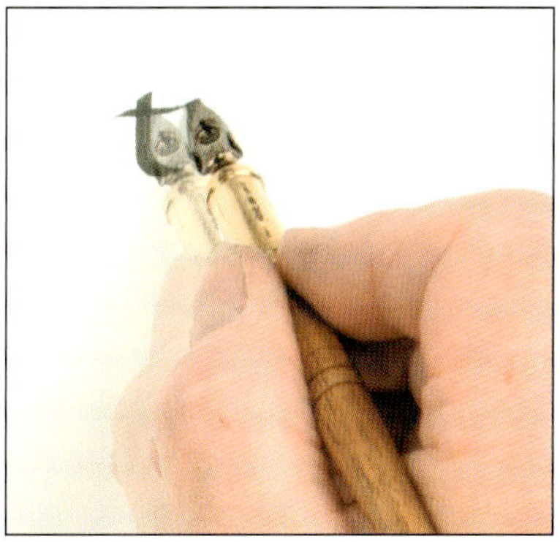

2 The top of crossbar sits immediately below the top line, just touching it. Keep your pen angle consistent.

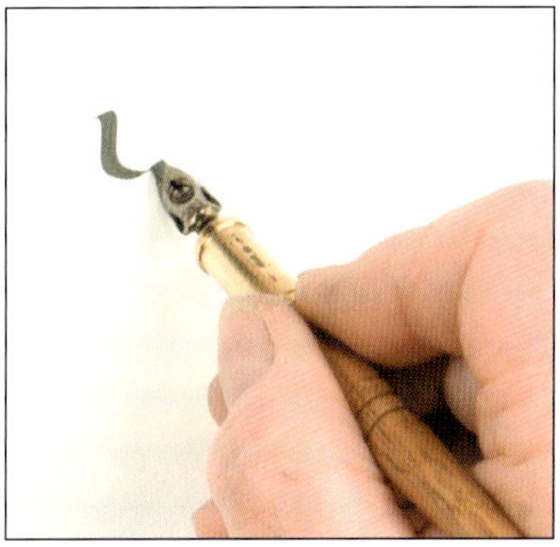

1 Start with a small serif and pull the pen down into an arch. The base of the 'u' relates to the arch of the 'n'.

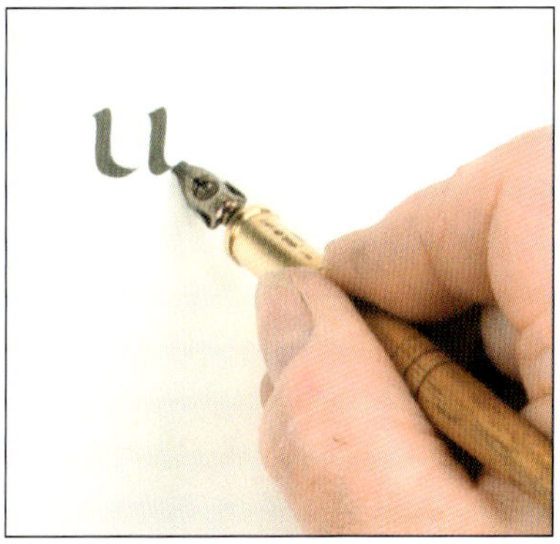

2 The second downstroke mirrors the first but, in this case, it ends with a serif.

Stroke reminder

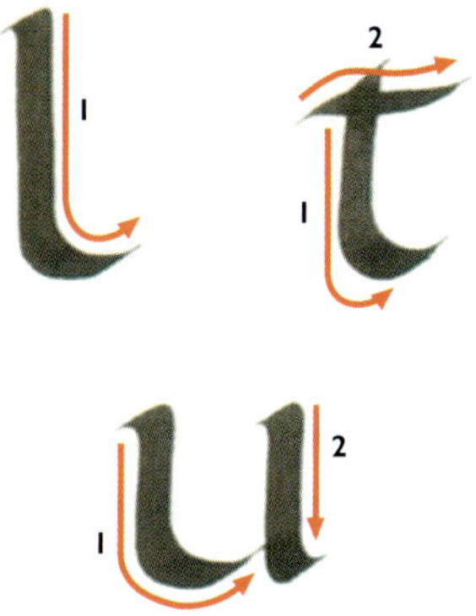

putting it all together

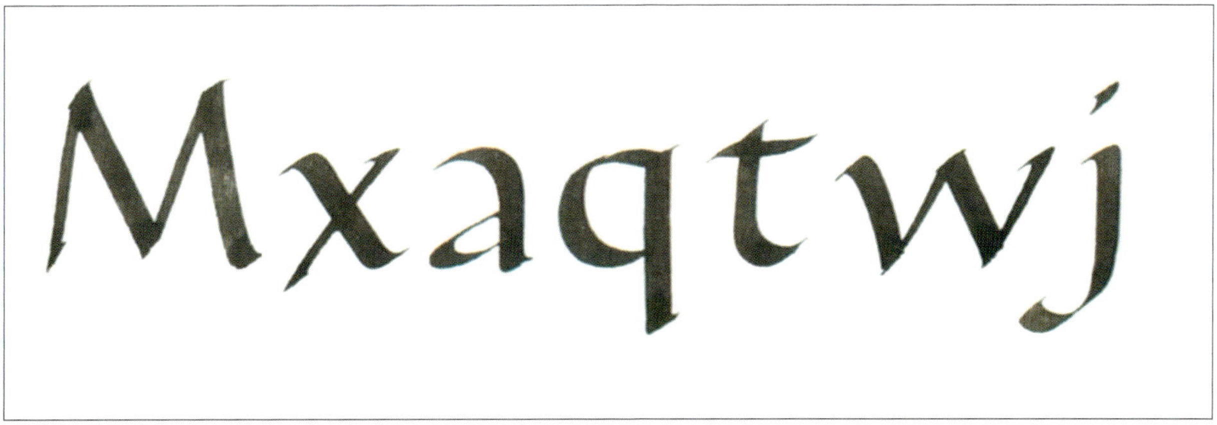

Roman capitals

Based on ancient Roman carved stone inscriptions, Roman capitals have elegant proportions constructed on the basis of the square and a circle within the square.

circular letters – O

'O' and 'Q' are circular letters. 'C', 'D' and 'G' are 7/8 width of a square containing the circle.

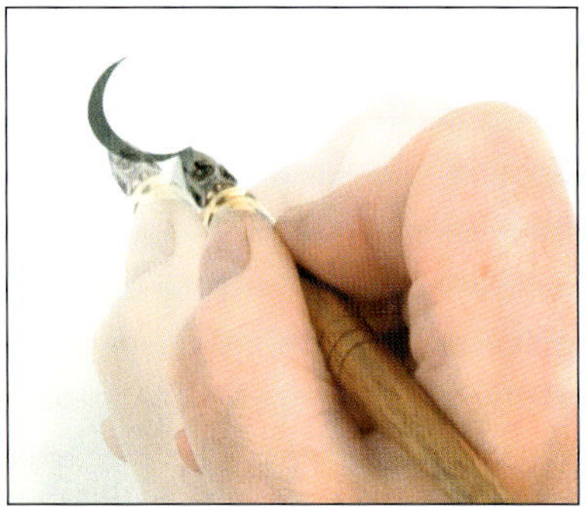

1 Start the stroke with the nib sitting just under the line. The top and bottom curves should both slightly cut the line.

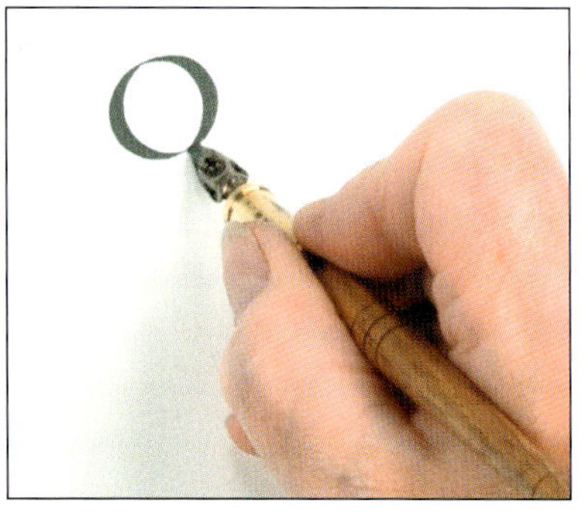

2 Mirror the same stroke in the opposite direction to create a smooth, circular shape.

Stroke reminder

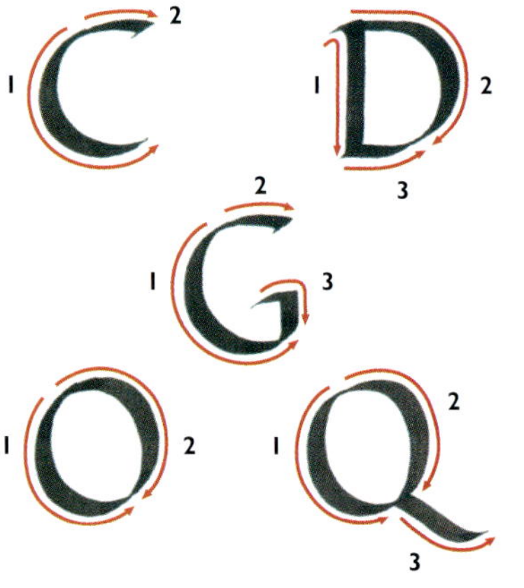

three-quarter width letters – A

The three-quarter width letters are 'A', 'H', 'N', 'T', 'U', 'V', 'X', 'Y' and 'Z'.

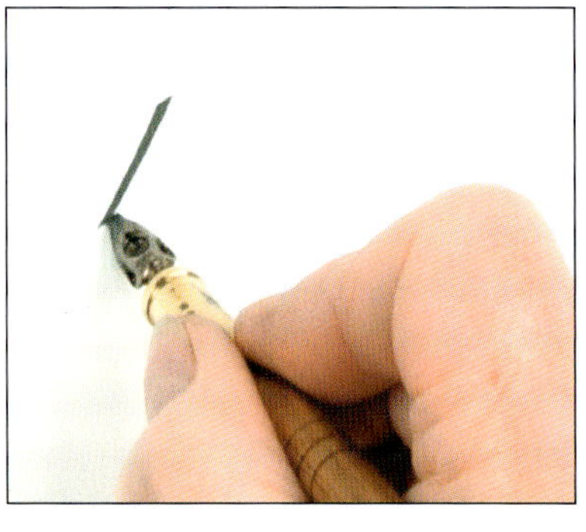

1 Steepen the pen angle to 45 degrees on the first downstroke.

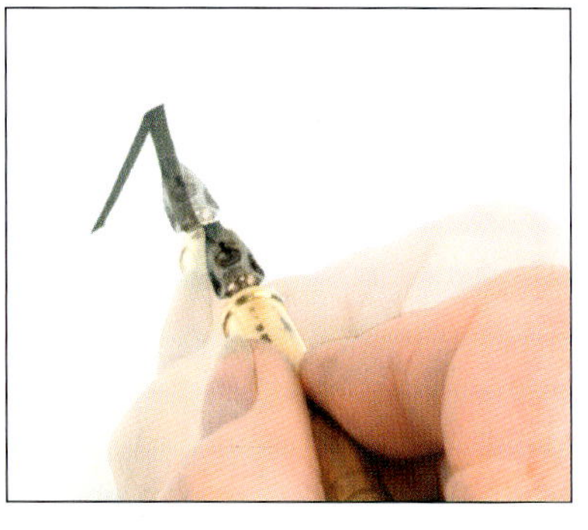

2 Hold the pen at the same angle for the second stroke, finishing with a serif.

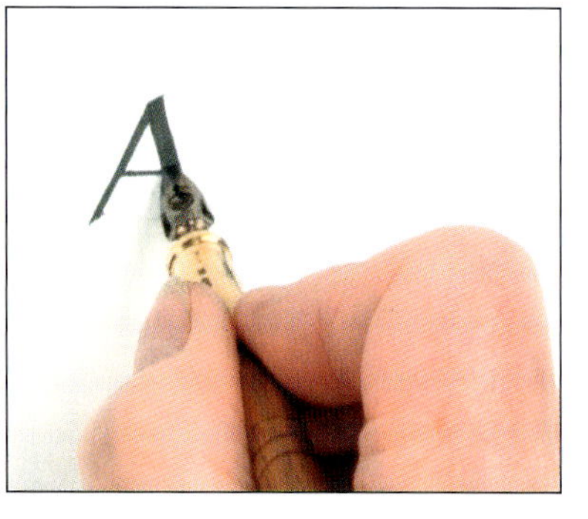

3 Complete the letter with a crossbar, slightly below half way.

Stroke reminder

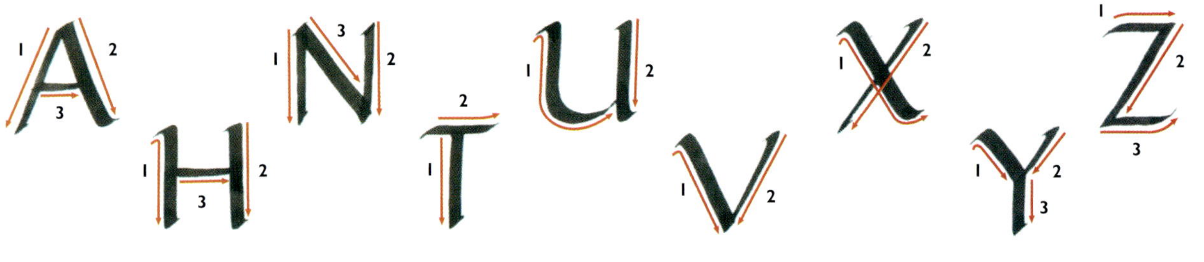

wide letters – W

The wide letters are 'M', which is the width of a square, and 'W', which is made from two 'V's.

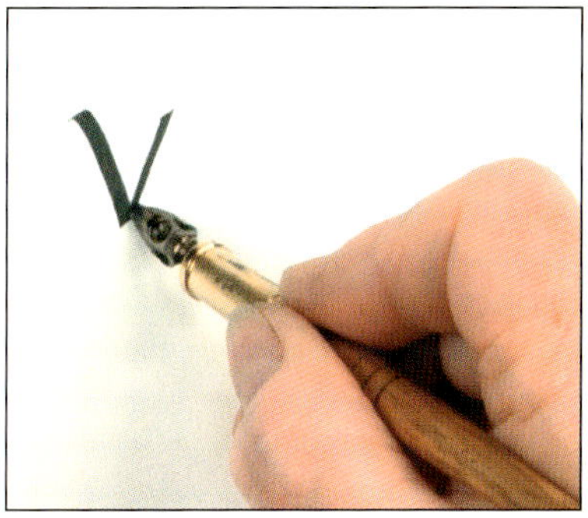

1 Make the first stroke with your pen at 45 degrees, starting with a lead-in serif. On the second stroke, pull the pen down, keeping a consistent angle, to join the bottom of the first stroke.

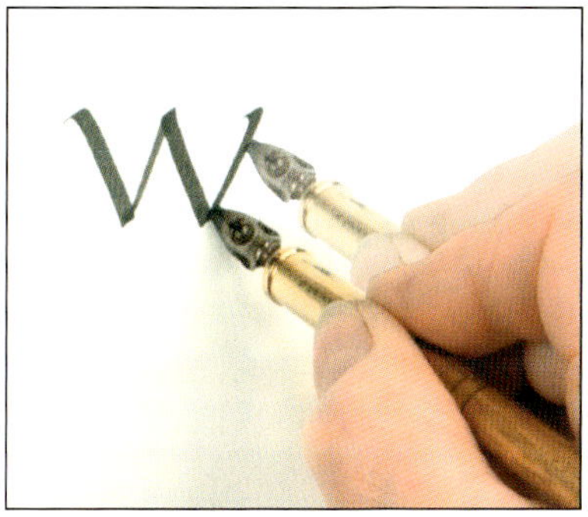

2 Repeat the first downstroke, making sure the angle of the line is consistent. The last downstroke starts with a small serif. This is a very wide letter – keep it upright.

Stroke reminder

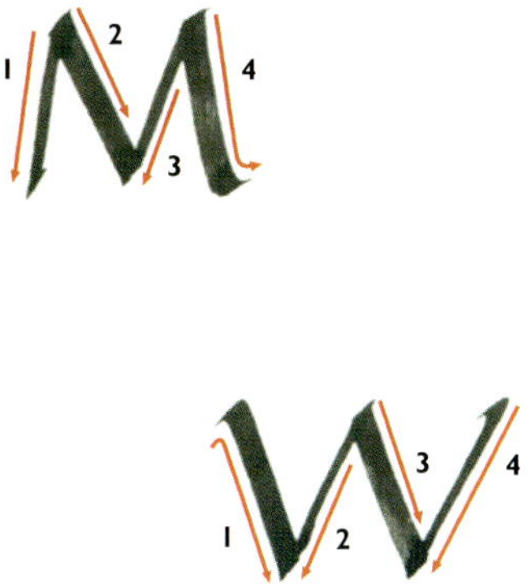

half-width letters – P

The half-width letters are 'B', 'E', 'F', 'K', 'L', 'P', 'R' and 'S'.

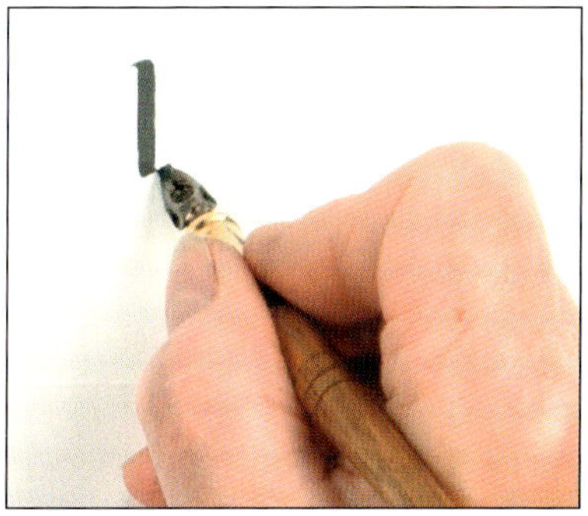

1 Start the stroke with a serif, then pull the pen down vertically to the line. Keep your pen angle at 30 degrees.

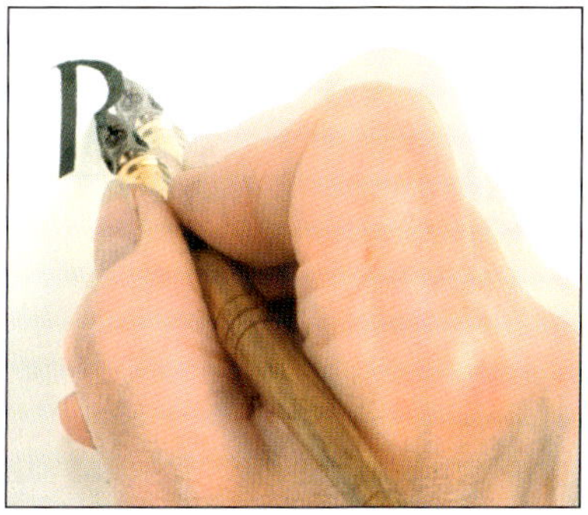

2 The bowl of the letter should be a smooth circular shape. Stop before reaching the first downstroke.

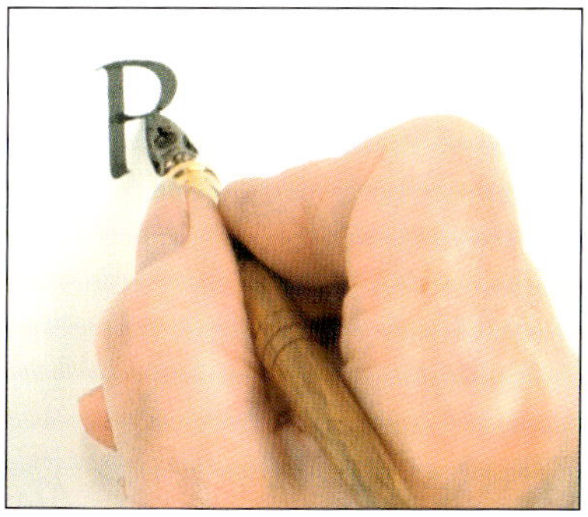

3 The base of the bowl is finished with a straight stroke, beginning at half way and curving smoothly to join the bowl.

Stroke reminder

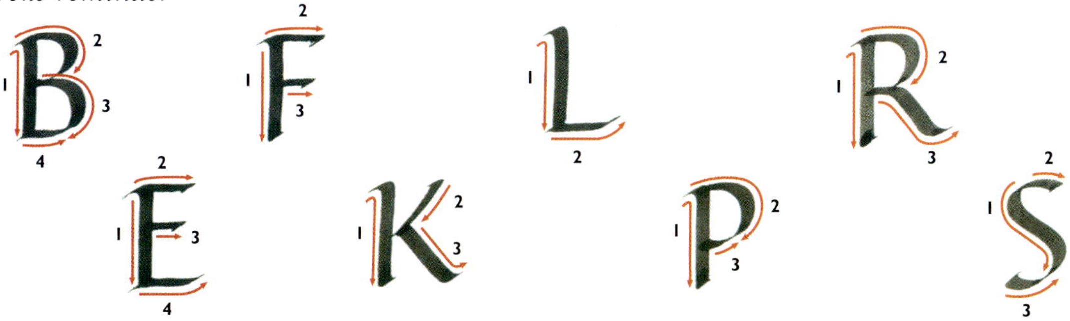

straight letters *continued*

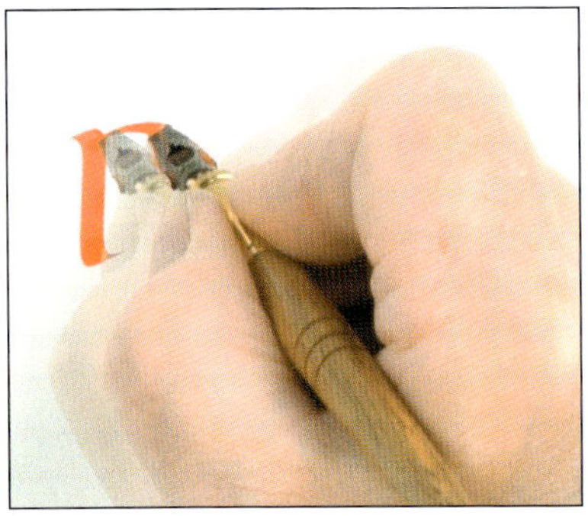

1 The first stroke descends below the baseline. The top is slightly curved and springs from the downstroke. The curve relates to the arched letters.

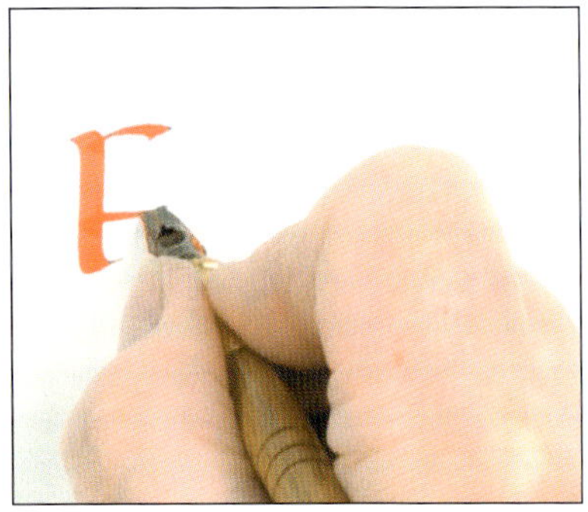

2 The third stroke sits above the baseline, creating a generous space between the arms.

Stroke reminder

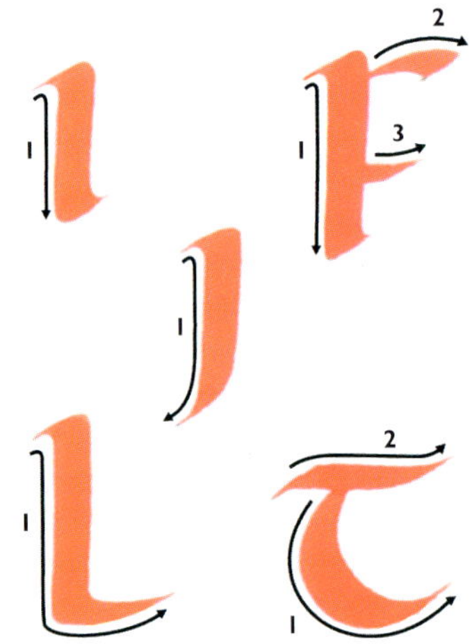

diagonal letters – k and n

The diagonal letters are 'a', 'k', 'n', 'v', 'w', 'x', 'y' and 'z'.

Stroke reminder

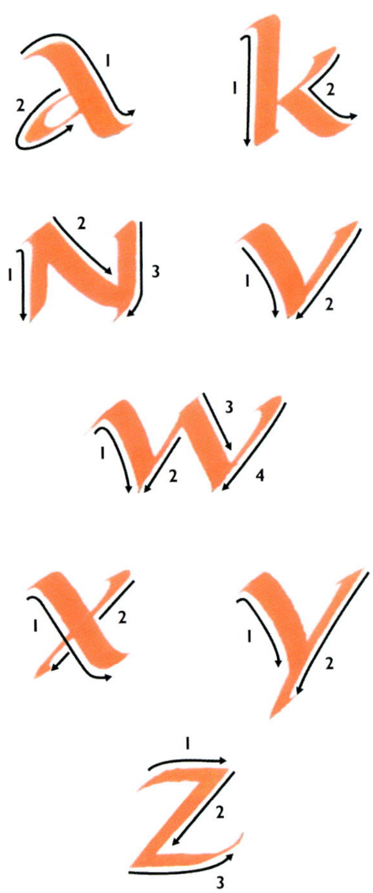

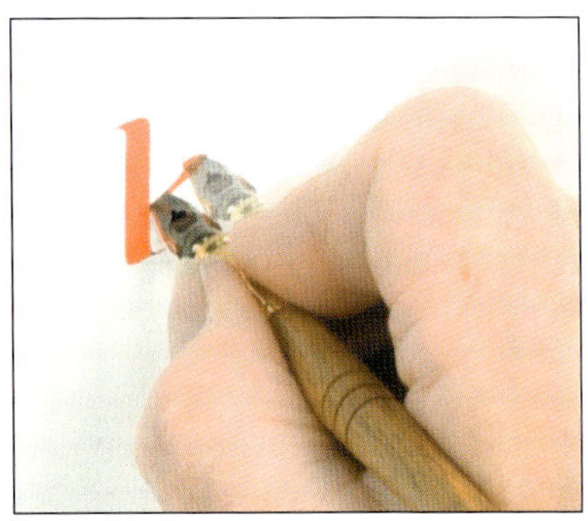

1 The downstroke is a vertical line, beginning with a serif at the top.

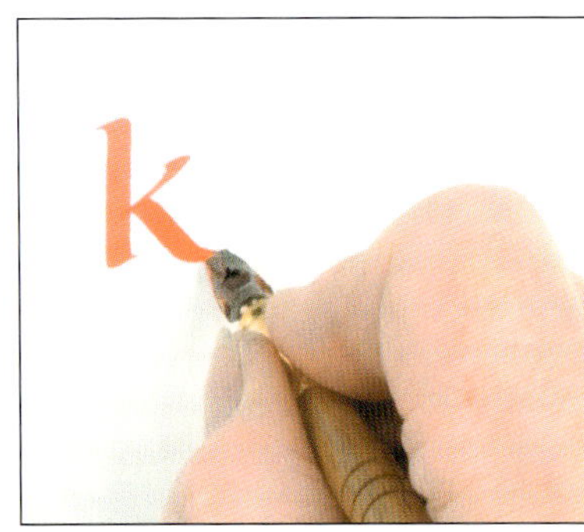

2 Keep the diagonals at 45 degrees to the downstroke and 90 degrees to each other. The second stroke just touches the downstroke.

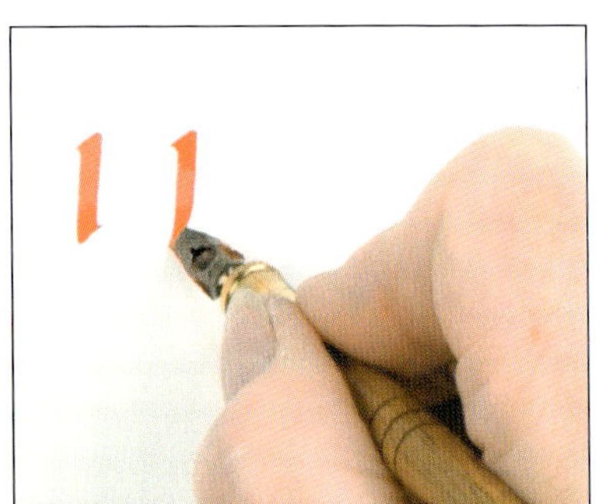

1 Start with two parallel downstrokes. The second one tapers slightly to the left.

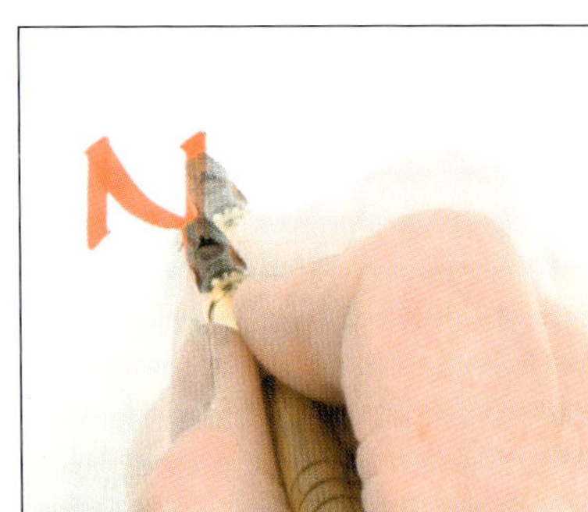

2 Join the two downstrokes with a diagonal, which curves slightly from top to bottom.

arched letters – h

There are only three arched letters – 'h', 'm' and 'u'.

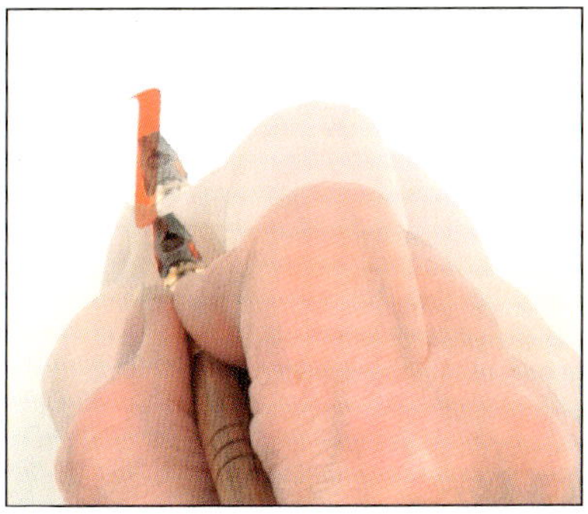

1 Begin the downstroke two nib widths above the line. Pull the pen straight down and finish with a serif.

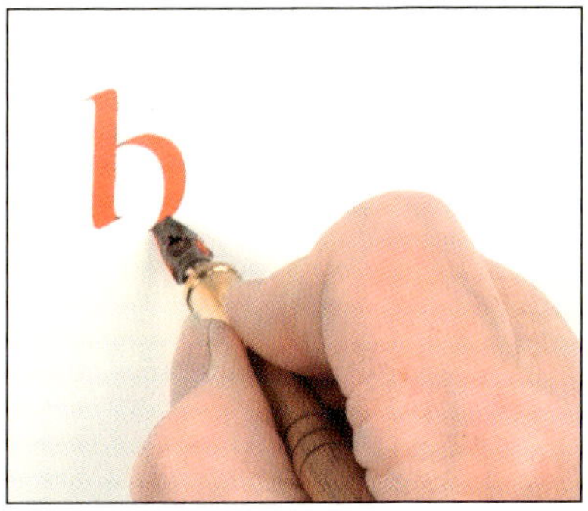

2 The arch springs from inside the downstroke and is smooth and round. It extends slightly below the line.

Stroke reminder

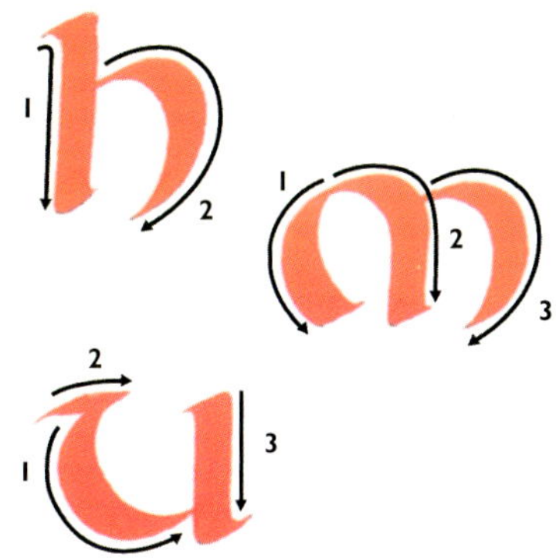

small-bowl letters – b

The three small-bowl letters are 'b', 'r' and 's'.

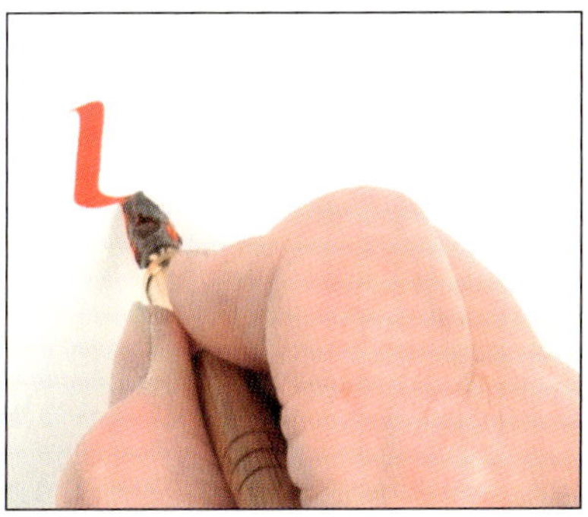

1 The first stroke extends above the line. Pull the pen down, then to the right, to form the base of the letter.

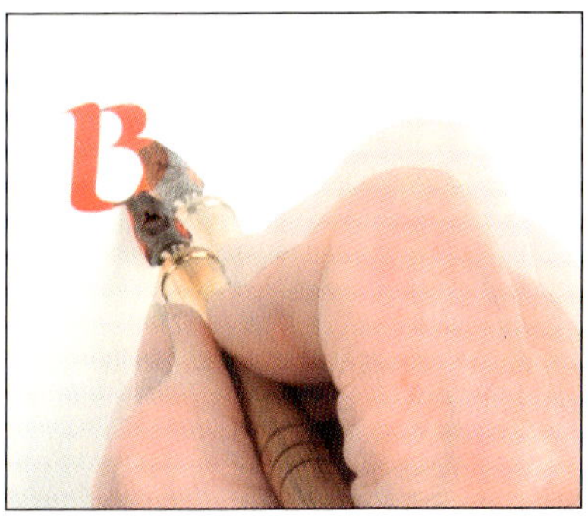

2 The top bowl is smaller than the bottom one. The second stroke is left open – it does not touch the downstroke.

Stroke reminder

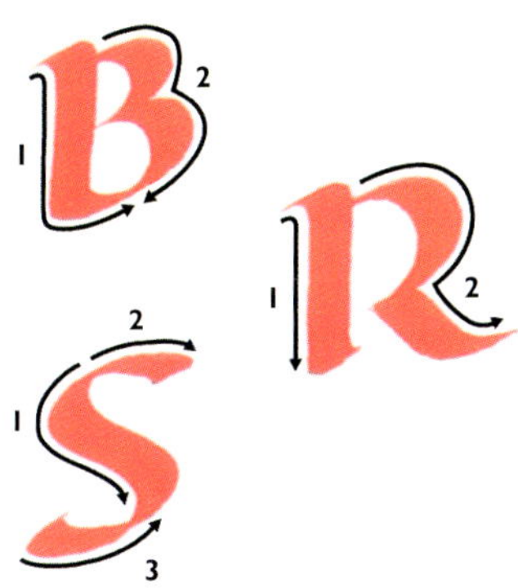

putting it all together

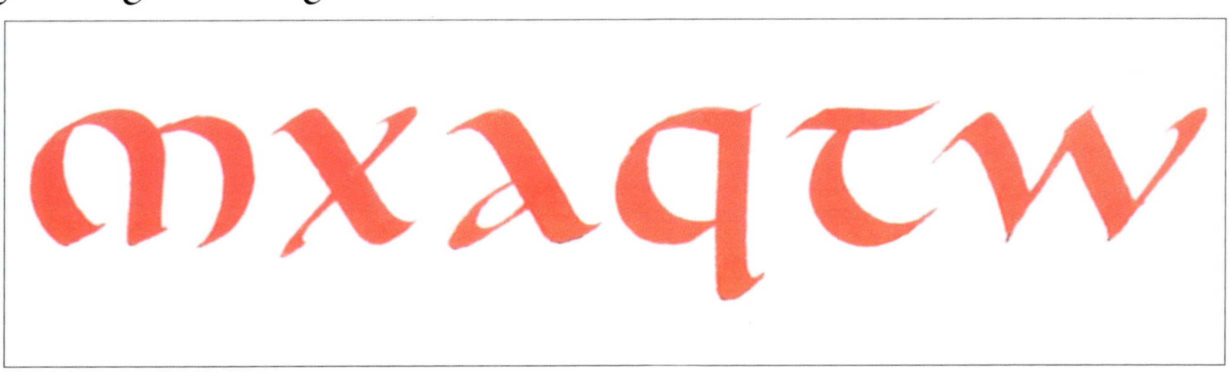

Gothic

Gothic blackletter was developed between the 12th and 15th centuries. Rounder scripts were gradually compressed and angularized to produce bold letterforms.

LOWER CASE

X-HEIGHT	5 nib widths
PEN ANGLE	45 degrees
LETTER SLOPE	Upright
FORM	Parallelogram O
ASCENDERS	2 nib widths
DESCENDERS	2 nib widths
SERIF STYLE	Angular
SPACING	Equal spacing between letters

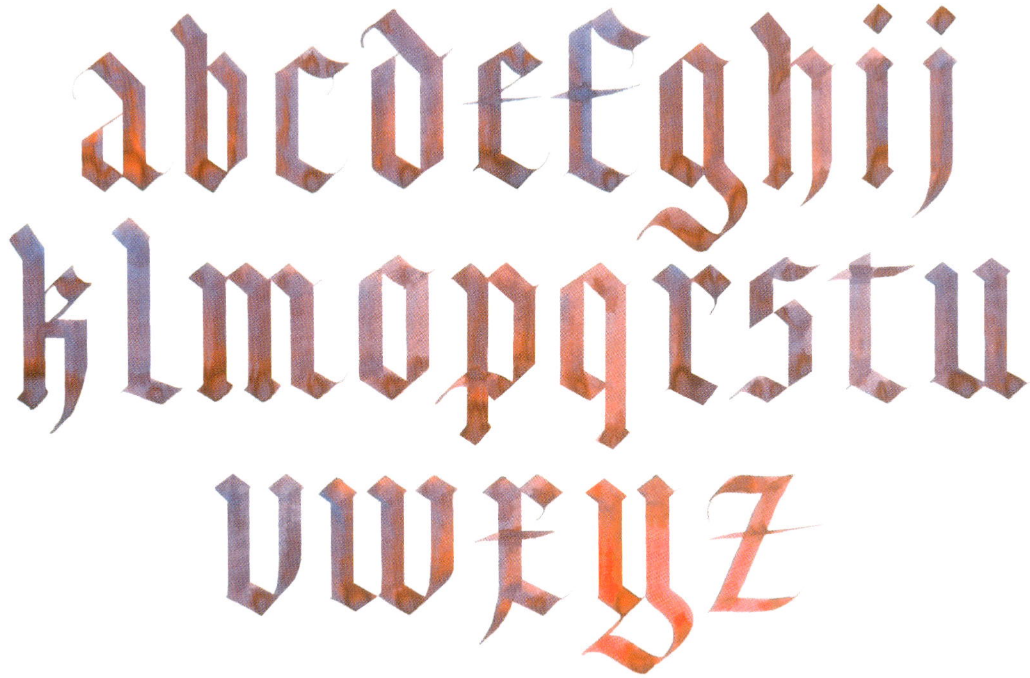

CAPITALS

X-HEIGHT	6 nib widths
PEN ANGLE	45 degrees
LETTER SLOPE	Upright
FORM	Circular and wide
ASCENDERS	1–2 nib widths
DESCENDERS	1–2 nib widths
SERIF STYLE	Hairlines and slab serifs
SPACING	Equal spacing between letters

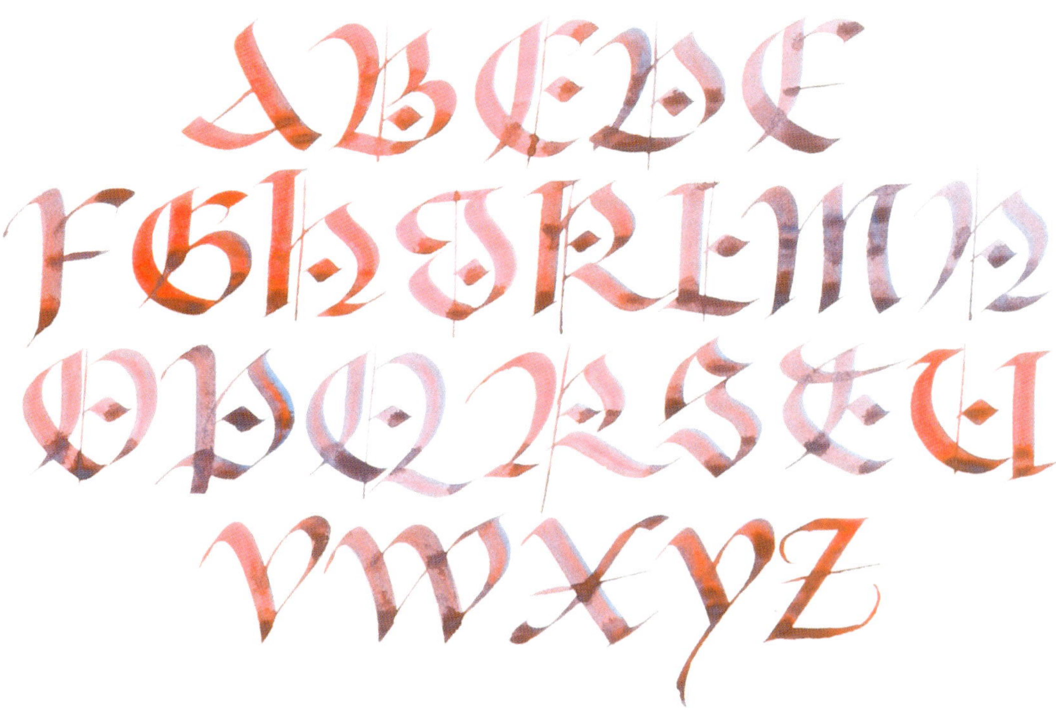

round letters – o, e, and q

The round letters are based on the 'o'. Also in this group are 'a', 'c', 'e', 'g', 'q' and 't'.

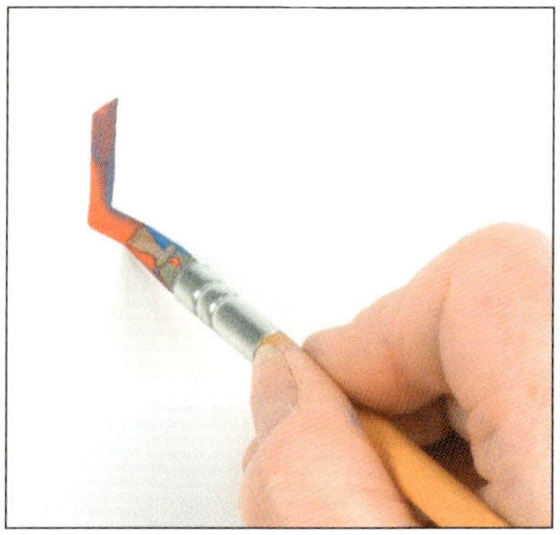

1 Starting from slightly below the top line, draw a downstroke that stops just above the baseline.

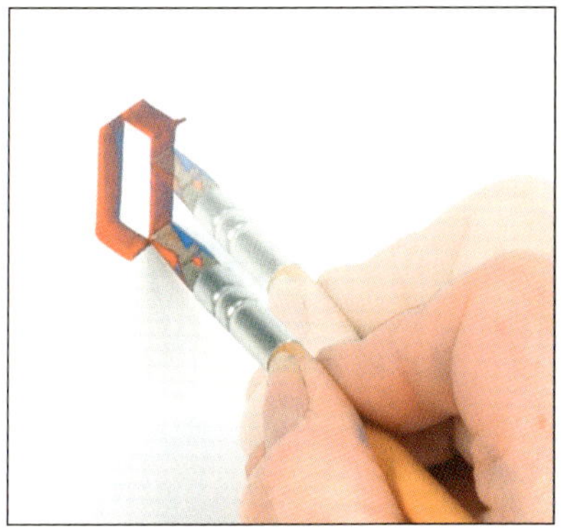

2 Mirror the first downstroke to complete the letter, adding a small hairline 'ear' on the shoulder.

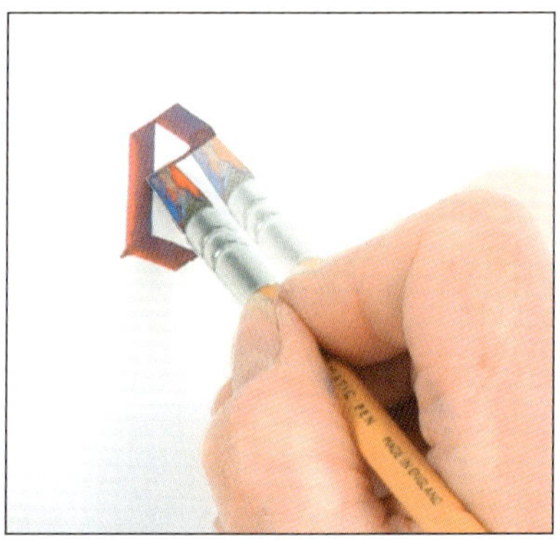

1 Start the downstroke below the top line. Then add the 'foot' with a hairline serif. Add the eye in one movement, placing it above half way.

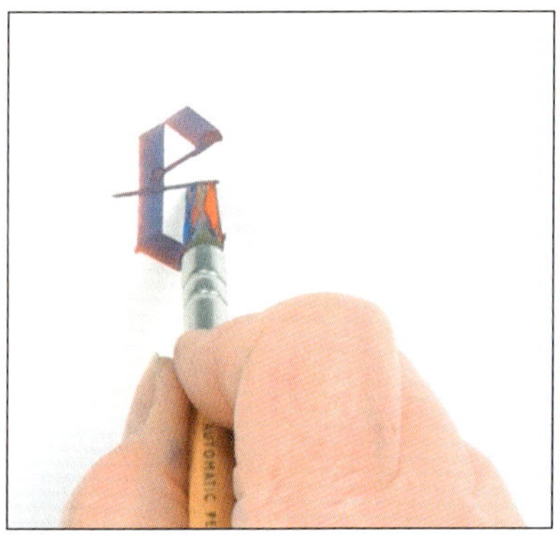

2 To finish, add a crossbar using a pen angle of zero degrees.

Stroke reminder

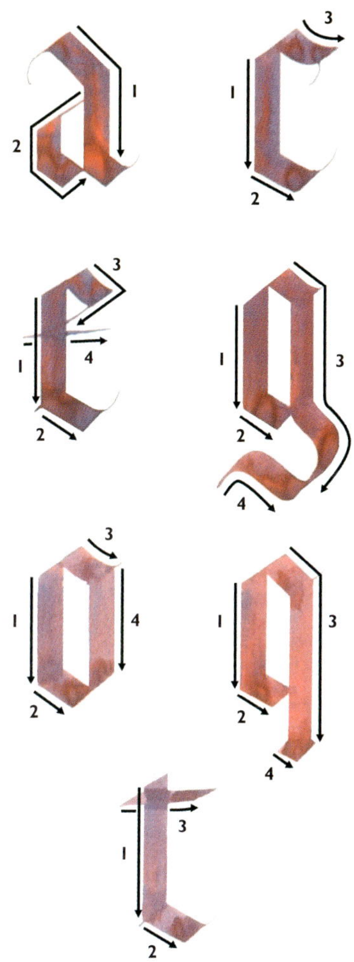

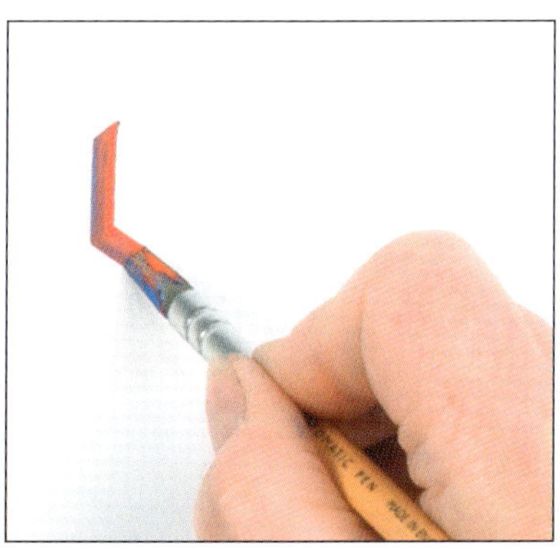

1 Starting from just below the top line, draw a downstroke that finishes just above the baseline. Add the foot.

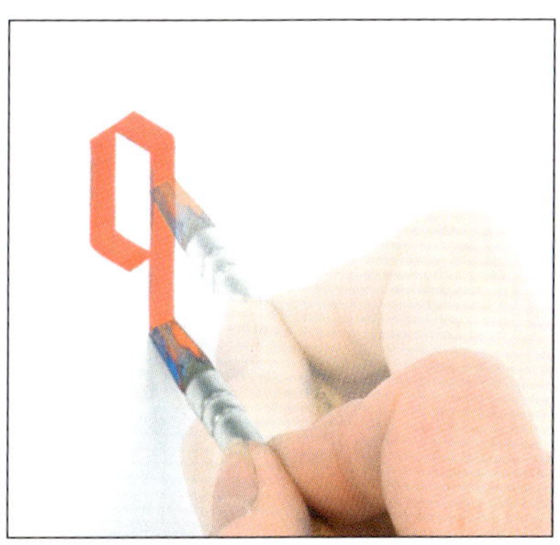

2 Add the second downstroke as for the 'o', but continue it below the baseline, finishing with a diamond serif.

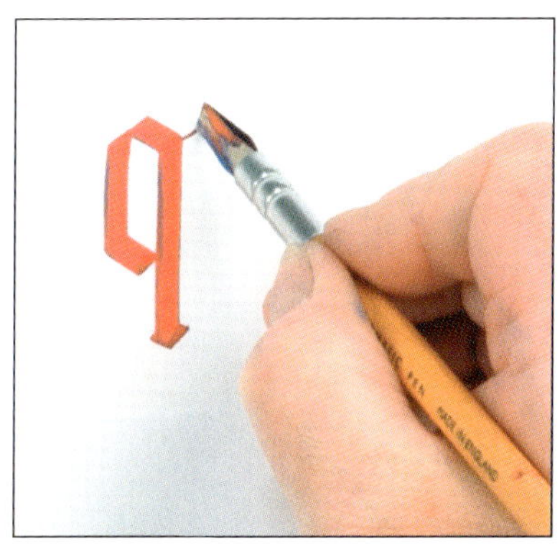

3 Add a hairline ear to the shoulder of the letter using the edge of the pen.

straight strokes with an arch – k and b

These letters have a vertical downstroke with an arch. They are 'b', 'h', 'k', 'm', 'n', 'p' and 'r'.

Stroke reminder

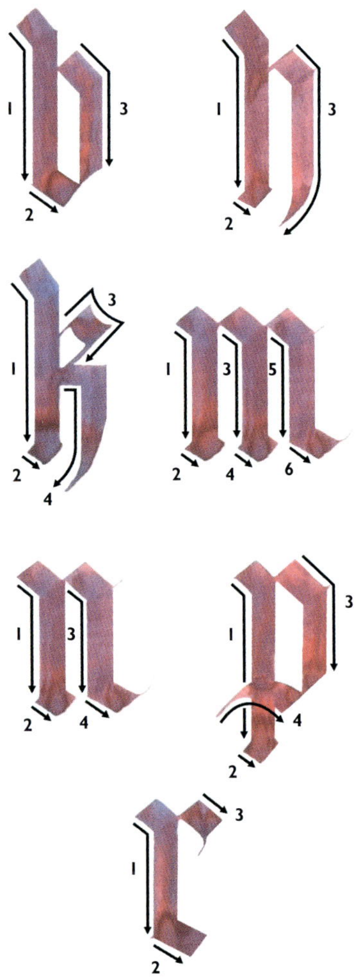

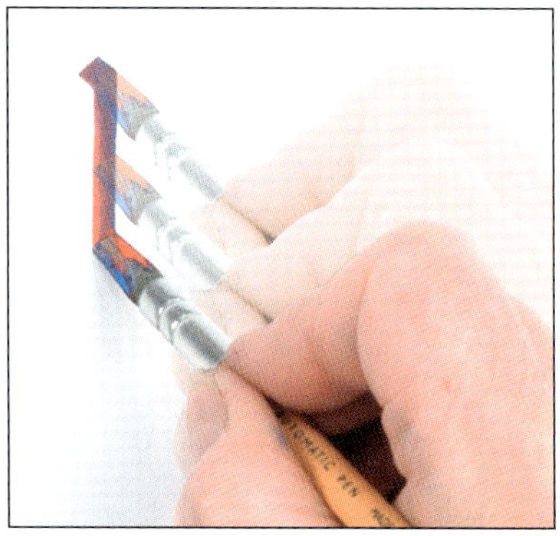

1 Start the ascender with a serif then pull the pen downwards to the baseline.

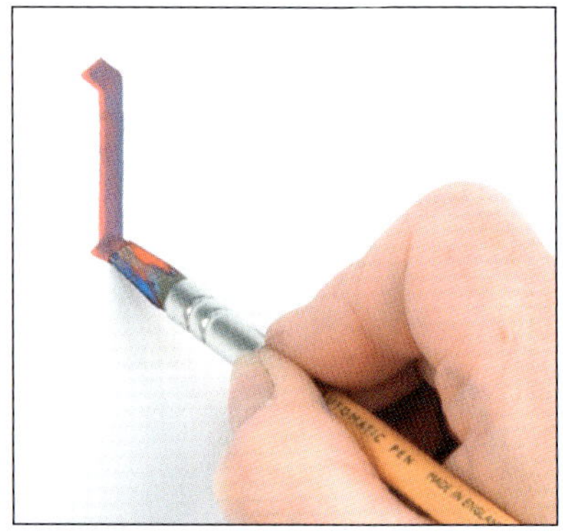

2 Finish the downstroke with a diamond serif.

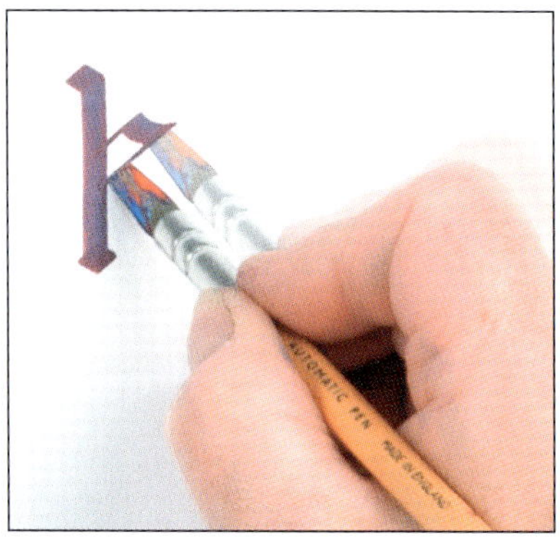

3 Form the counter by keeping the pen angle at 45 degrees. Notice the slight curve in the thick edge.

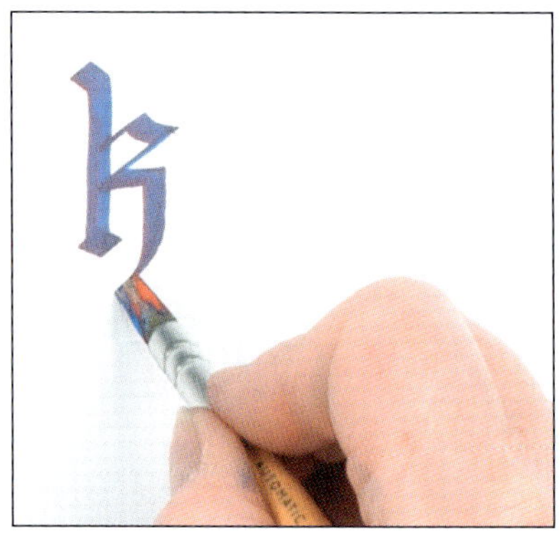

4 With the pen at the same angle, pull it to the right then downwards. Taper slightly to the left to achieve a softer tail.

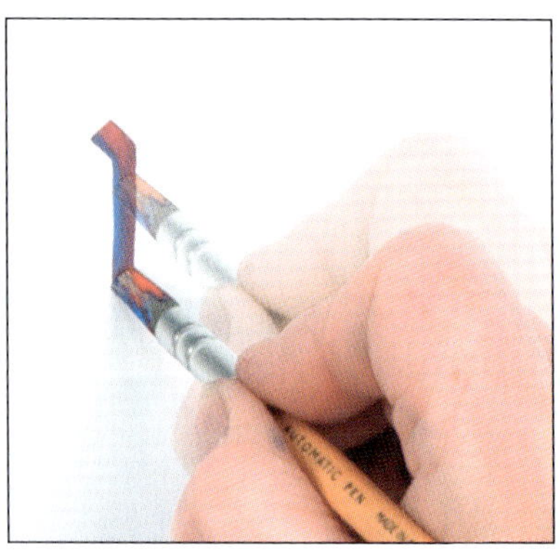

1 Start the ascender with a serif, pulling the pen from left to right. Stop the downstroke above the baseline.

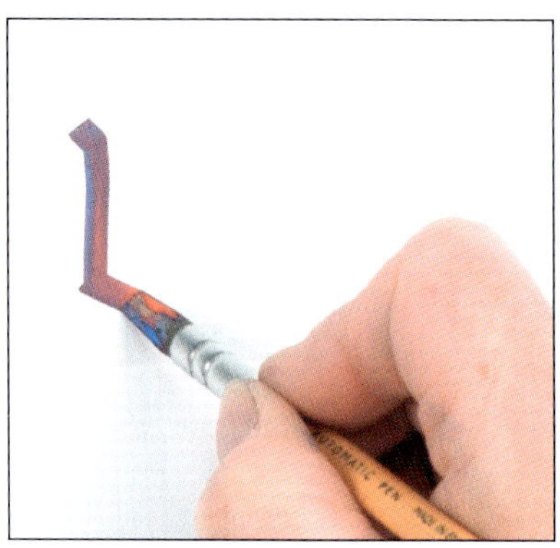

2 Make a long foot for the base of the bowl, stopping on the baseline.

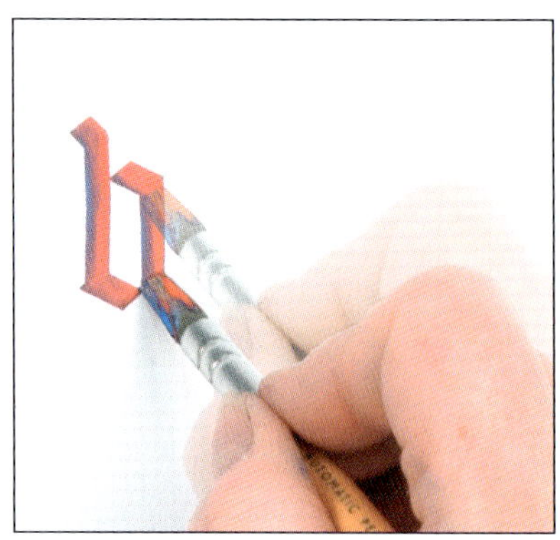

3 Working from above half way, complete the bowl. This should relate to the 'o'.

straight-stroke letters – i

The letters in this group are based around a vertical downstroke. They are 'f', 'i', 'j' and 'l'.

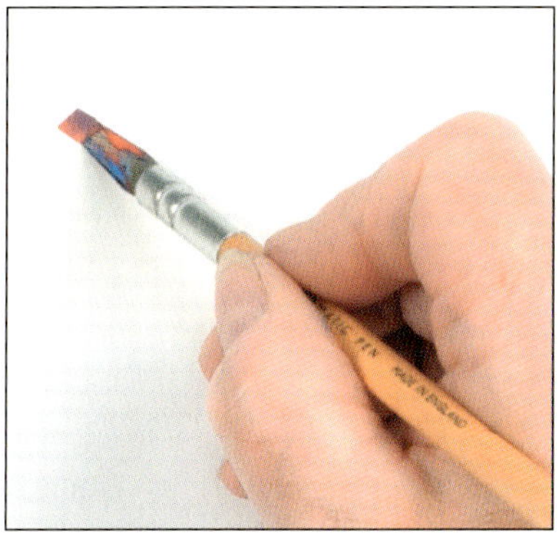

1 Start the letter with a 45-degree pen angle to make a diamond serif.

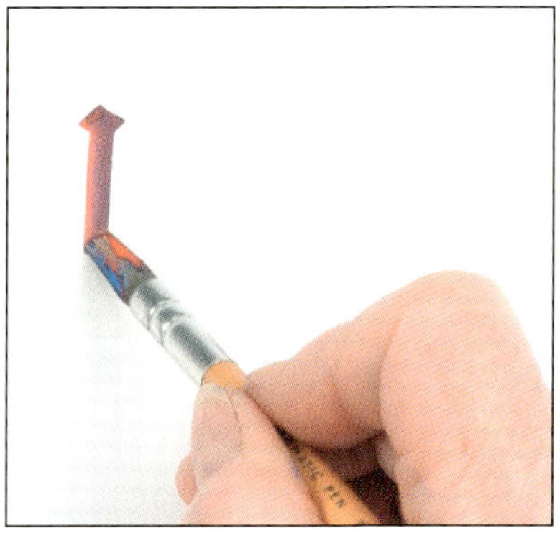

2 Place the nib in the centre of the serif and pull the pen straight down to just above the baseline.

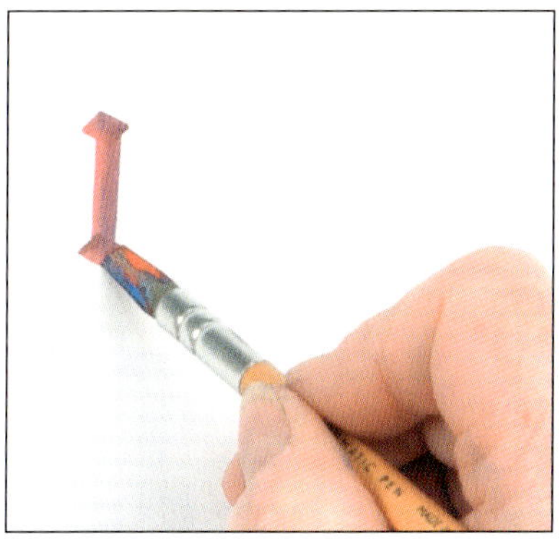

3 Add another diamond serif to finish the downstroke, again at 45 degrees.

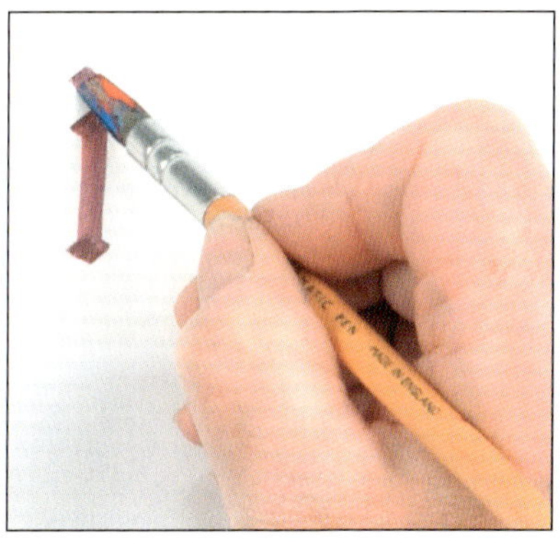

4 Finish the letter by adding a diamond-shaped dot at the same angle as the serifs.

Stroke reminder

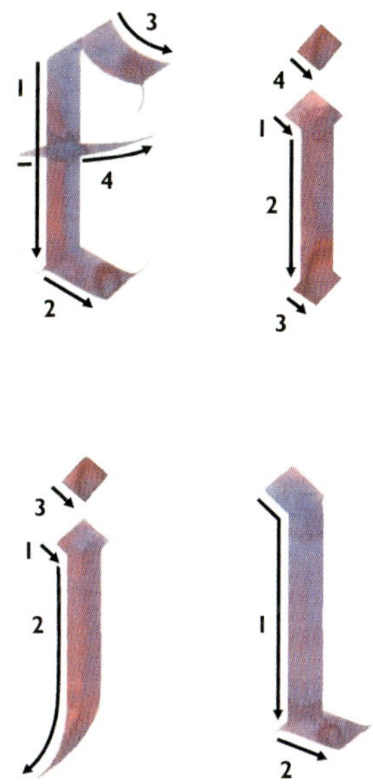

putting it all together

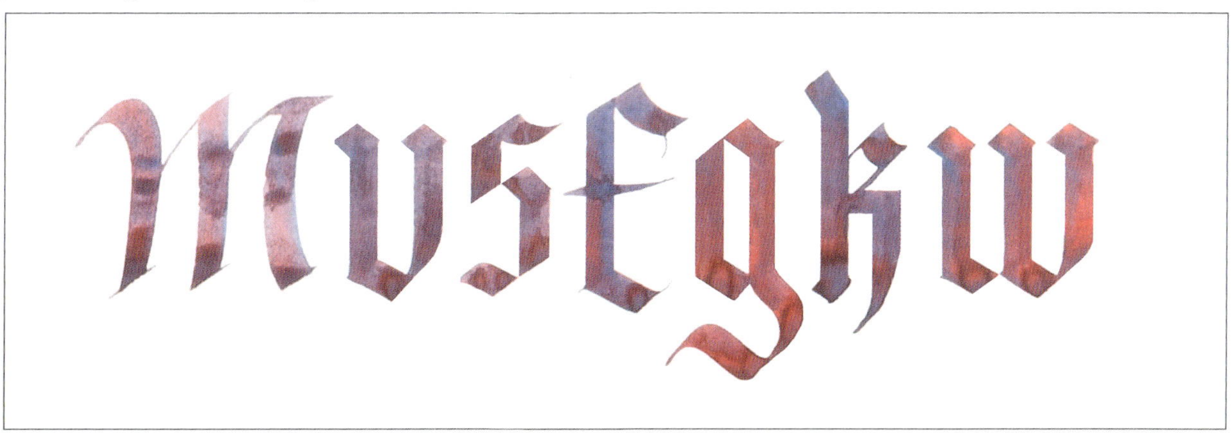

exceptions – s

Some letters belong to no particular group. They are 's', 'x' and 'z'.

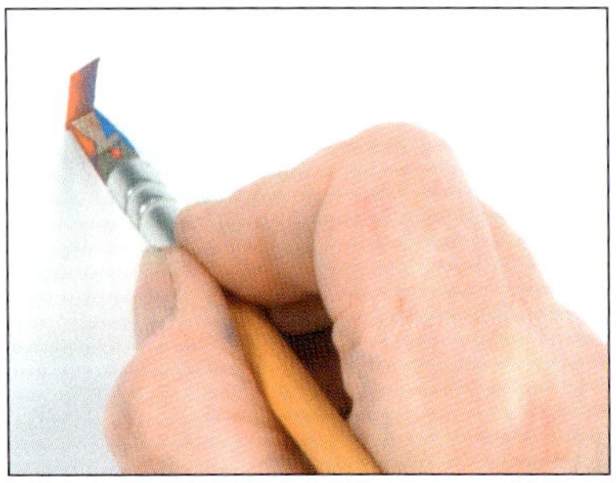

1 Start the stroke on the first 'curve' of the 's', just below the top line.

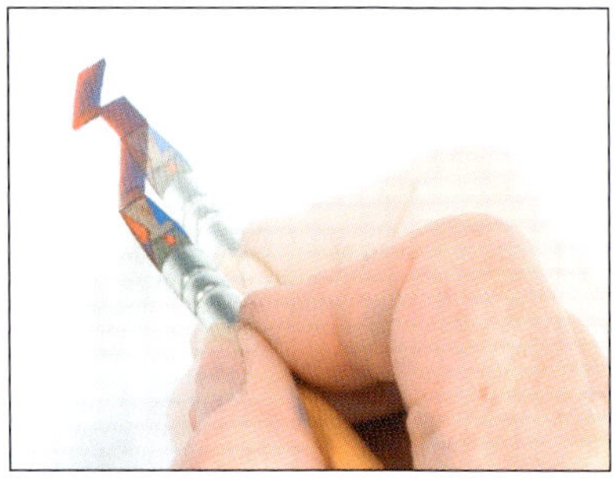

2 Push the pen diagonally upwards, followed by two downstrokes.

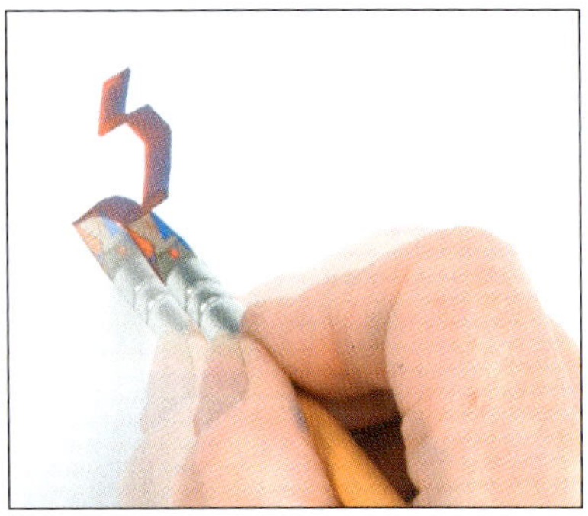

3 Draw the bottom stroke, finishing just above the baseline. Work from the left to add the bottom curved stroke.

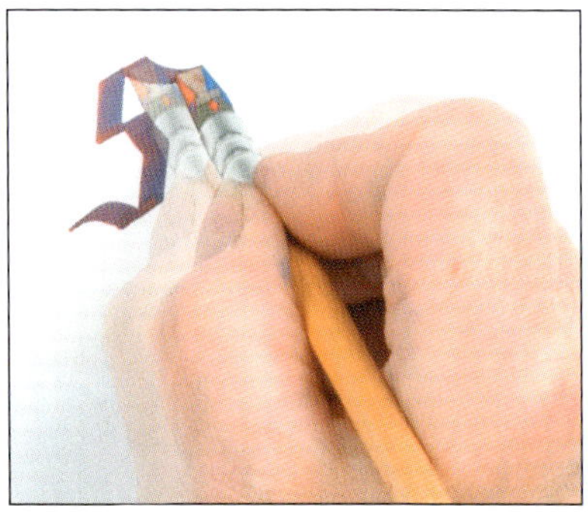

4 The top of the letter is also curved. Work from the left to draw this. Align the letter at the front.

Stroke reminder

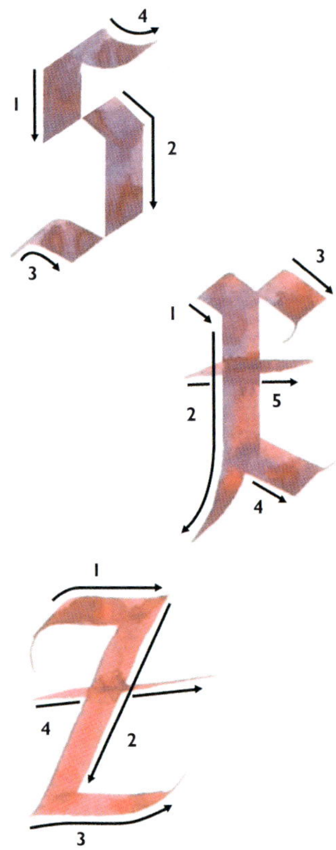

letters based on 'u' – v

The letter 'u' forms the basis for the group comprised of 'u', 'v', 'w' and 'y'.

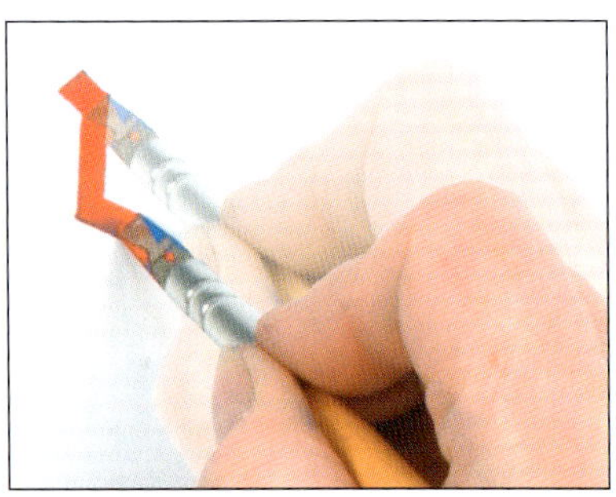

1 Start the letter with a serif then add a downward stroke to just above the baseline. Finish the first half of the letter with an elongated serif to form the long foot.

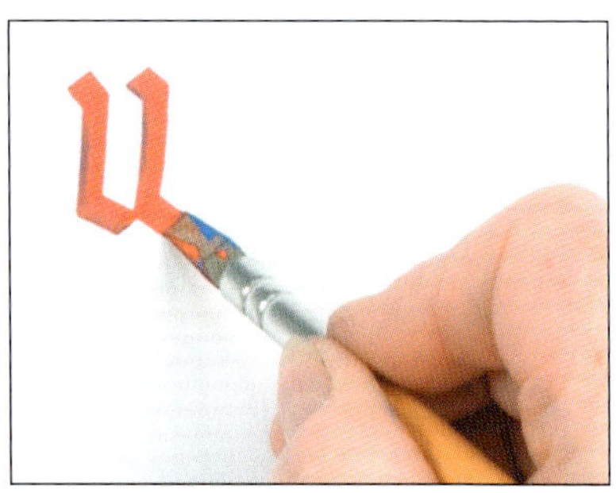

2 Repeat the downstroke, bringing the pen down to touch the edge of the foot of the first downstroke.

Stroke reminder

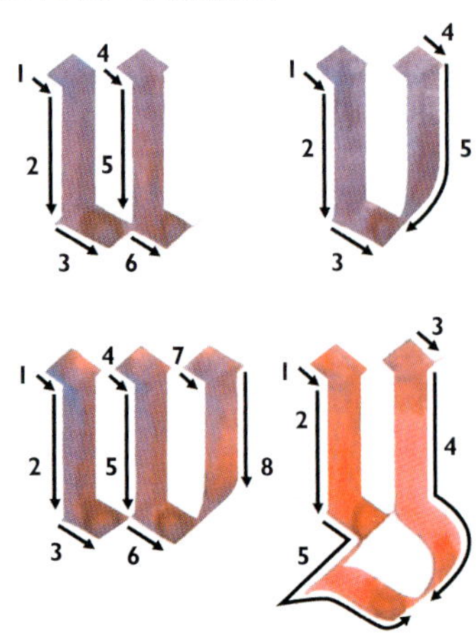

Gothic capitals

The capital letters in the Gothic hand are also known as 'majuscules'. The letters have more strokes than the lower case letters (the 'minuscules'), which produces a decorative script.

rounded letters – Q and E

The rounded letters are based on the 'O' and are 'C', 'E', 'G', 'O', 'Q' and 'T'.

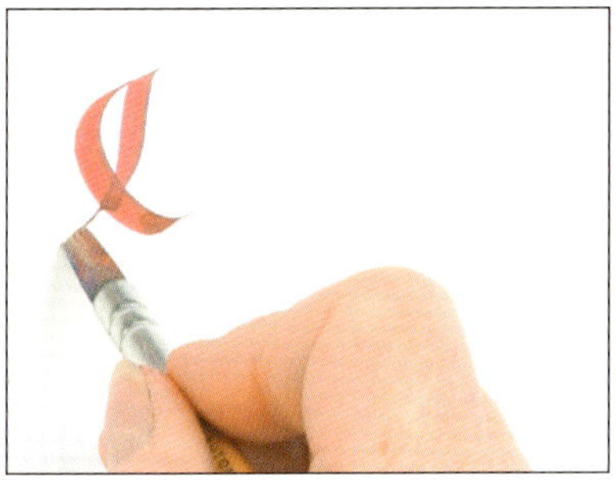

1 Make a wide, generous arc for the first stroke. Add a second stroke from the top, tapering to the left.

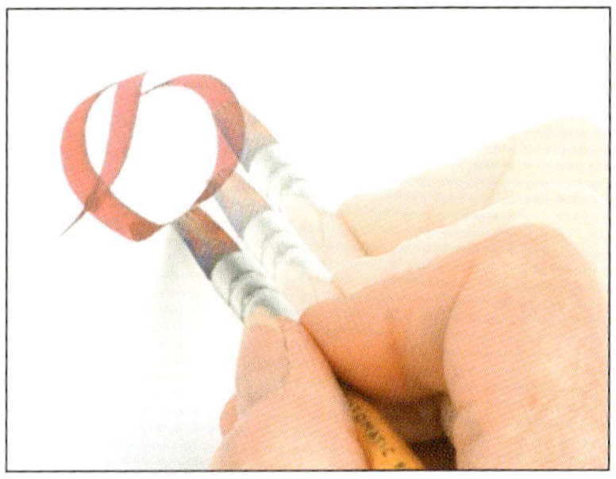

2 Add another wider, rounded arc. This stroke is left open – it does not touch the first arc.

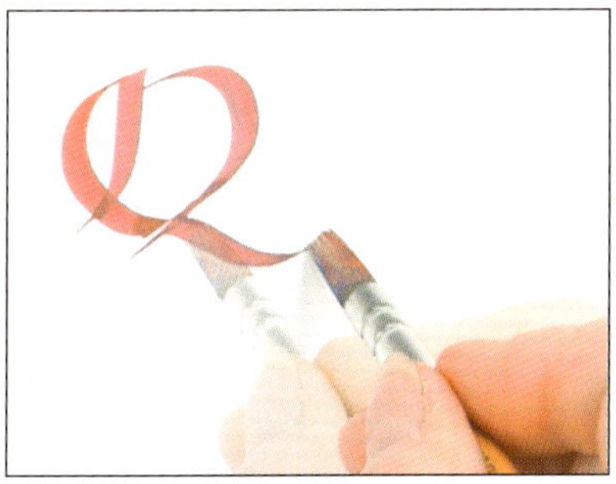

3 Add a long tail, which continues the line of the first arc, then tapers upwards.

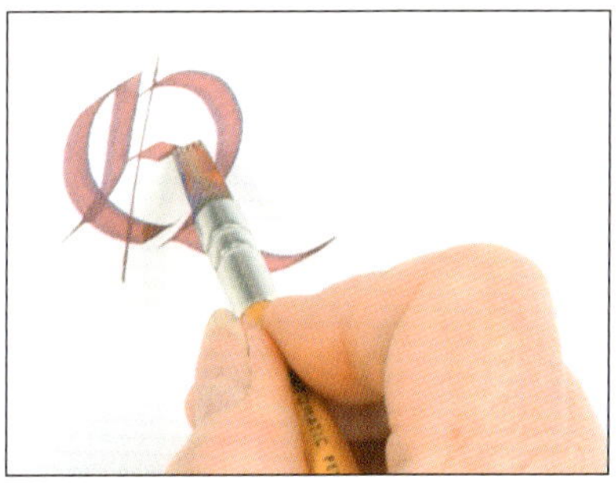

4 To finish the letter, add a vertical hairline and then a diamond that touches it, both in the middle of the bowl.

Stroke reminder

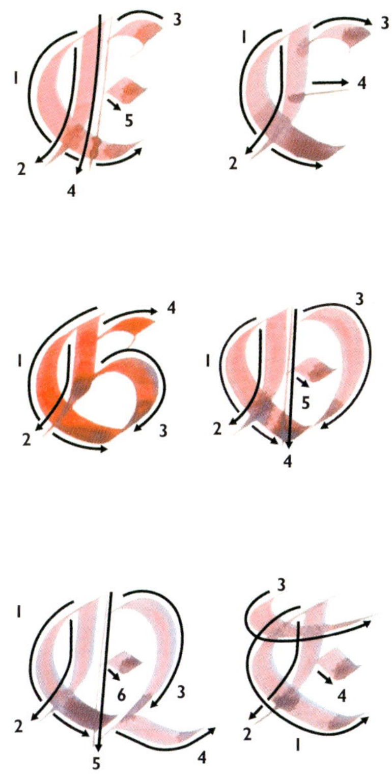

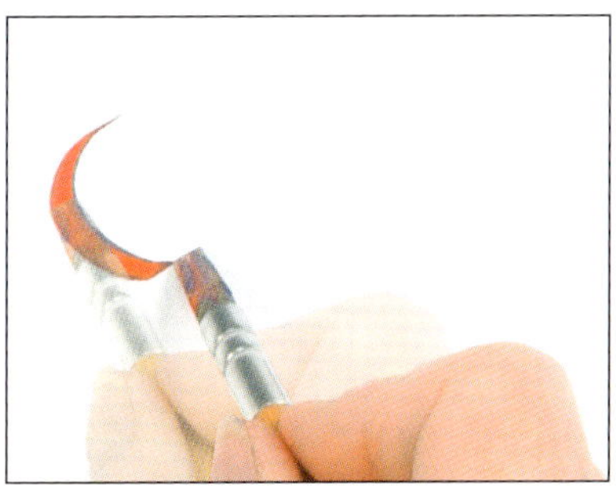

1 As with the 'Q', make a wide, generous arc to complete the first stroke.

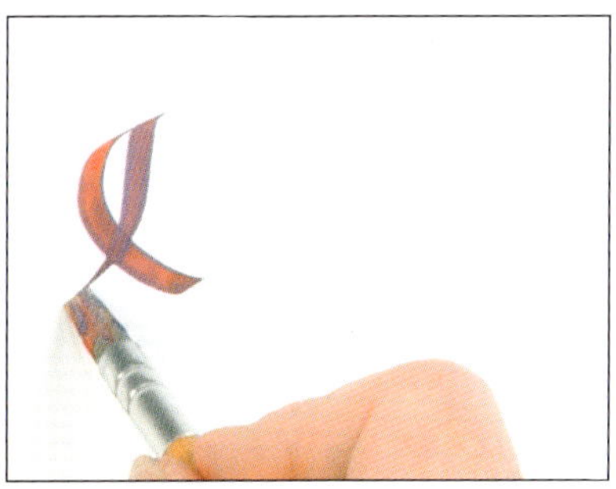

2 Starting from the top, pull the pen straight down, then taper to the left just before you cross the first arc.

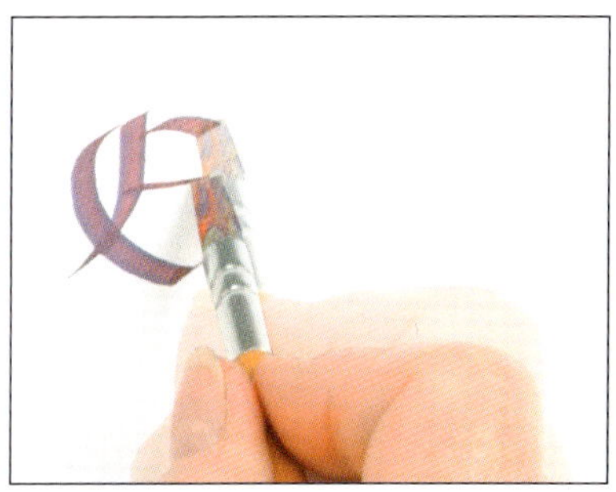

3 The top stroke is curved and the crossbar is straight. Both extend beyond the first arc.

diagonal letters – W

The diagonal letters are 'A', 'V', 'W', 'X', 'Y' and 'Z'.

Stroke reminder

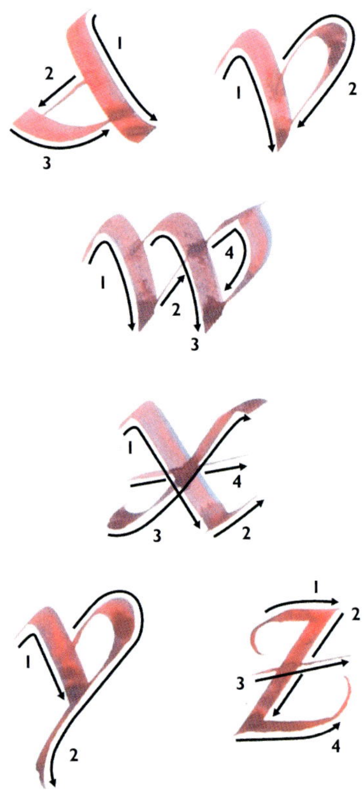

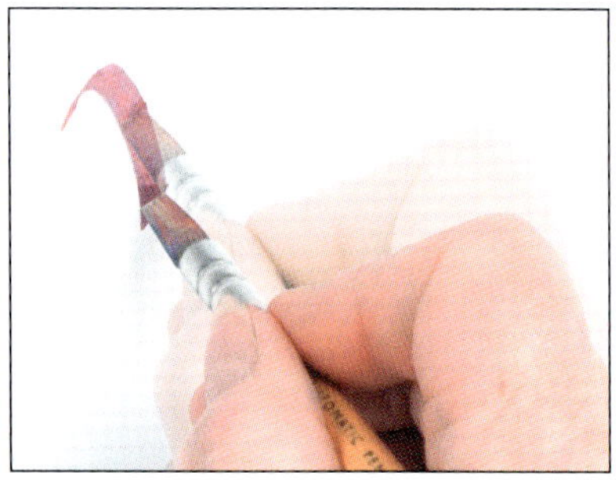

1 With the pen at 45 degrees, sweep the pen up then pull it down in a slight curve to the baseline.

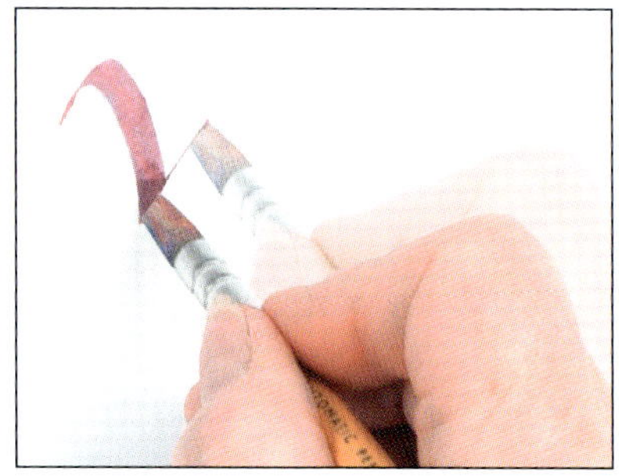

2 Add the second thin stroke, starting below the top line.

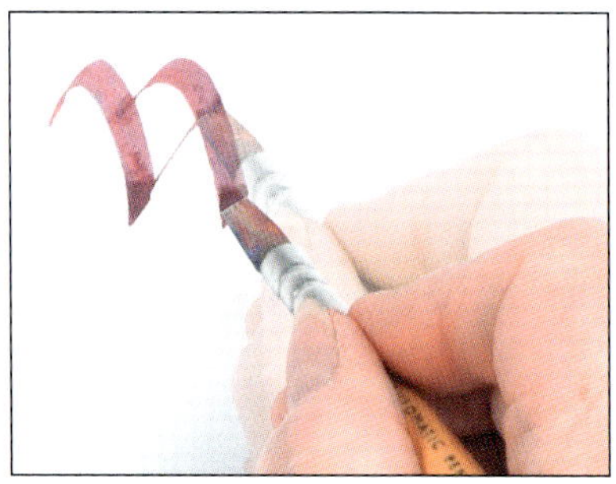

3 Repeat the first stroke so that it just touches the top of the second stroke on the way down.

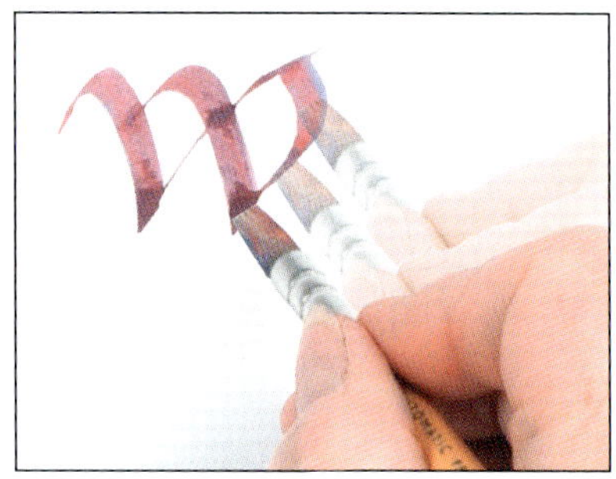

4 Without stopping, push the pen up then pull it down in a wide arc.

straight strokes with an arch – H

The letters in this group are 'F', 'H', 'K' and 'L'.

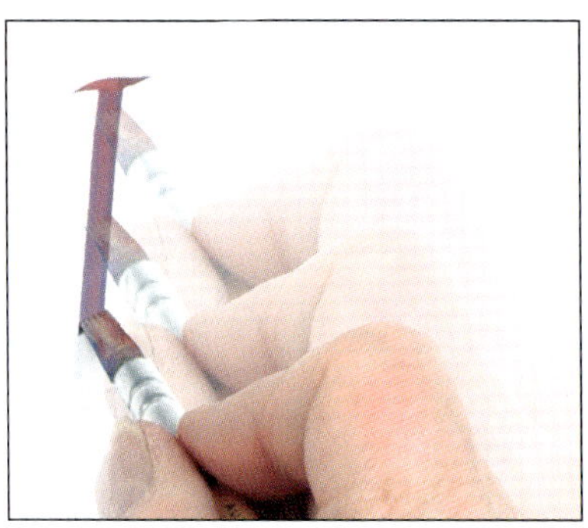

1 Start with a serif and from the mid-point, pull the pen down to the baseline.

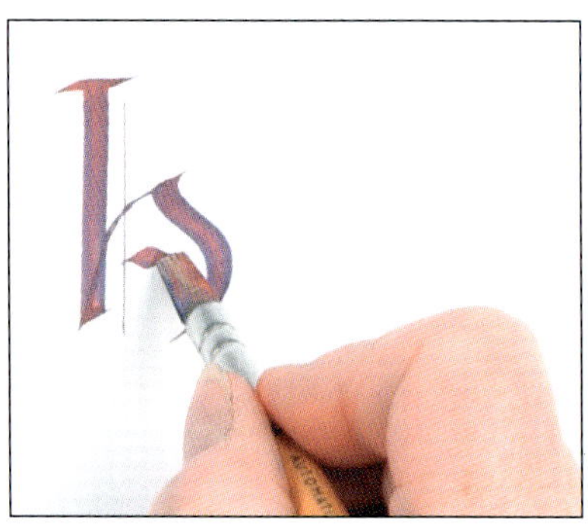

2 Draw a hairline arch, then add a wide curve to just below the baseline. Finish the letter by adding a vertical hairline together with a touching diamond.

Stroke reminder

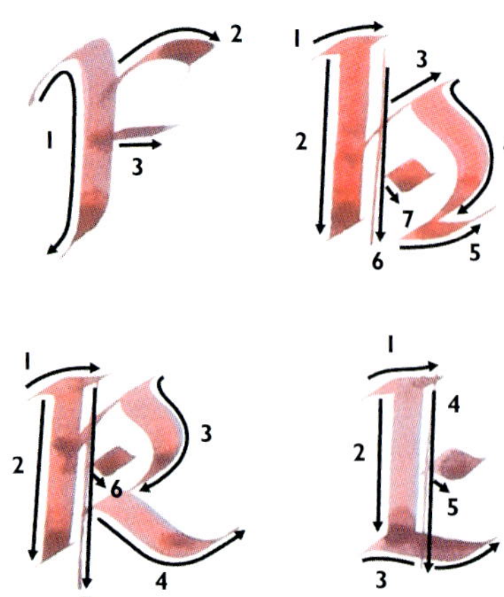

combinations – B

The combination letters are 'B', 'D', 'M', 'N', 'P', 'R' and 'U'.

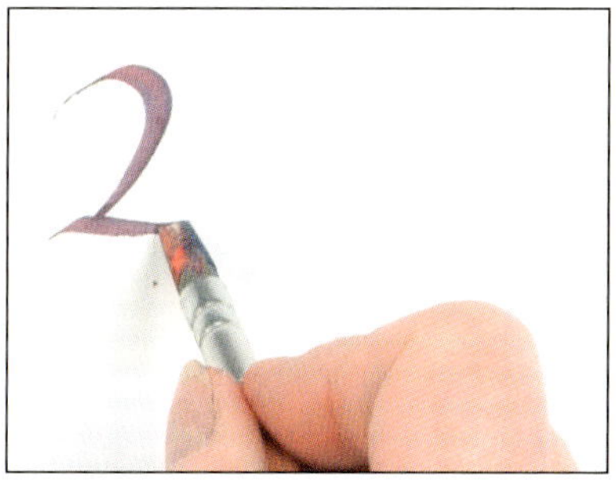

1 Sweep the pen around in a generous arc to the baseline. Make the baseline stroke.

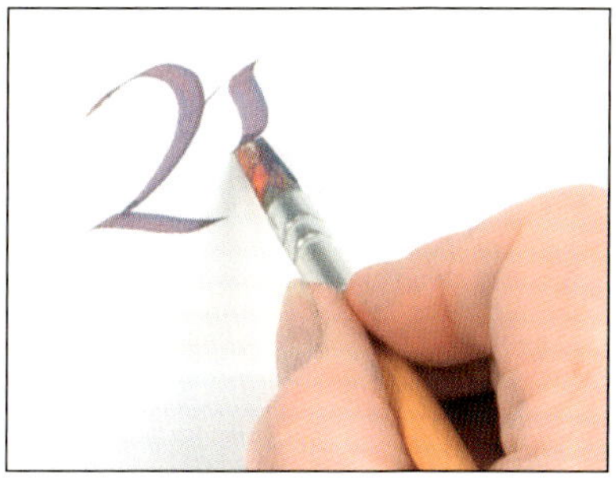

2 Work upwards then curve the pen down, tapering inwards slightly.

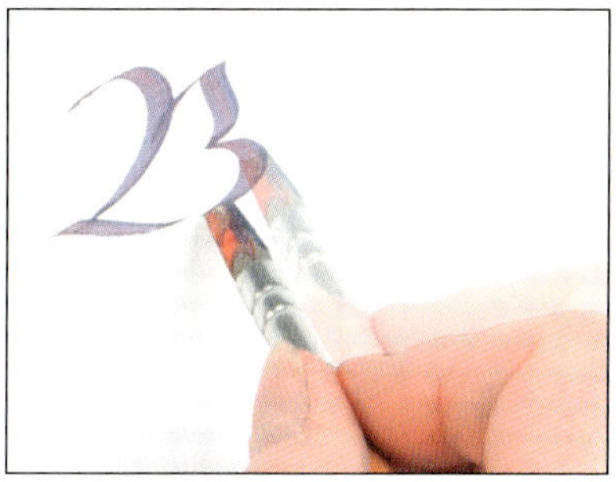

3 Then form a wide arc for the bottom bowl.

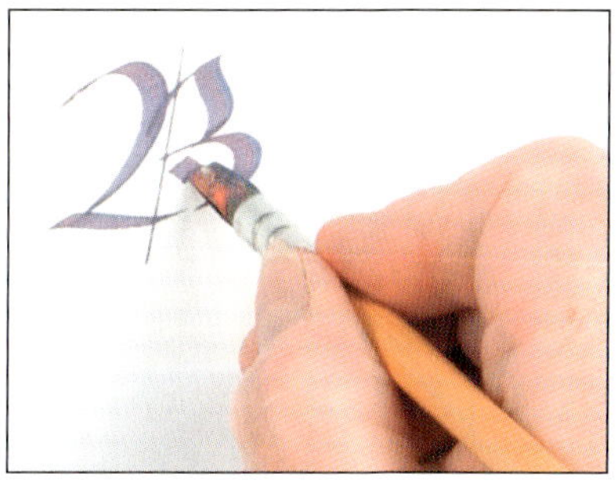

4 Add a hairline extending above and below the x-height and a diamond that just touches the hairline.

Stroke reminder

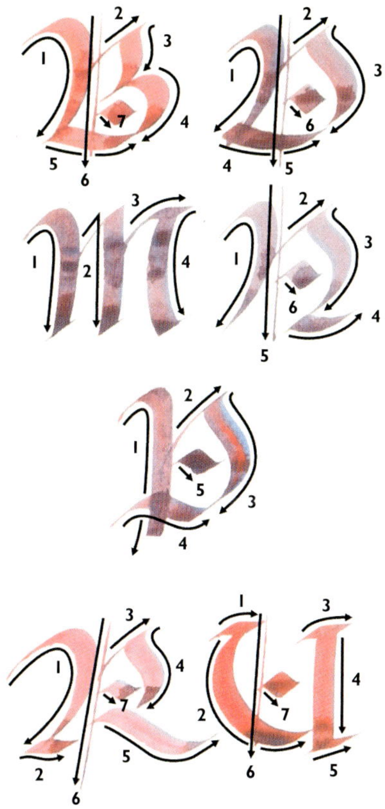

variants – S

The variants on the letterforms are 'I', 'J' and 'S'.

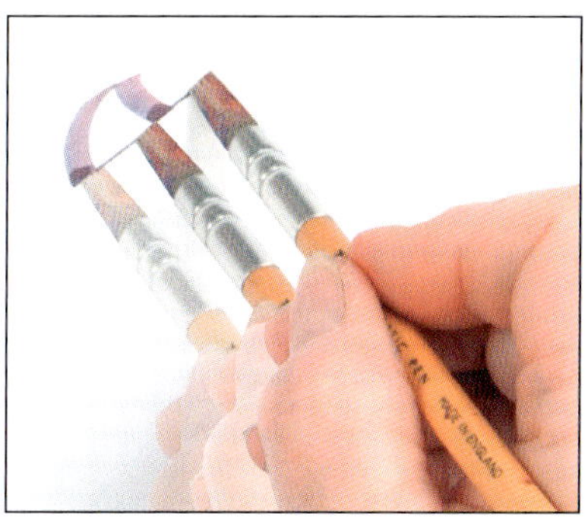

1 Form the top bowl by making a short curved stroke from the top line, then a wider one. Join the two with a hairline stroke.

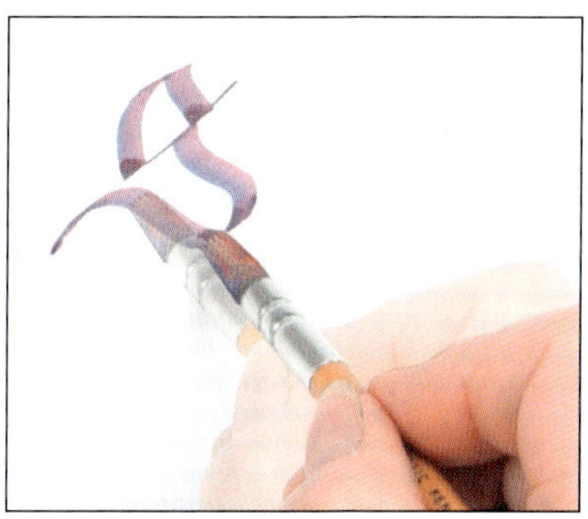

2 Next add a wide curve to form the first part of the tail. Finish the tail with a long curve. Then join this second half of the letter neatly to the first half.

Stroke reminder

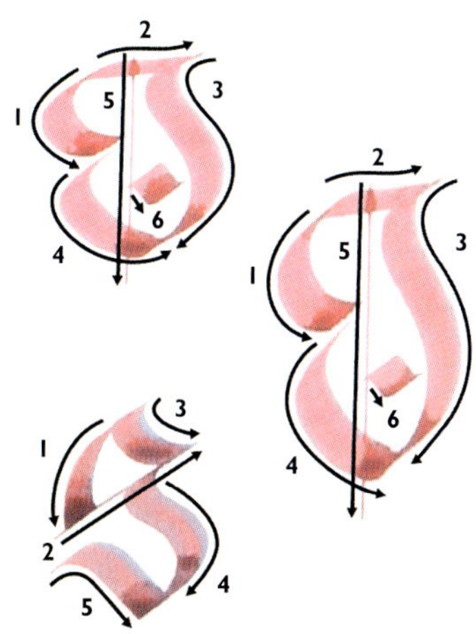

Italic

Italic is a flowing, rhythmical script developed during the Renaissance. It is a versatile, forward-sloping script that uses few pen lifts.

LOWER CASE

X-HEIGHT	5 nib widths
PEN ANGLE	45 degrees
LETTER SLOPE	5–10 degrees
FORM	Oval o
ASCENDERS	3–4 nib widths
DESCENDERS	3–4 nib widths
SERIF STYLE	Oval
SPACING	Equal spacing between letters. NI distance is almost the width of an N counter

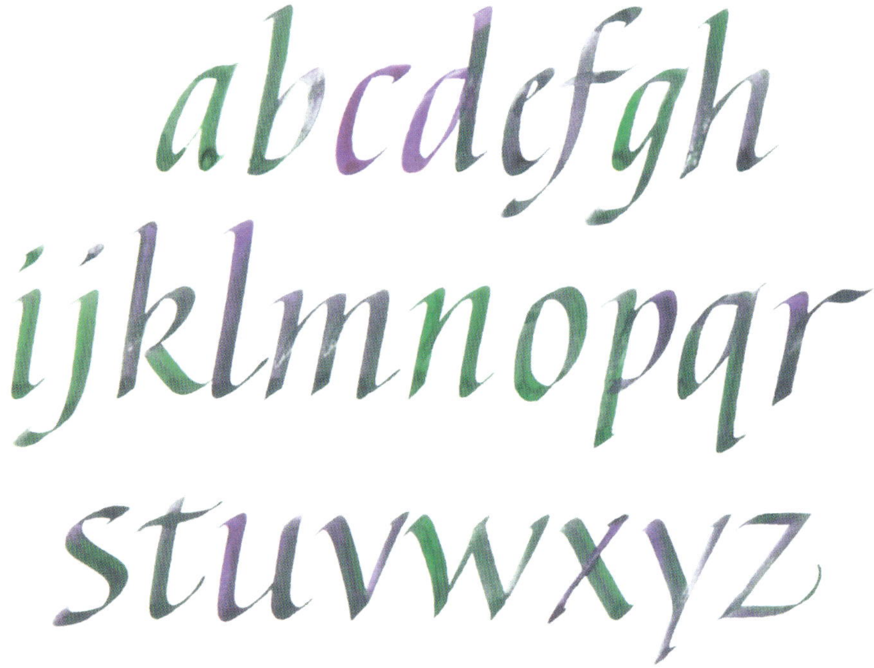

CAPITALS

X-HEIGHT	8 nib widths
PEN ANGLE	45 degrees
LETTER SLOPE	5–10 degrees
FORM	Oval O
ASCENDERS	3–4 nib widths
DESCENDERS	3–4 nib widths
SERIF STYLE	Oval
SPACING	Equal spacing between letters. N I distance is almost the width of an N counter

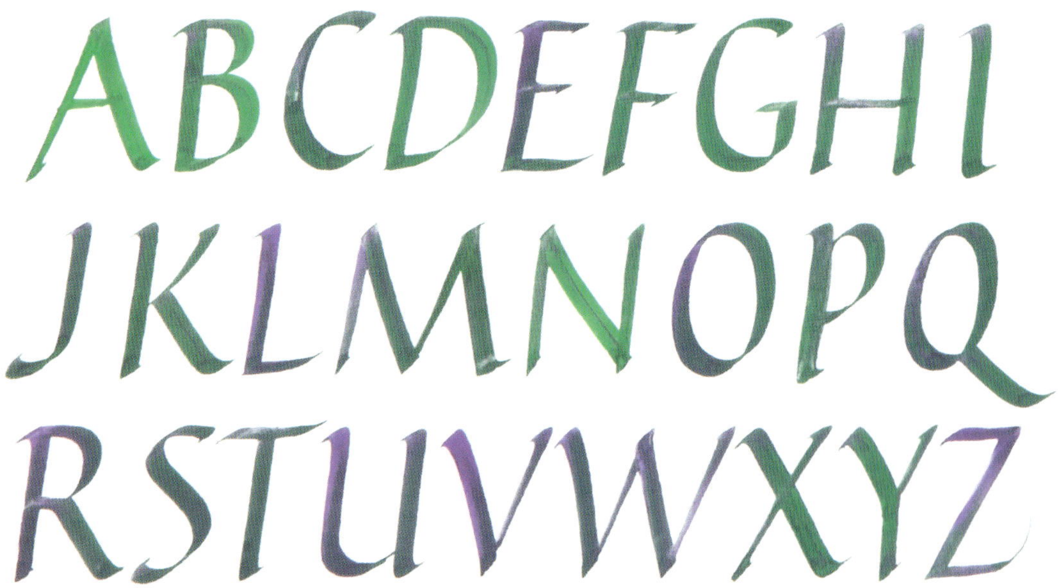

oval letters – o, c and e

The oval letters are based on the 'o'. The other letters in this group are 'c' and 'e'.

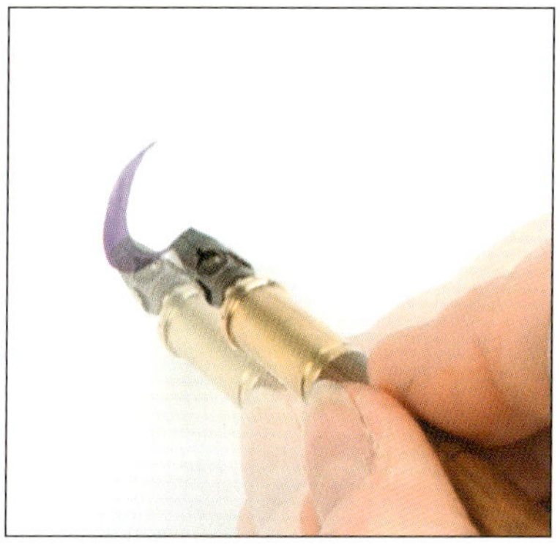

1 Start the first stroke with the nib at 45 degrees. The sides of the letter should be fairly flat curves.

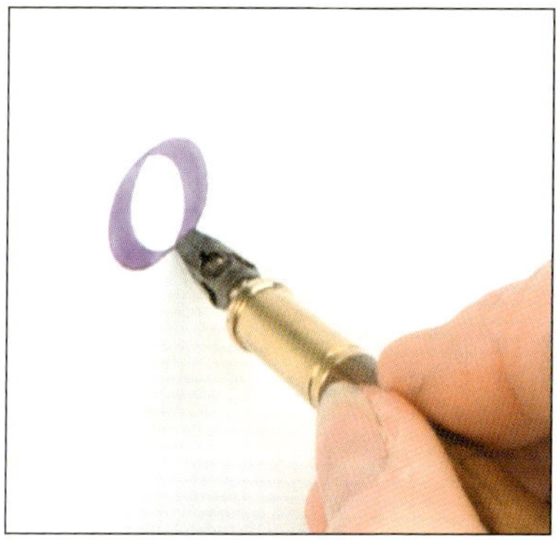

2 Mirror the same stroke on the other side, working clockwise and keeping the joins neat.

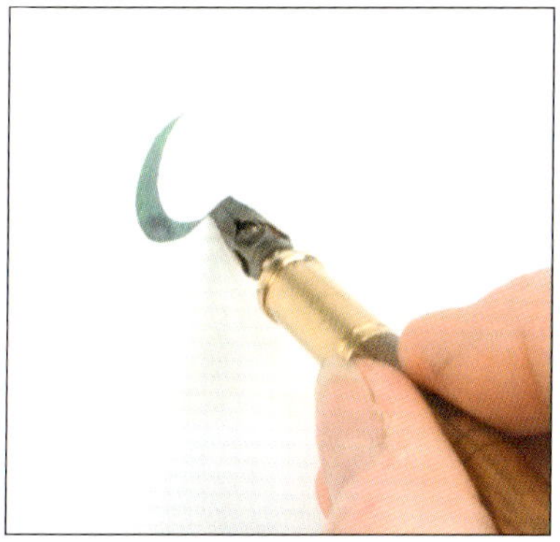

1 The first stroke of the 'c' is the same as the first stroke of the 'o', with a flattened back.

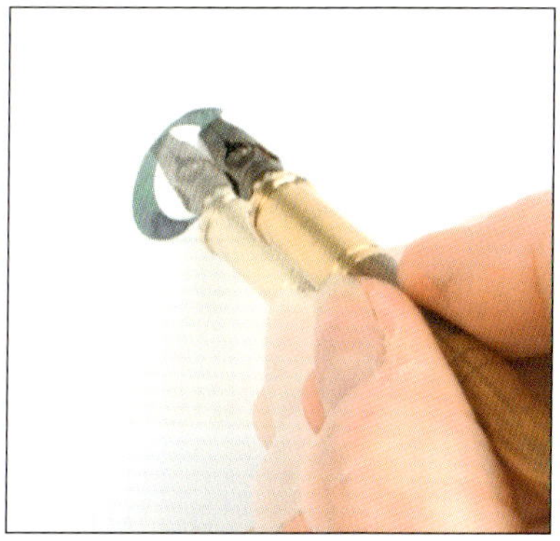

2 Add a stroke to form the top of the letter, which is almost flat.

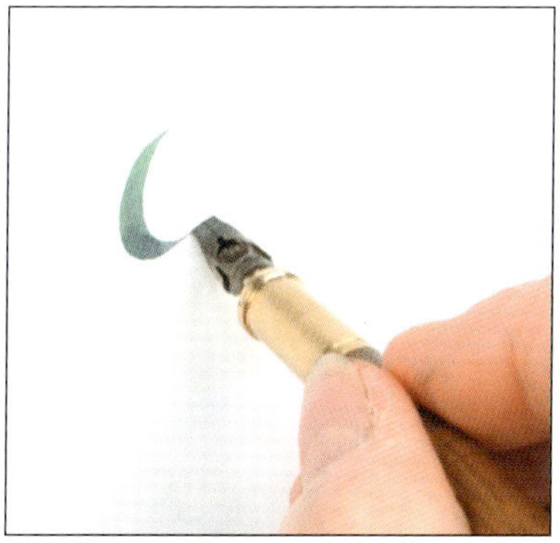

1 The first stroke of the 'e' starts in the same way as the 'o' and the 'c', with the pen at 45 degrees.

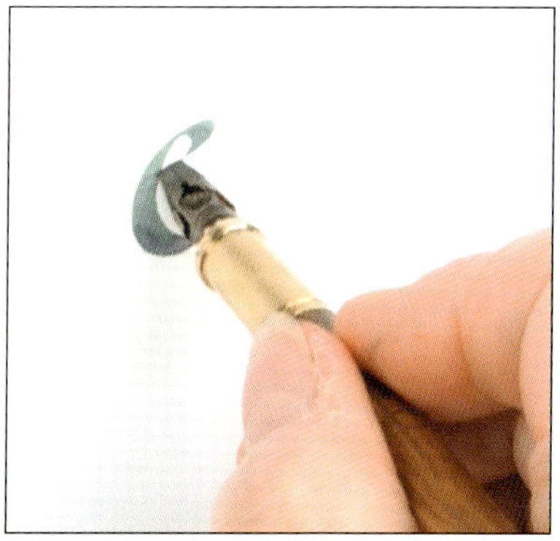

2 Working from the top, add the eye of the letter with a small, smooth loop. Keep the bowl above half way.

Stroke reminder

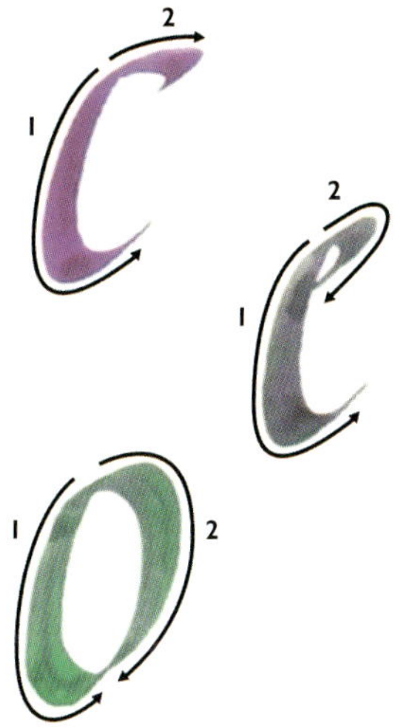

triangular letters – g and a

The letters in the triangular group are 'a', 'd', 'g' and 'q'.

Stroke reminder

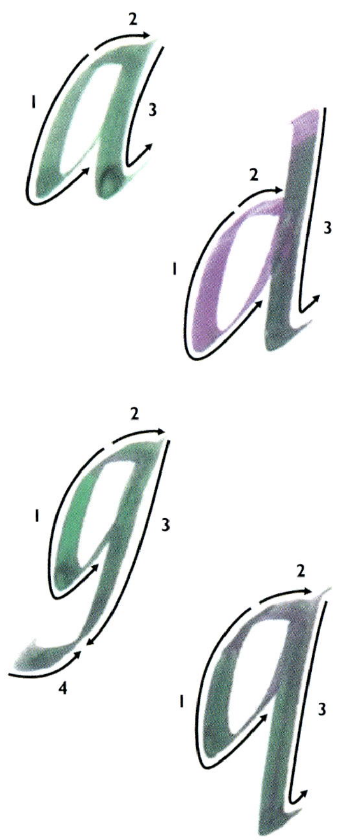

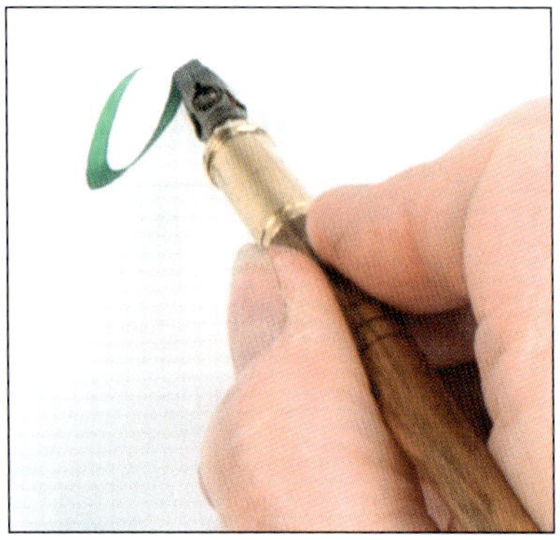

1 The first stroke is a subtle curve followed by a vertical downstroke. The upstroke is a mirror image.

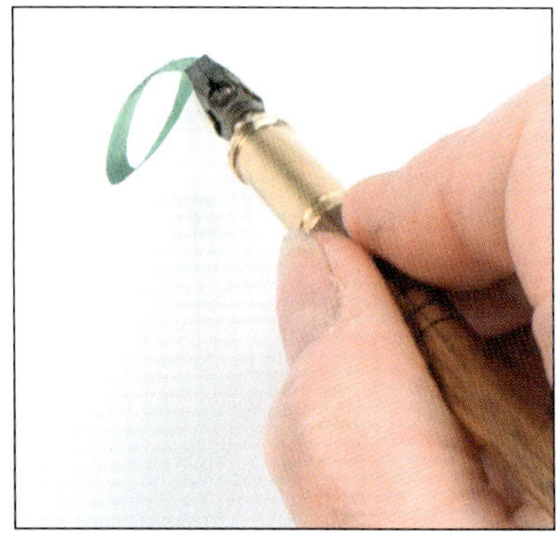

2 Add the top of the letter, which should be a flattened curve, starting at the top of the first stroke.

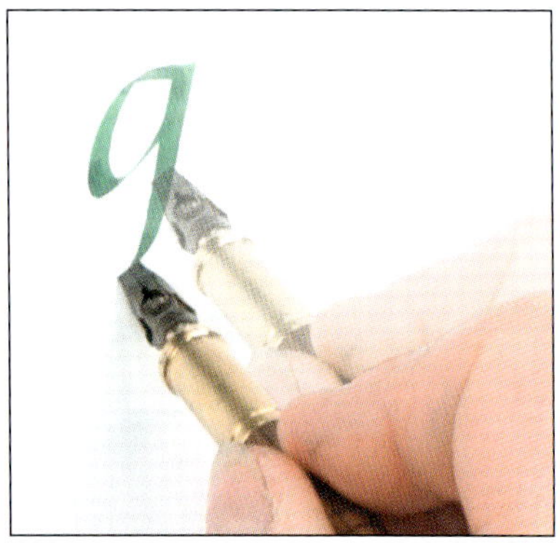

3 Pull the pen down at a slight angle to form the descender. Taper the stroke to the left.

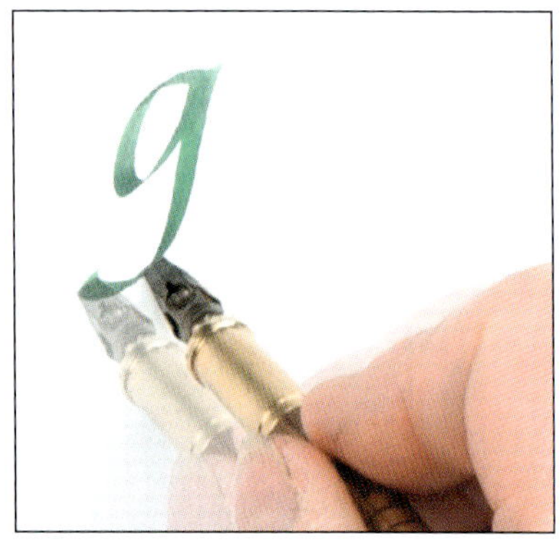

4 Working from left to right, finish the tail, starting with a serif and joining it to touch the end of the previous stroke.

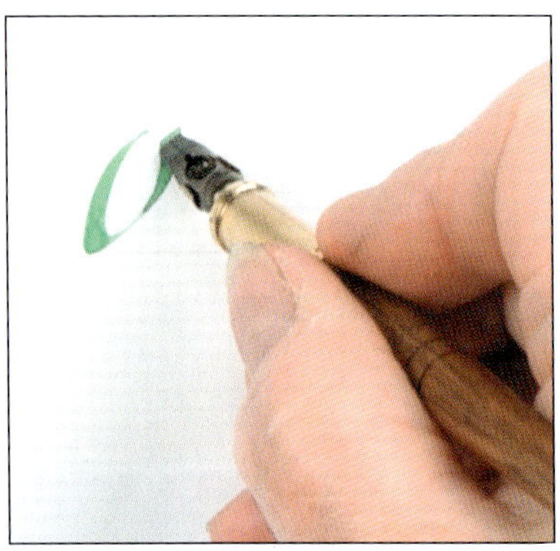

1 The first stroke of the letter is the same as the letter 'g', with a subtle curve, downstroke and upstroke.

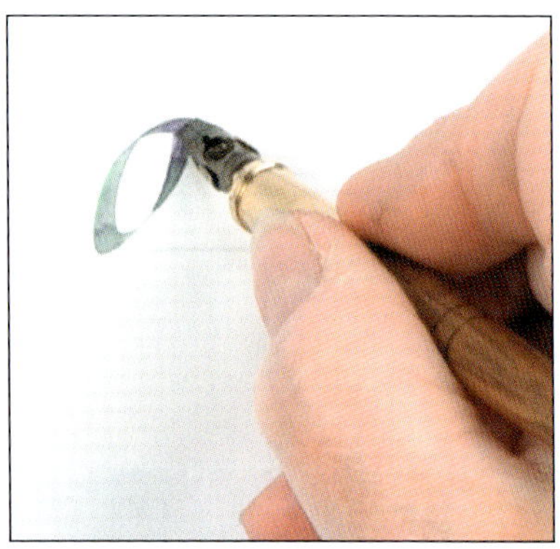

2 Add in the top of the letter, which should be a flattened curve. Start at the top of the first stroke.

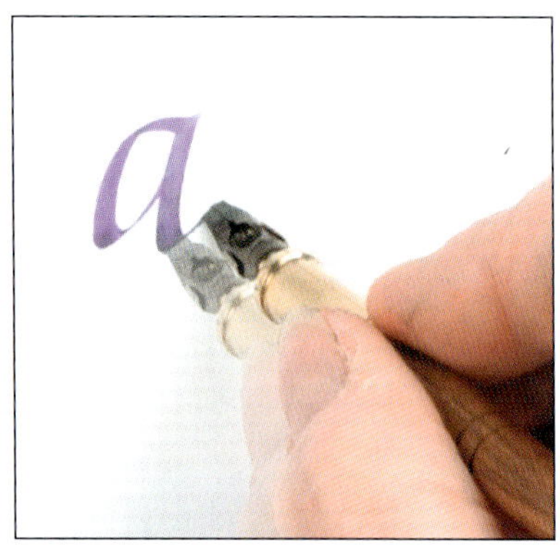

3 Add the downstroke to the baseline, followed by a smooth upstroke to finish.

clockwise arches – b, h and m

The clockwise arches are 'b', 'h', 'i', 'k', 'm', 'n', 'p' and 'r'.

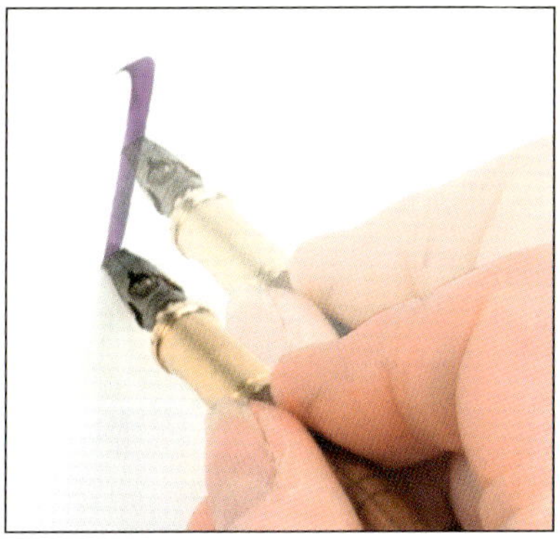

1 Start the downstroke with an oval serif. Pull the pen down to the baseline.

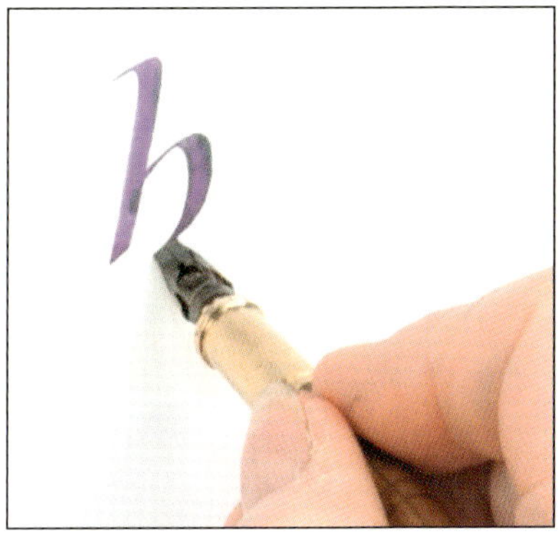

2 Spring the arch upwards then flatten the curve as you bring the pen down. Relate the width of the arch and curve to the 'n'.

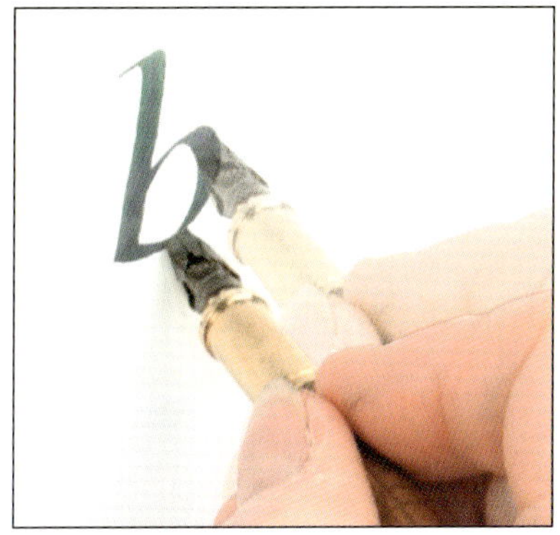

3 Working from the bottom of the first downstroke, complete the bowl with a follow-through curve.

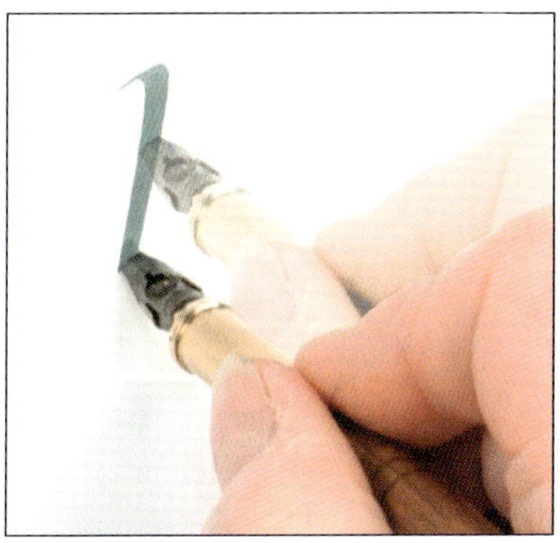

1 Like the 'b', start the downstroke with an oval serif.

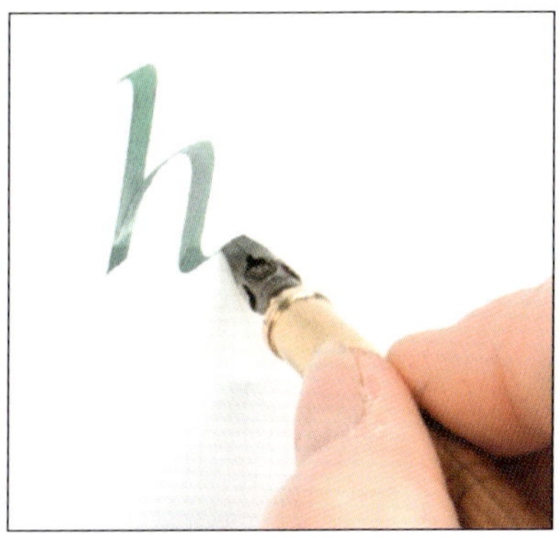

2 Keep your pen on the paper as you form the springing arch, then pull the pen downwards. Finish with a serif.

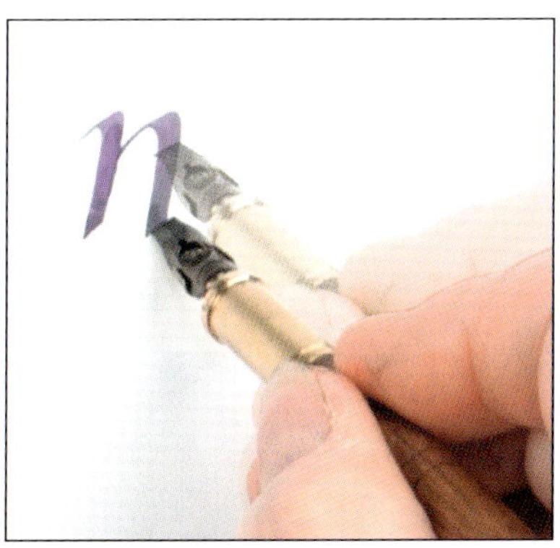

1 Start the first downstroke with a serif. Spring the arch upwards then pull the pen down parallel to the first stroke.

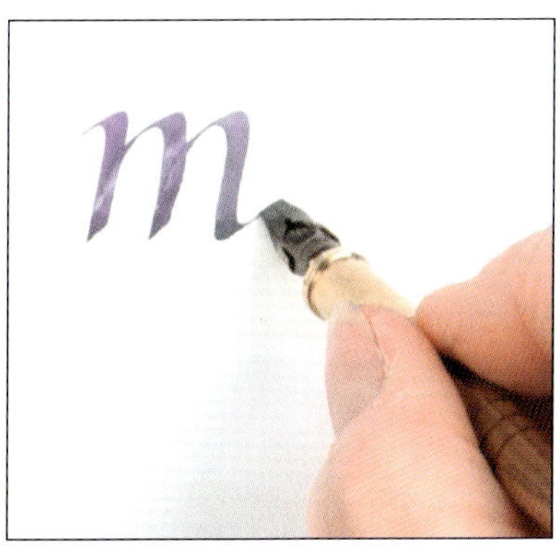

2 In the same movement, spring the second arch to look the same as the first. Finish with a serif.

Stroke reminder

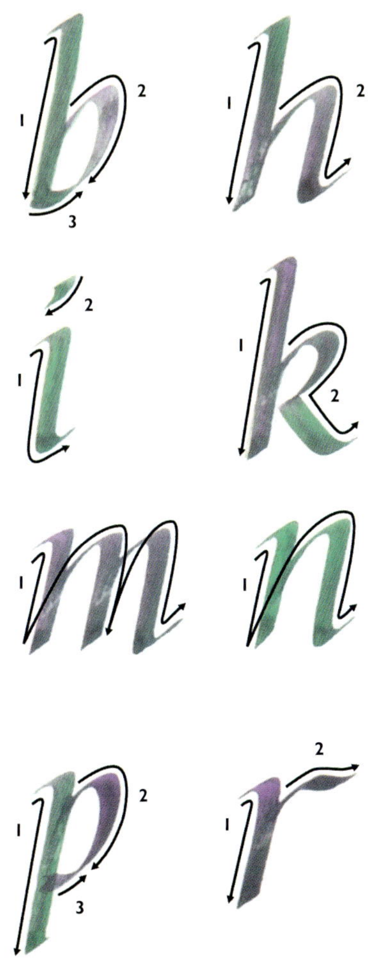

anti-clockwise arches – u

There are only three anti-clockwise arches – 'l', 't' and 'u'.

Stroke reminder

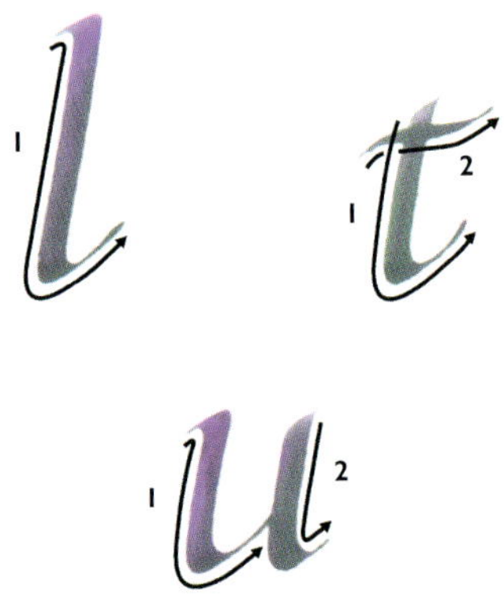

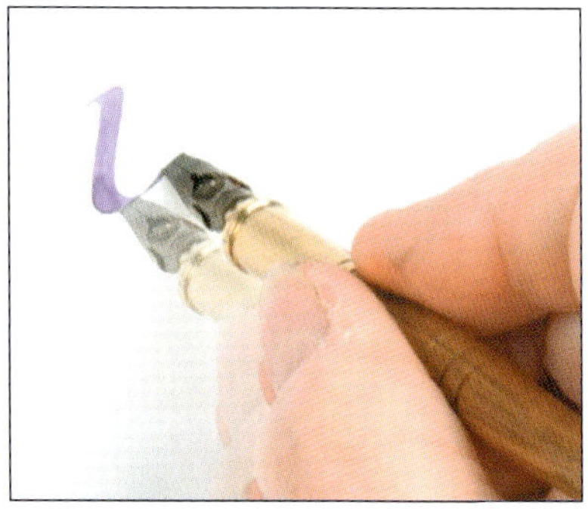

1 Start the stroke with a serif, pull the pen downwards then curve upwards, all in one movement.

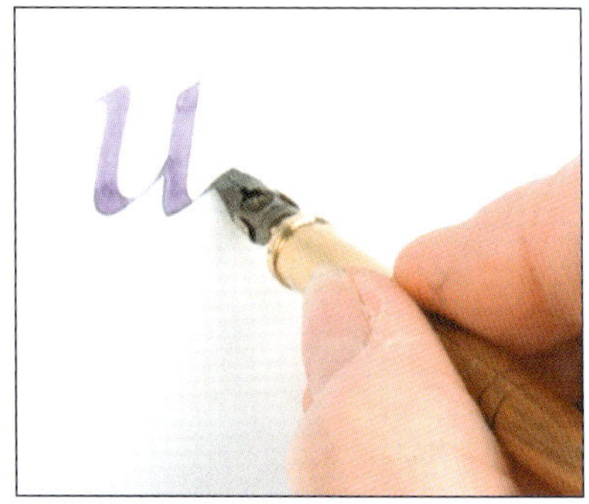

2 Start the second stroke at the top of the line. Keep the stroke parallel to the first. Finish with a serif.

related tops and base curves – f

The three letters in this group are 'f', 'j' and 's'.

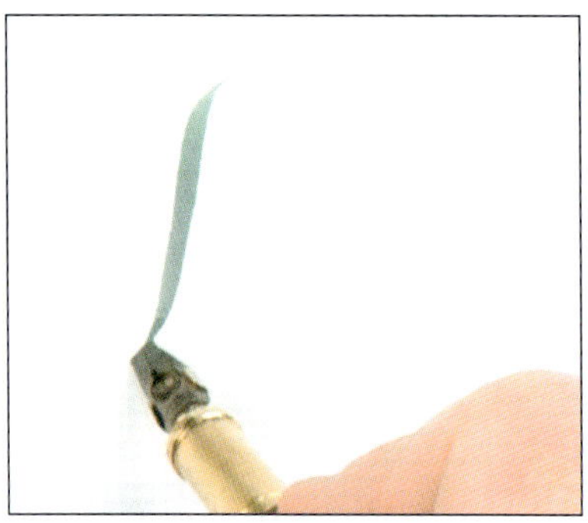

1 Start the downstroke with the pen at 45 degrees. Pull the pen down smoothly to form a slight curve.

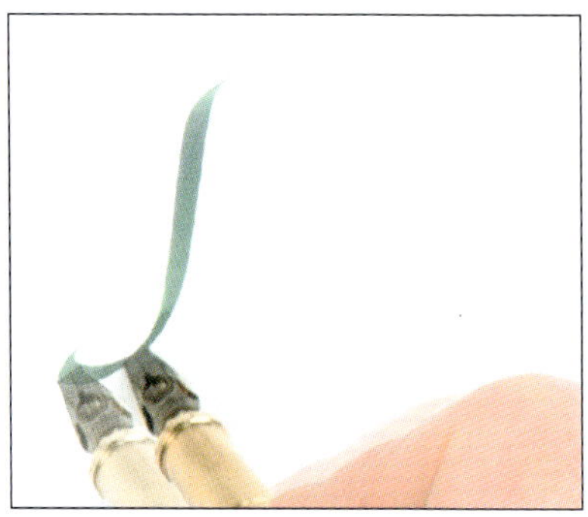

2 Working from left to right, start with a serif then join the tail to the end of the downstroke.

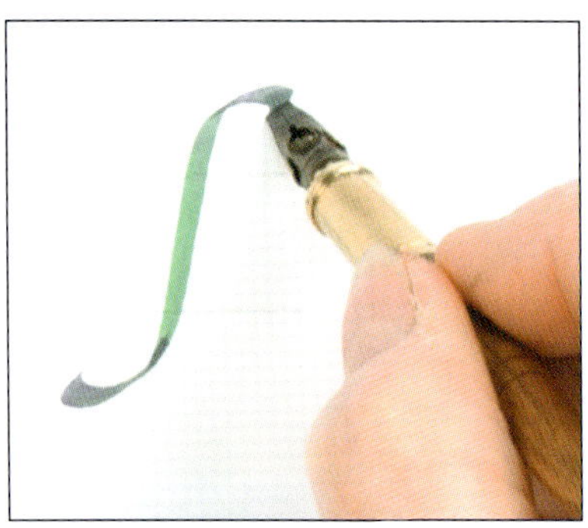

3 Create the top counter, making a spacious, flowing join. Make sure that your pen angle is consistent.

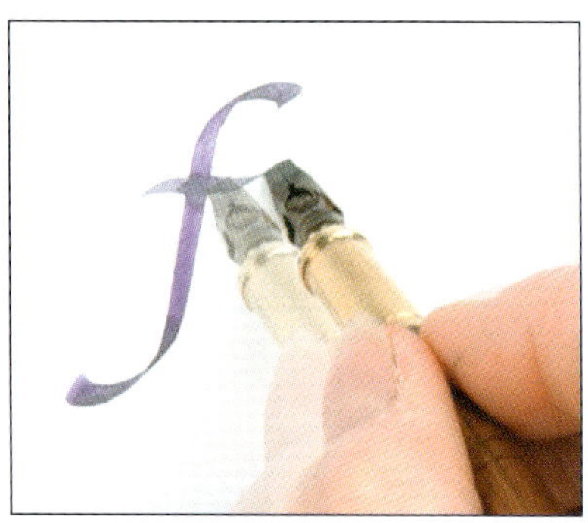

4 Finish the letter with the crossbar that comes on, or slightly below, the line.

Stroke reminder

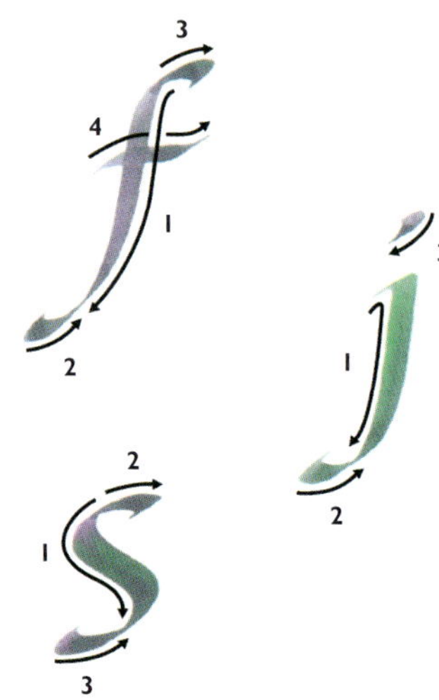

diagonal letters – y and x

The last five letters in the alphabet – 'v', 'w', 'x', 'y' and 'z' – make up this group.

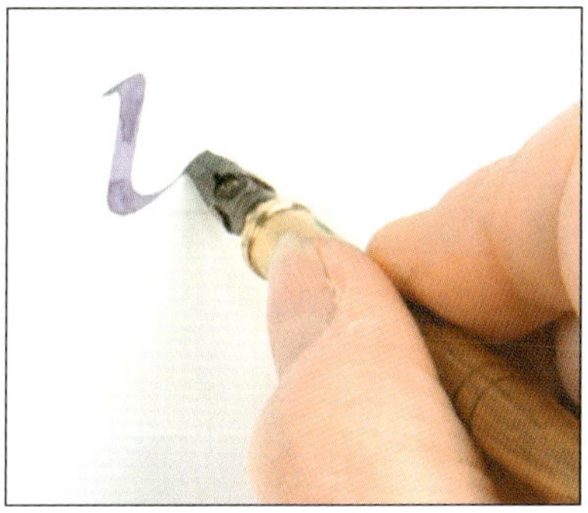

1 As with the 'u', start the stroke with a serif, pull the pen downwards then curve upwards, all in one movement.

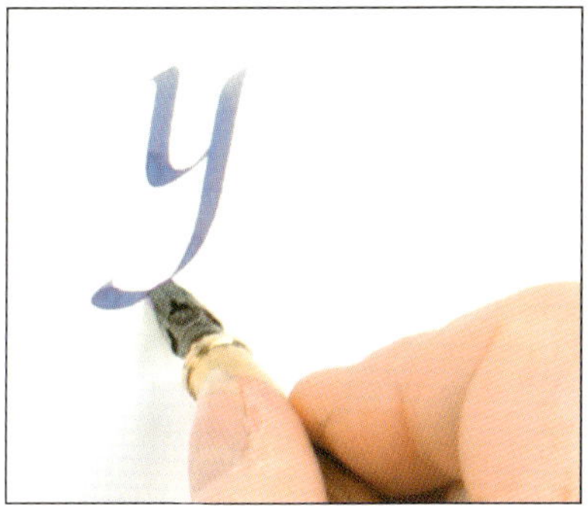

2 The next stroke is parallel to the first, and tapers below the baseline. Finish the tail with a serif and a flattened curve.

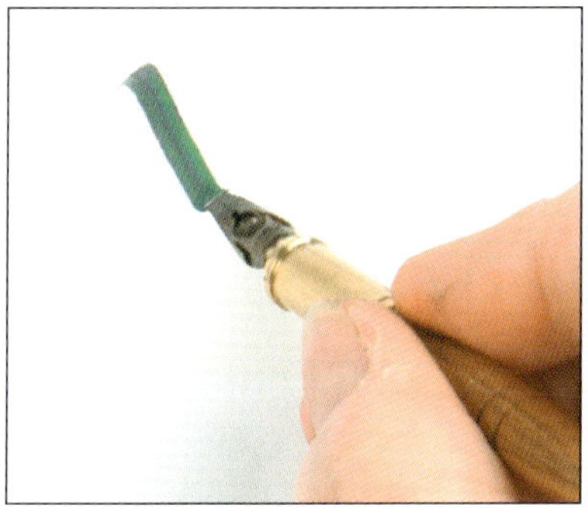

1 With the pen at 45 degrees, start with a small serif then pull down, finishing with another small serif.

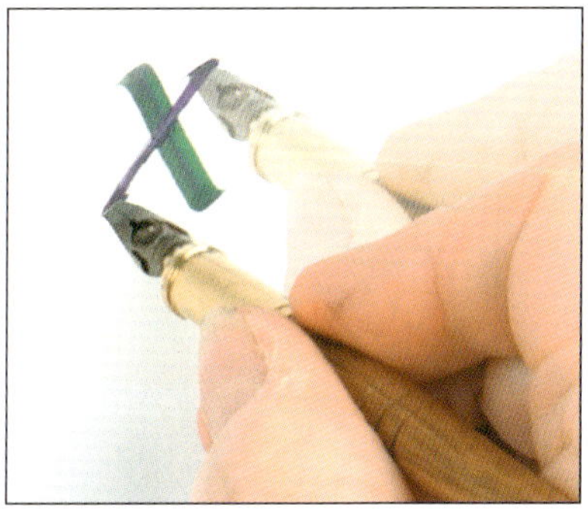

2 The second, slightly flatter, stroke should cross the first stroke just above the half-way point.

Stroke reminder

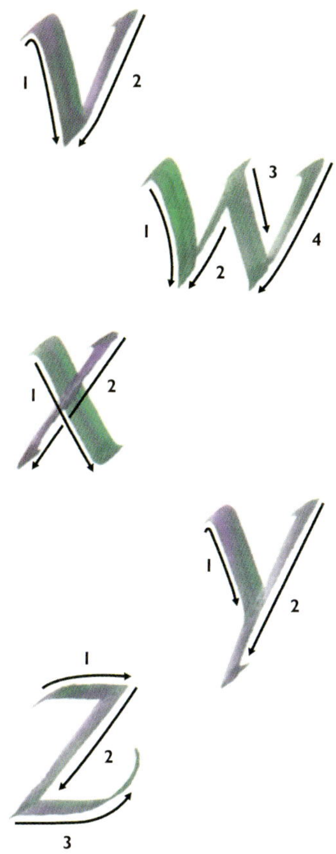

putting it all together

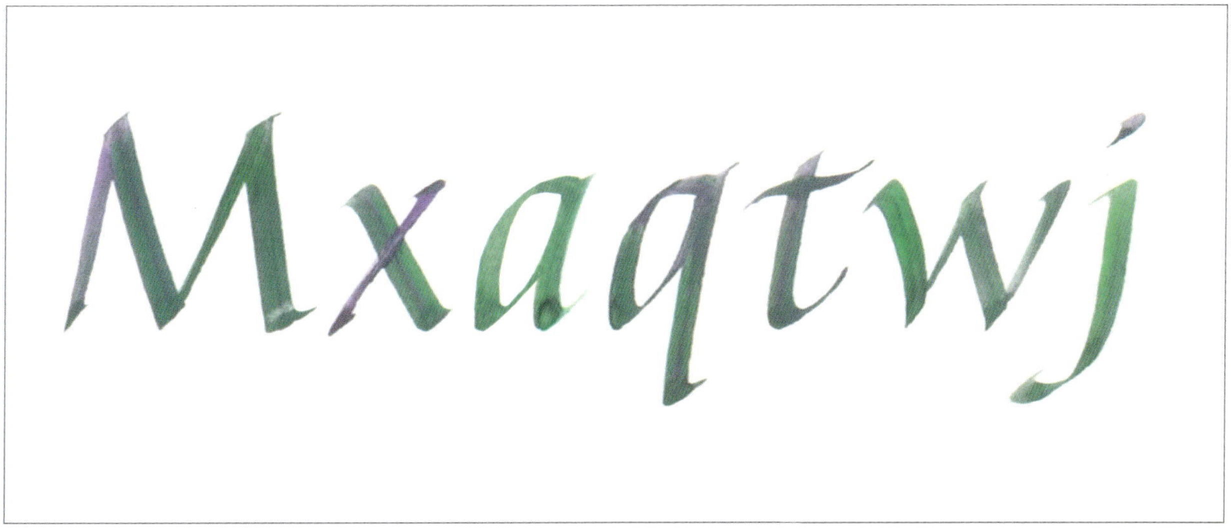

Italic capitals

Italic capitals are a compressed version of Roman capitals with a forward slope. They are based on an oval of the same shape found in the italic lower case (minuscule) letters.

oval letters – D

The oval letters are based on the 'O' and also include 'C', 'D,' 'G' and 'Q'.

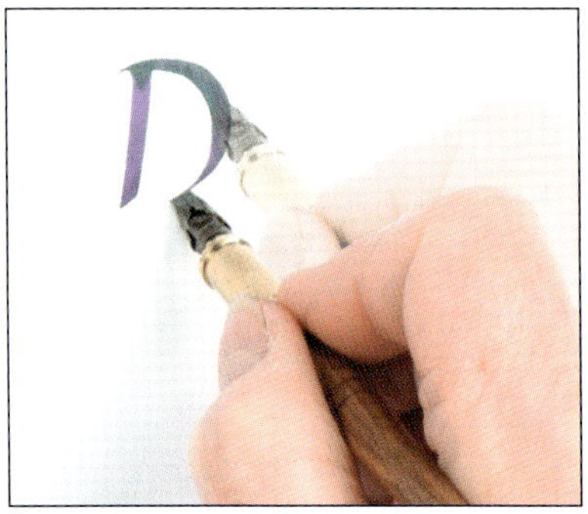

1 Make the downstroke. Then starting at the top of the downstroke, pull the pen round in wide arc.

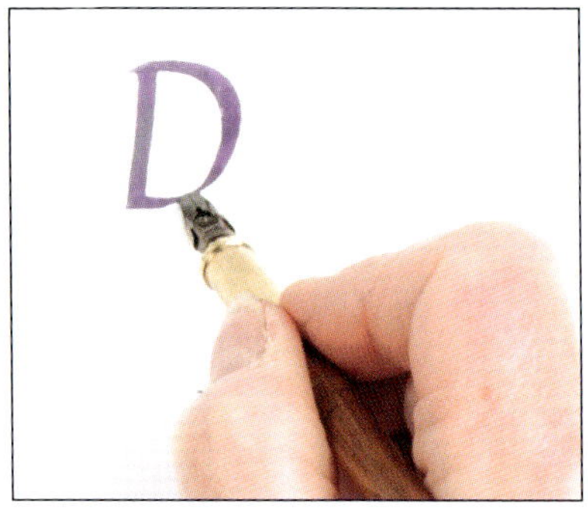

2 Finish the bowl with a flattened curve. The letter should be the same width as 'C' and 'G'.

Stroke reminder

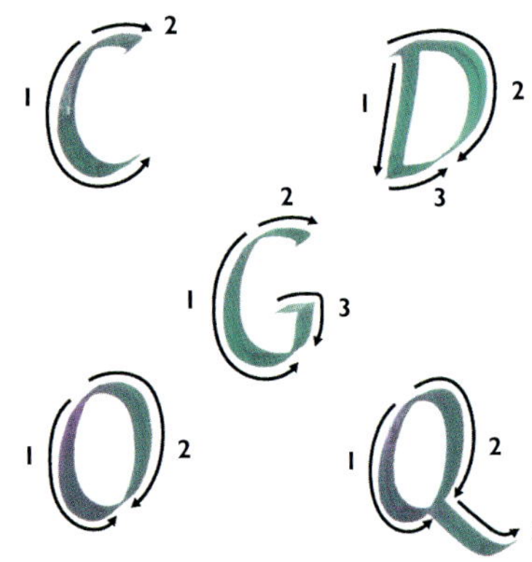

rectangular letters – H

These letters are three-quarters of the width of the oval and are 'A', 'H', 'N', 'T', 'U' and 'V'.

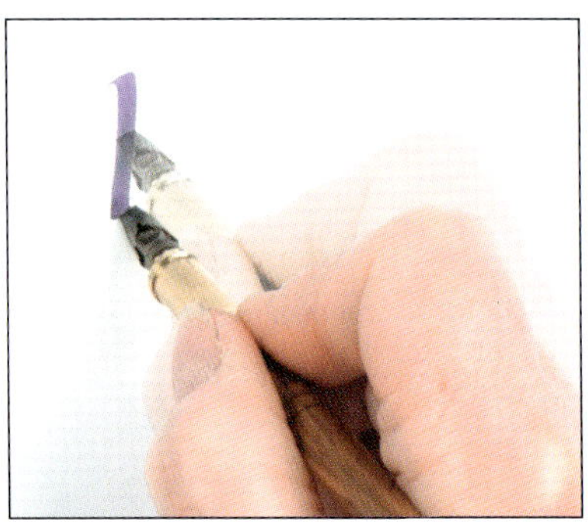

1 Start the letter with a serif, followed by a downstroke.

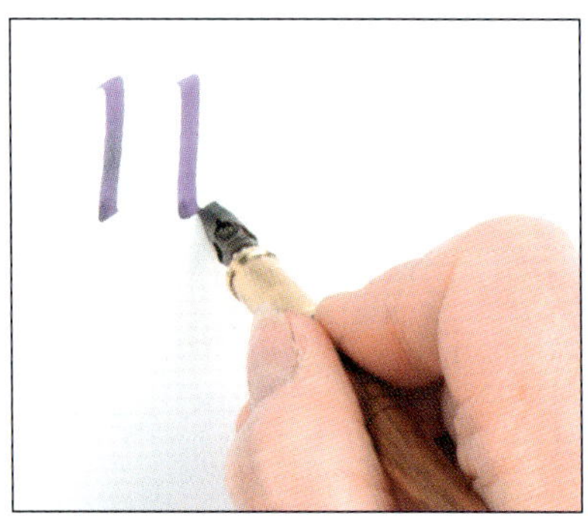

2 Repeat the same stroke for the second downstroke. Finish this one with a small serif.

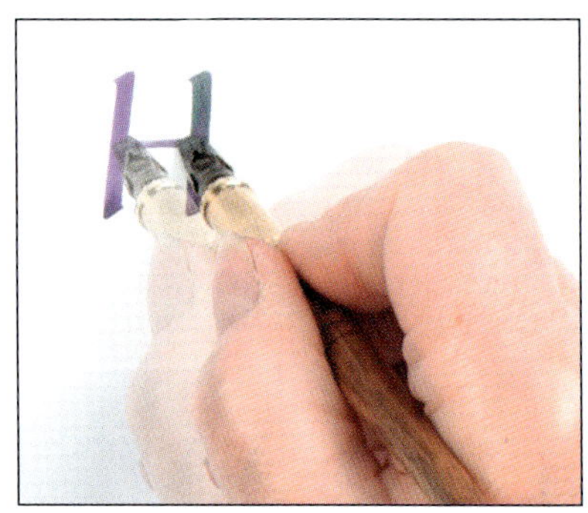

3 Add a crossbar just above half way to complete the letter.

Stroke reminder

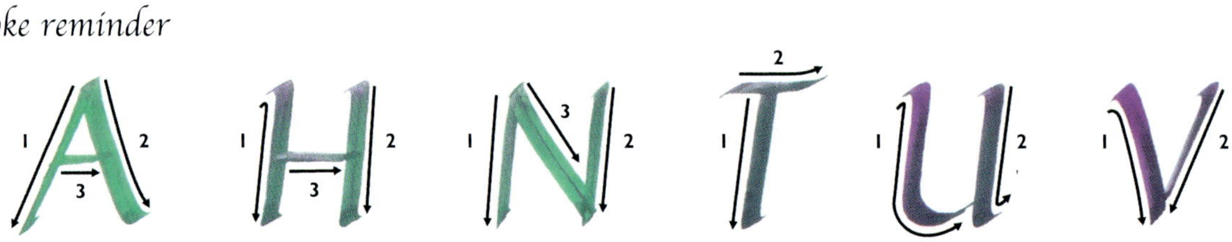

half-width letters – E

'B', 'E', 'F', 'K', 'L', 'P', 'R' and 'S' are the letters in this group. 'I' and 'J' are also included.

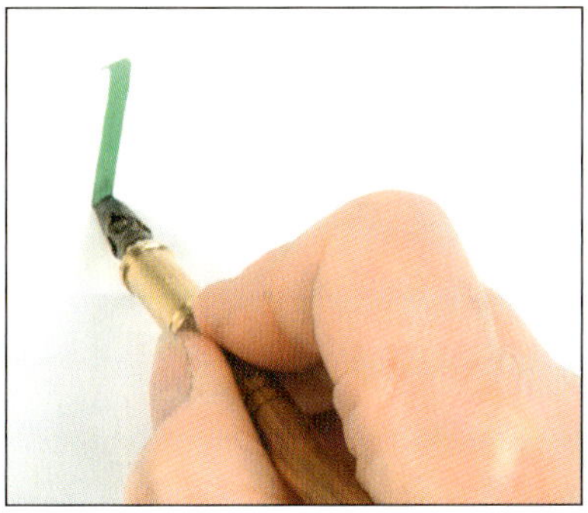

1 Make the first downstroke, starting with a serif.

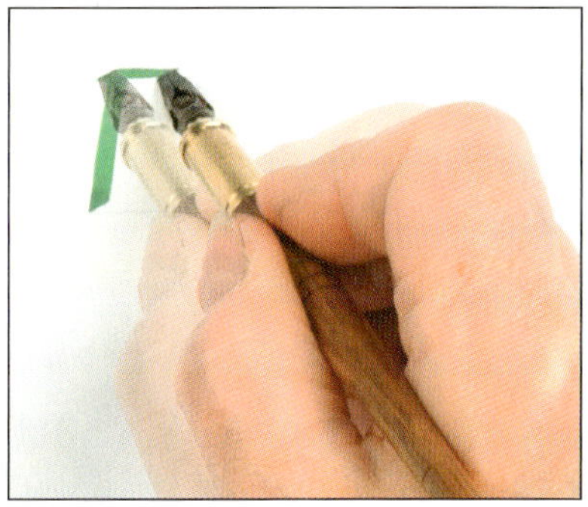

2 Then add the top arm, keeping your pen angle at 45 degrees. The arm touches the downstroke.

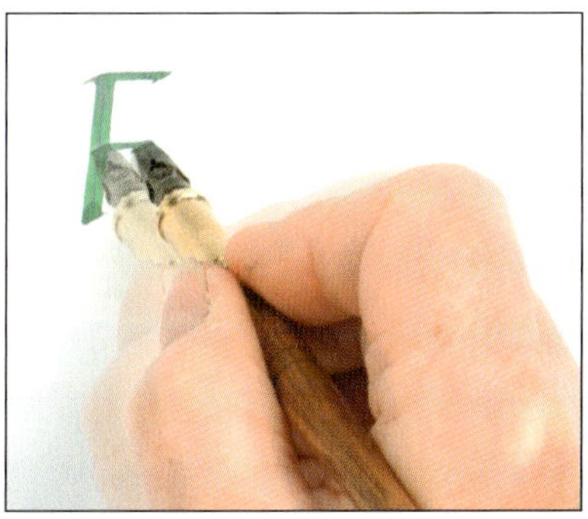

1 Add the middle arm, just above half way. It is slightly shorter than the top one.

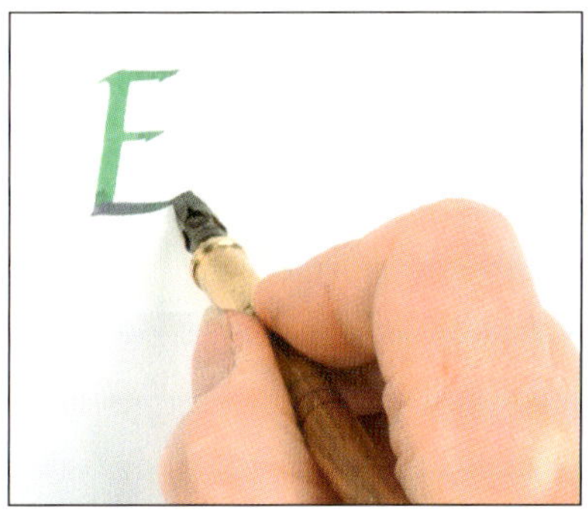

2 Add the base arm. This should be slightly longer than the top arm, and tapers upwards slightly.

Stroke reminder

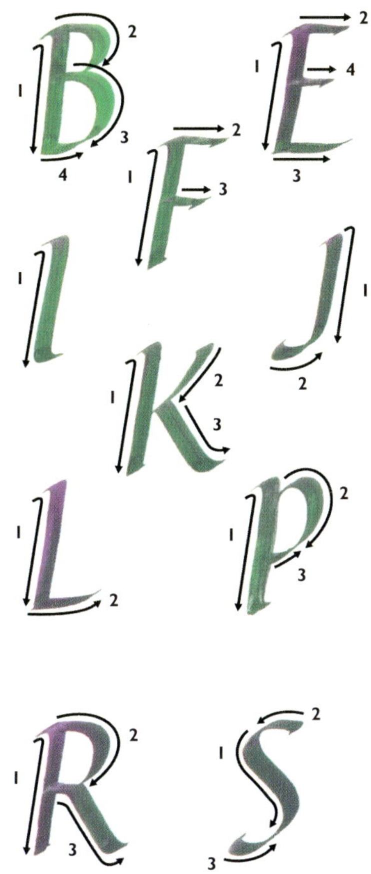

wide letters – W

There are only two wide letters – 'M' and 'W'.

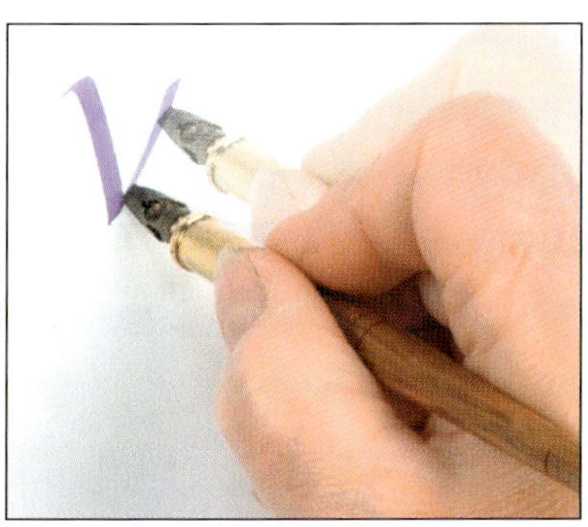

1 Start with a serif and a slightly curved downstroke to the baseline. Make the second stroke from the top down.

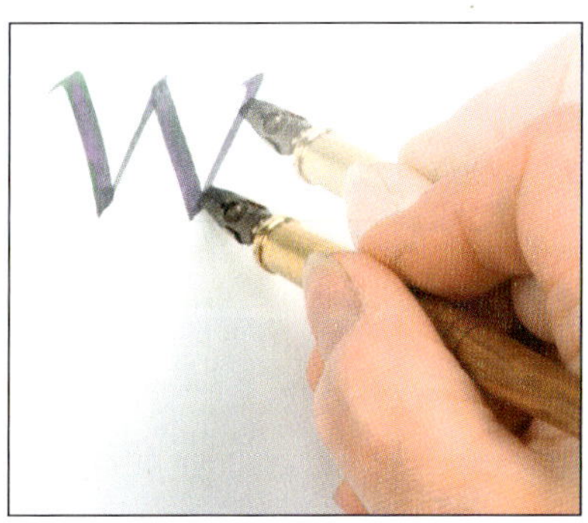

2 Repeat the first two strokes to form the second half of the letter. Keep the spacing consistent.

Stroke reminder

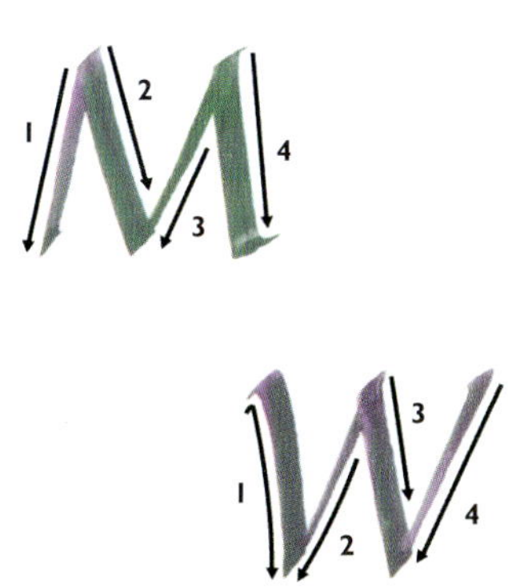

Sharpened italic

Sharpened italic is one of the many variations on the classic italic hand. The main features of this hand are the triangular arches and the sharpened serifs.

X-HEIGHT
5 nib widths
PEN ANGLE
45 degrees
LETTER SLOPE
12–70 degrees
FORM
Triangular o
ASCENDERS
3–4 nib widths
DESCENDERS
3–4 nib widths
SERIF STYLE
Sharpened
SPACING
Equal spacing between letters. NI distance is almost the width of an N counter

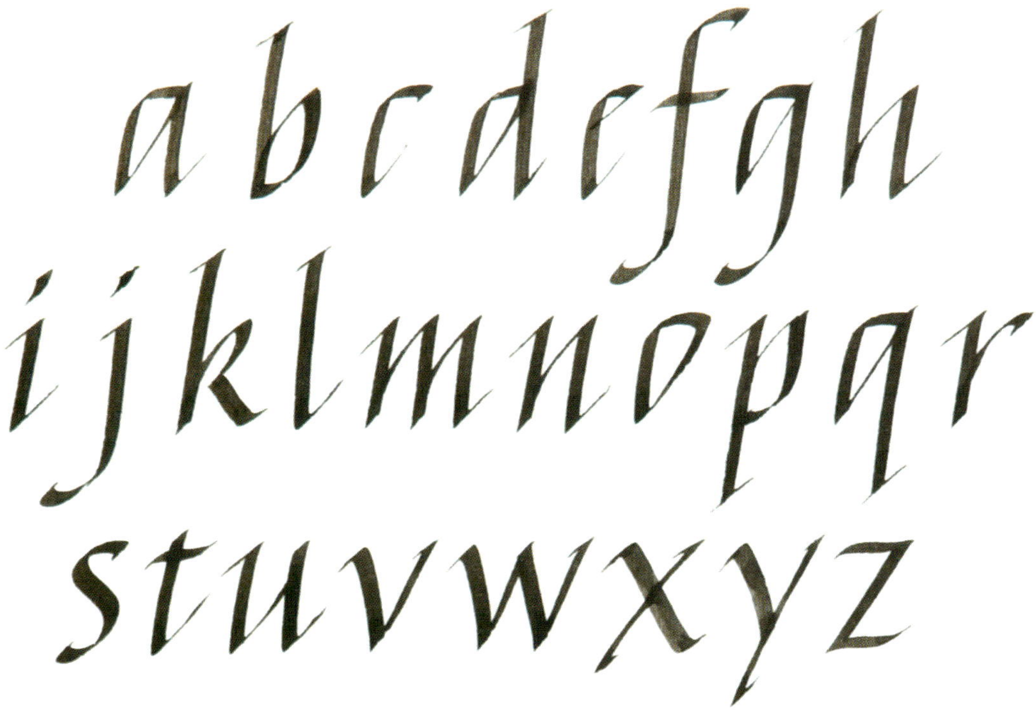

triangular letters – o, a and g

The triangular letters are based on 'o'. The other letters in this group are 'a', 'c', 'd', 'e', 'g' and 'q'.

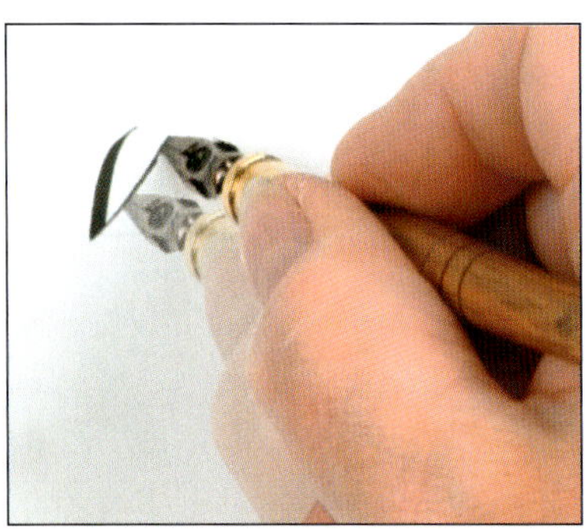

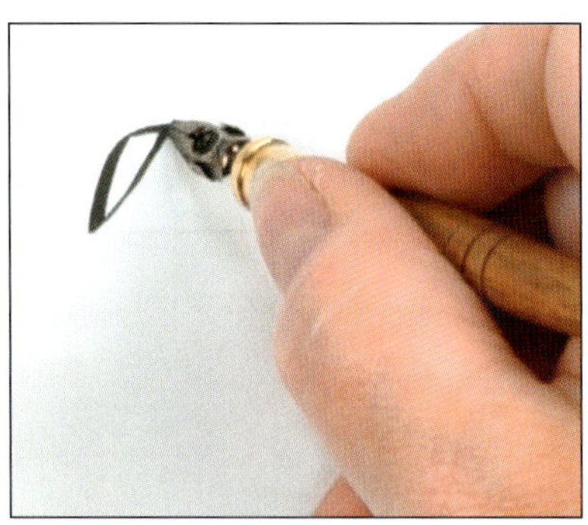

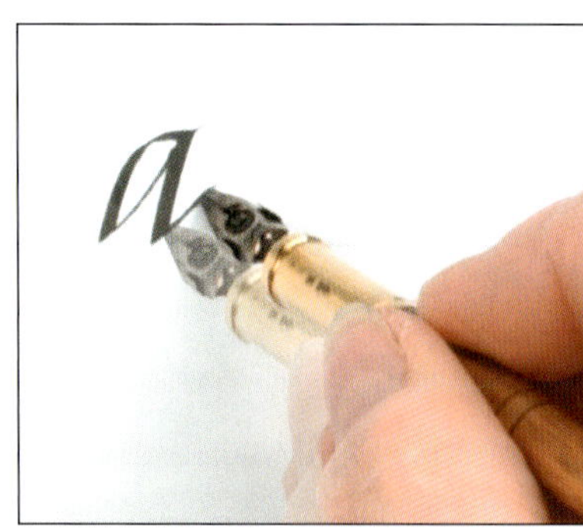

1 With your pen at 45 degrees, pull it down. Without lifting the nib, continue in an upward movement.

2 Take the pen off the paper and replace it accurately where you started the stroke, keeping the nib at 45 degrees. Pull the pen across the paper to meet the top of the upstroke.

1 The first three strokes for the 'a' are the same as for the 'o'. To finish the 'a', add a downstroke parallel to the first stroke, then add a final upstroke, keeping the upward turn sharp.

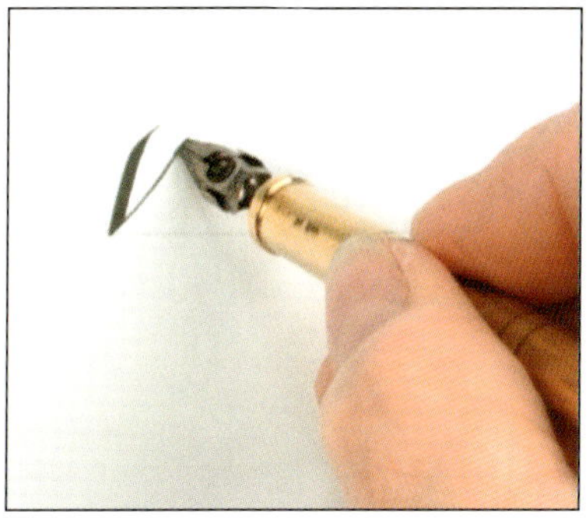

1 As for the 'o', make a downstroke and in one movement, move the pen upwards.

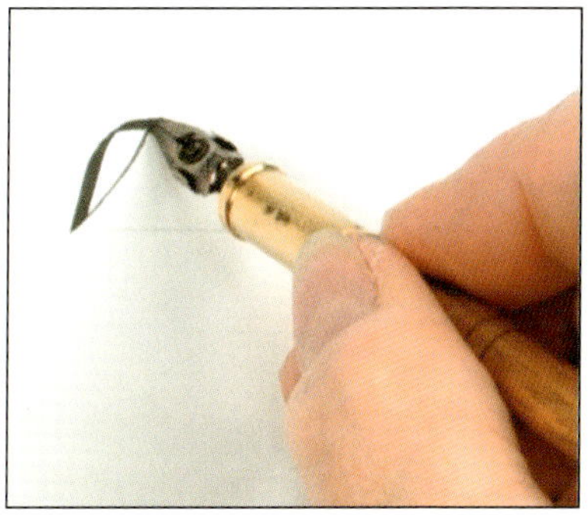

2 Take the pen off the paper and place it at the top of the first stroke. Pull the pen across the paper.

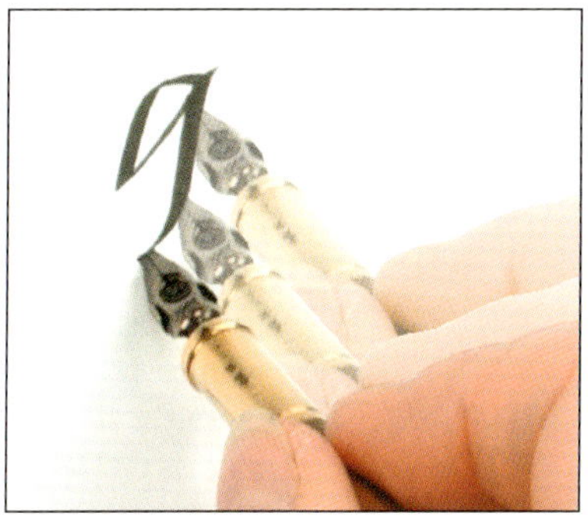

3 Add a small hairline 'ear' to the shoulder of the letter, then pull the pen downwards, tapering below the baseline.

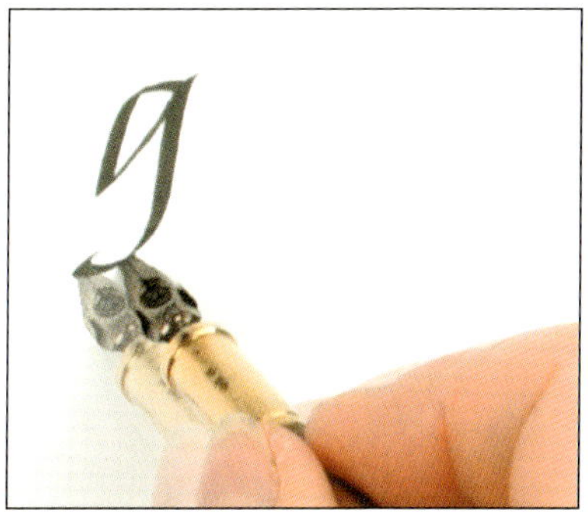

4 Finish the letter with a serif followed by a flattened curve to join up with the previous stroke.

Stroke reminder

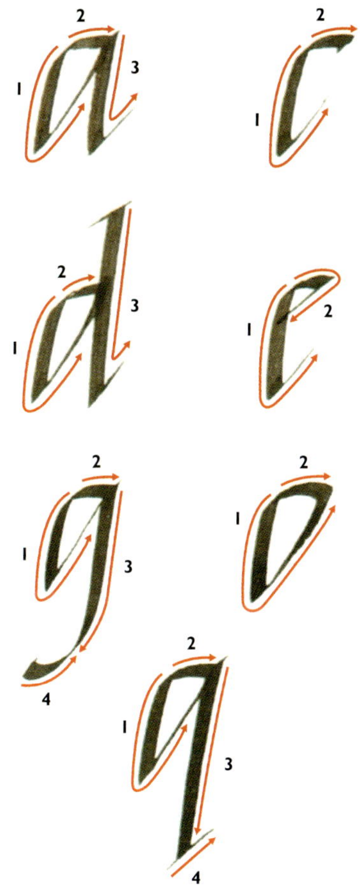

clockwise arches – m and k

There are four clockwise arches – 'b', 'k', 'm' and 'n'.

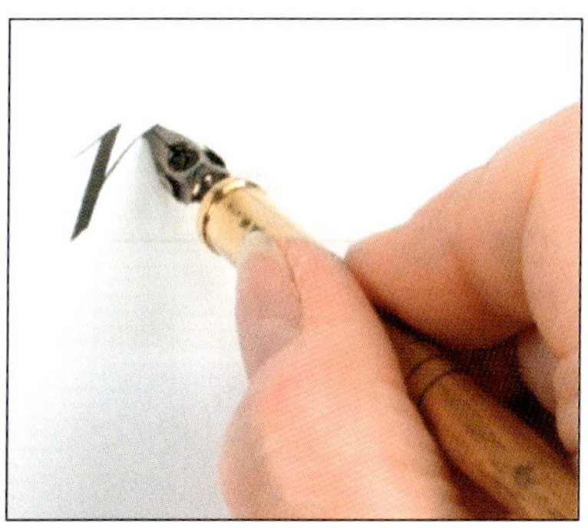

1 Make a sharpened serif then pull the pen downwards. Spring upwards for the angular arch.

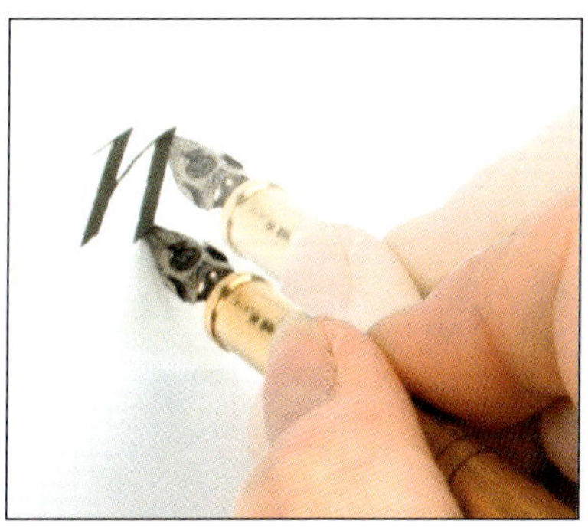

2 Pull the pen straight down to the baseline for the second downstroke. Keep the turn sharp.

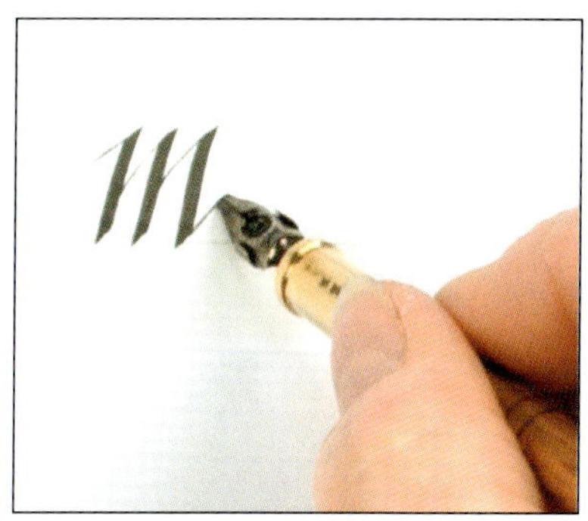

3 Repeat the angular arch and downstroke to form the second half of the letter. Keeping the pen on the paper, finish the letter by adding a sharpened serif.

clockwise arches continued

Stroke reminder

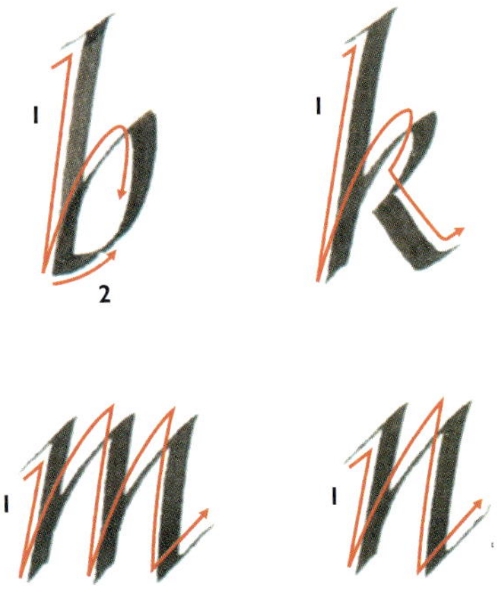

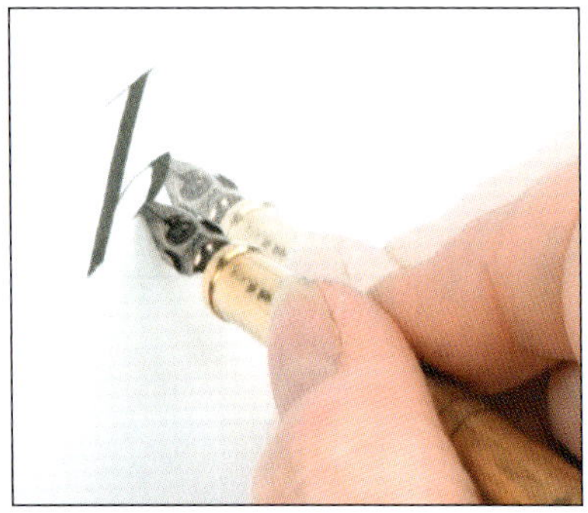

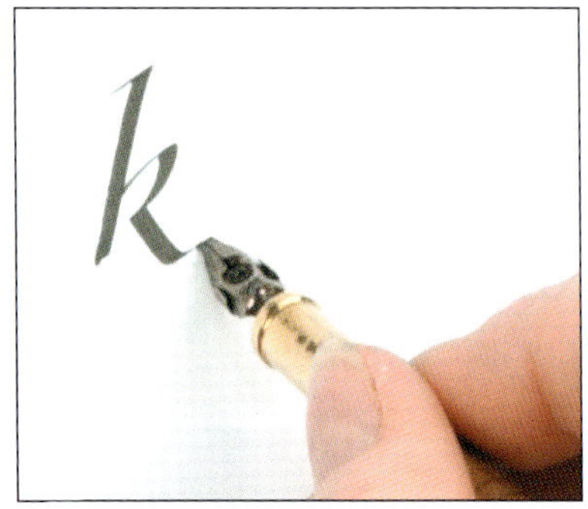

1 Create a long ascender three or four nib widths above the x-height. Start with a serif then pull the pen down. Draw a springing arch and finish the bowl and tail in one movement.

2 Keep the bowl sharpened and finish with a serif. Notice that the bowl is open and does not touch the downstroke.

anti-clockwise arches – t and u

The anti-clockwise arches are 'l', 't' and 'u'.

Stroke reminder

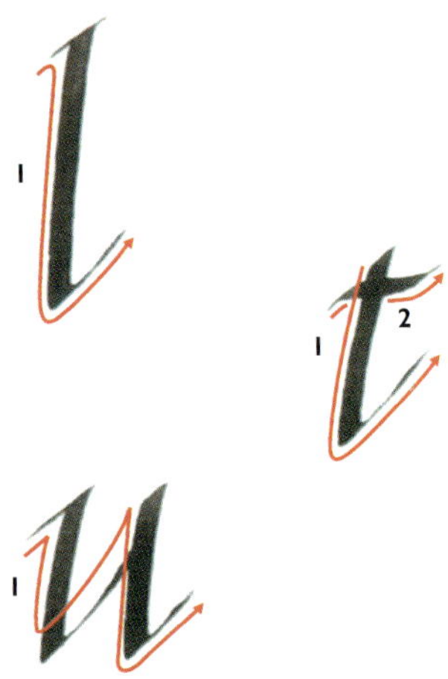

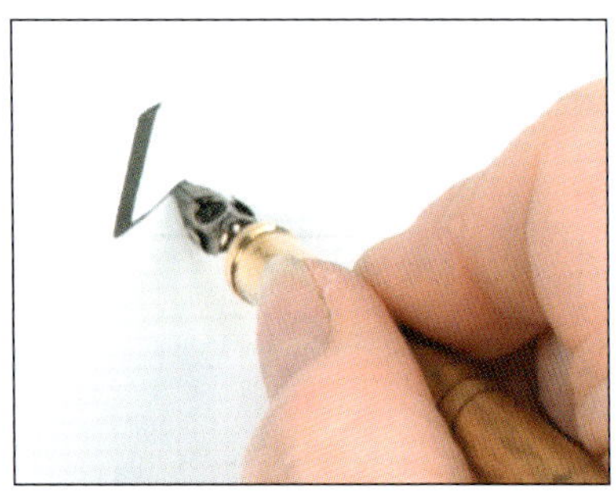

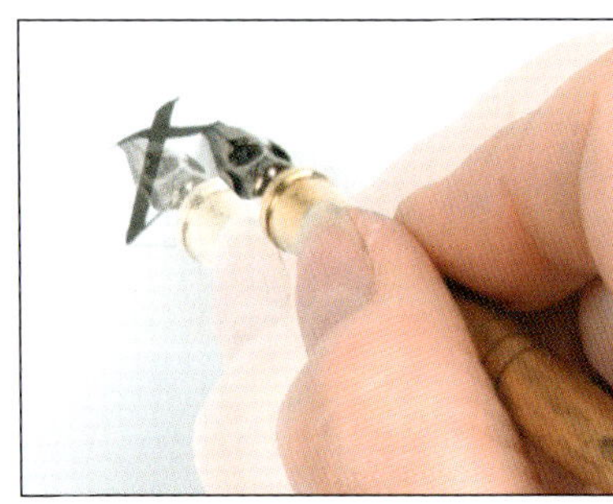

1 Start with an upward stroke for the sharpened serif. The downstroke ends with an upward movement.

2 Add the crossbar, placing it on the line. Keep the pen angle consistent.

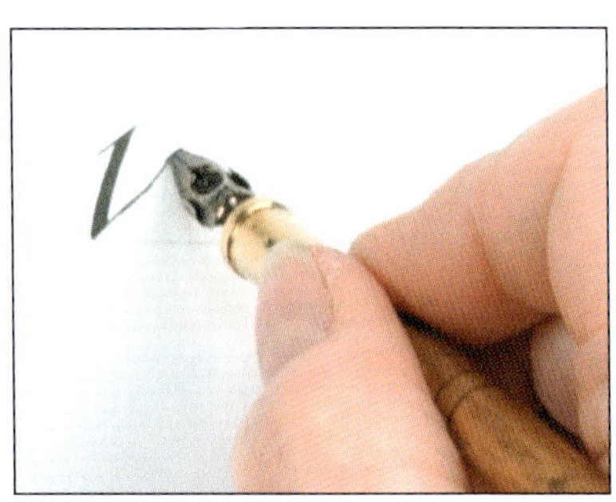

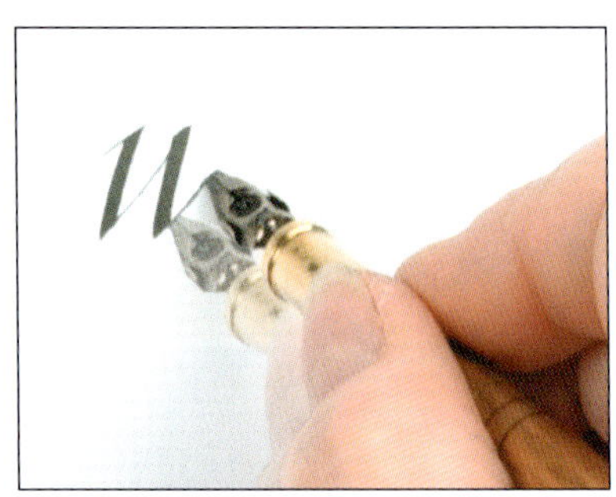

1 Make a serif, then pull the pen down. Push the pen upwards to create the second stroke.

2 The final stroke is parallel to the first. Make sure your pen angle is 45 degrees.

related tops and base curves – s

There are three letters in this group – 'f', 'j' and 's'.

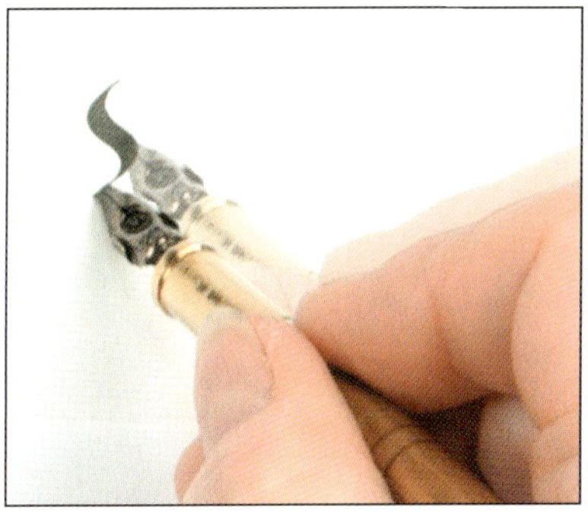

1 Make the centre stroke first, keeping it angular. The curves of the stroke are flattened.

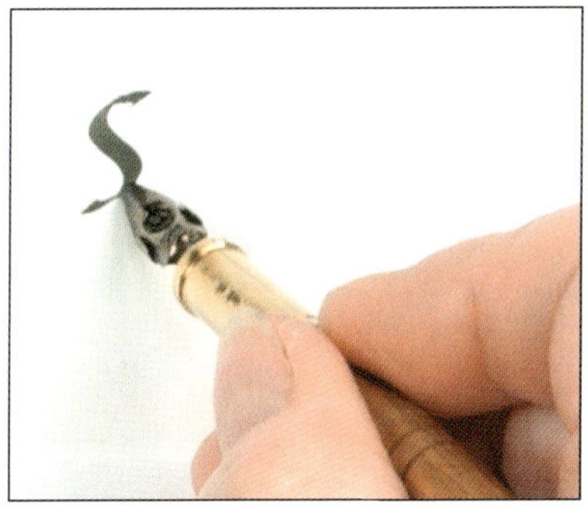

2 Go back to the top of the stroke and add the top of the letter, which is almost flat. Then add the bottom stroke.

Stroke reminder

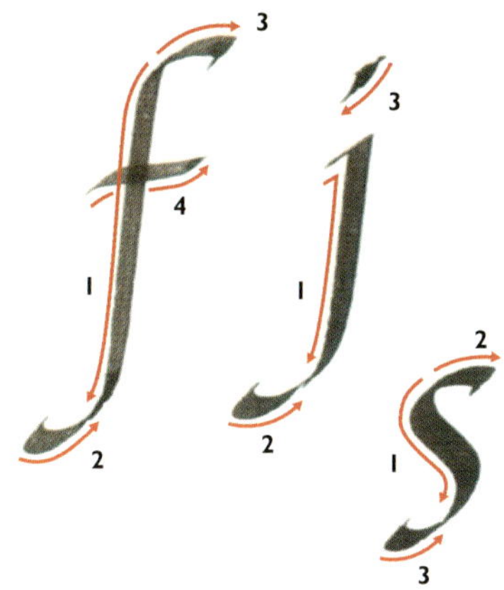

diagonal letters – x

The last five letters of the alphabet – 'v', 'w', 'x', 'y' and 'z' – make up this group.

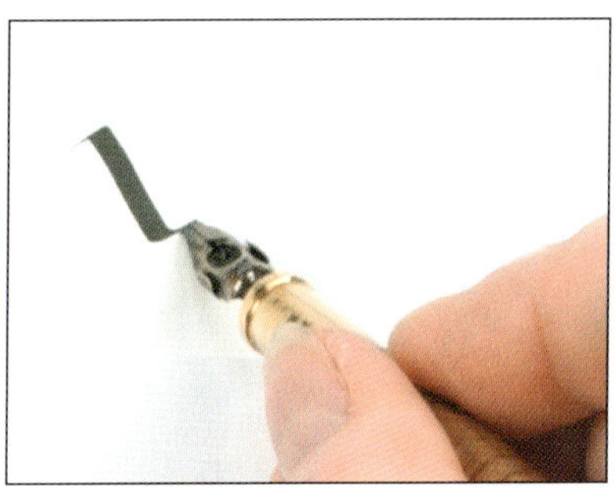

1 Make a serif, then pull the pen down to make the first diagonal stroke.

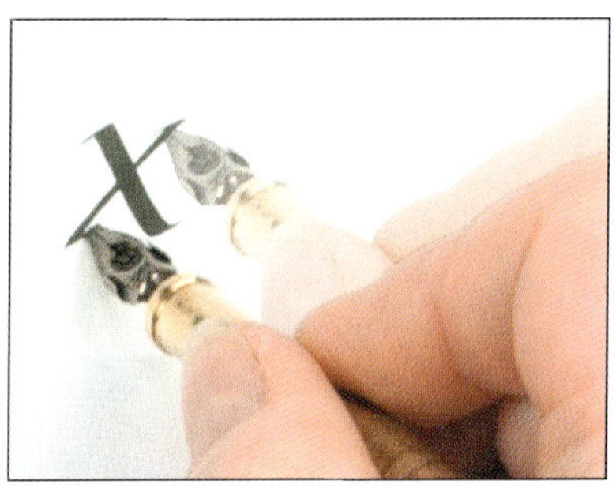

2 The second diagonal crosses the first just above half way.

Stroke reminder

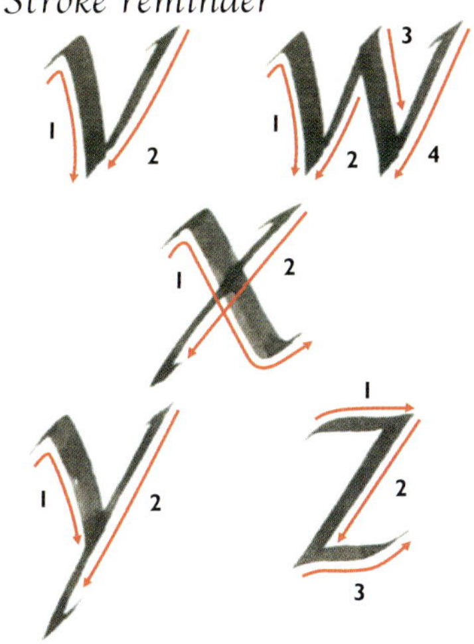

putting it all together

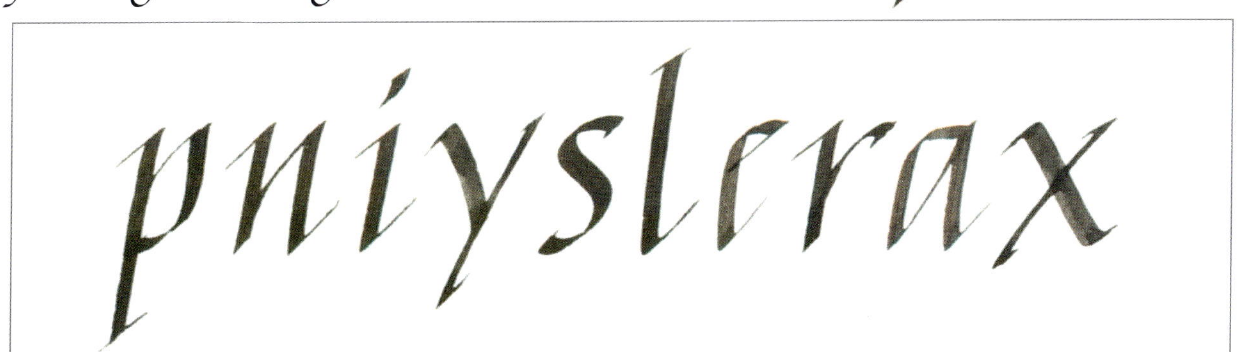

Copperplate

All copperplate scripts are created using a pointed nib. Different line weights are created by varying the pressure on the nib rather than by altering the pen angle.

LOWER CASE

X-HEIGHT
None (height for body of letter optional)

PEN ANGLE
None (pointed nib)

LETTER SLOPE
54 degrees

FORM
Oval

ASCENDERS
Same height as for body of letters

DESCENDERS
Same height as for body of letters

SPACING
Equal spacing between letters

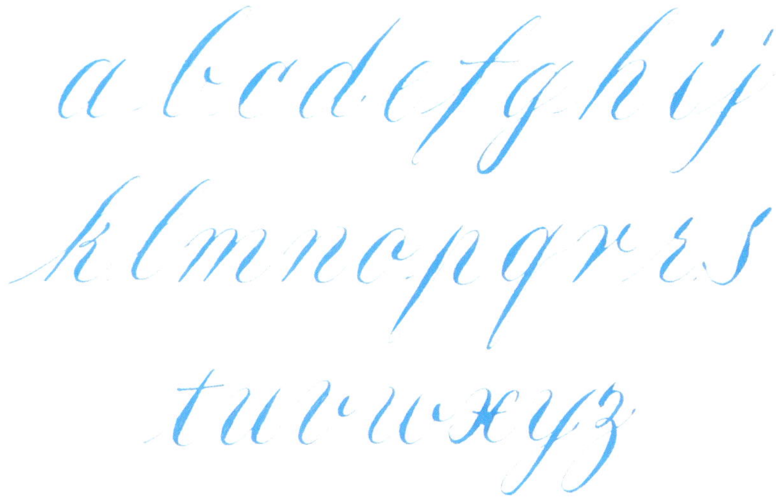

CAPITALS

X-HEIGHT
None (height for body of letter optional)

PEN ANGLE
None (pointed nib)

LETTER SLOPE
54 degrees

FORM
Oval

ASCENDERS
None

DESCENDERS
For G and Y: as for body height

SPACING
Equal area

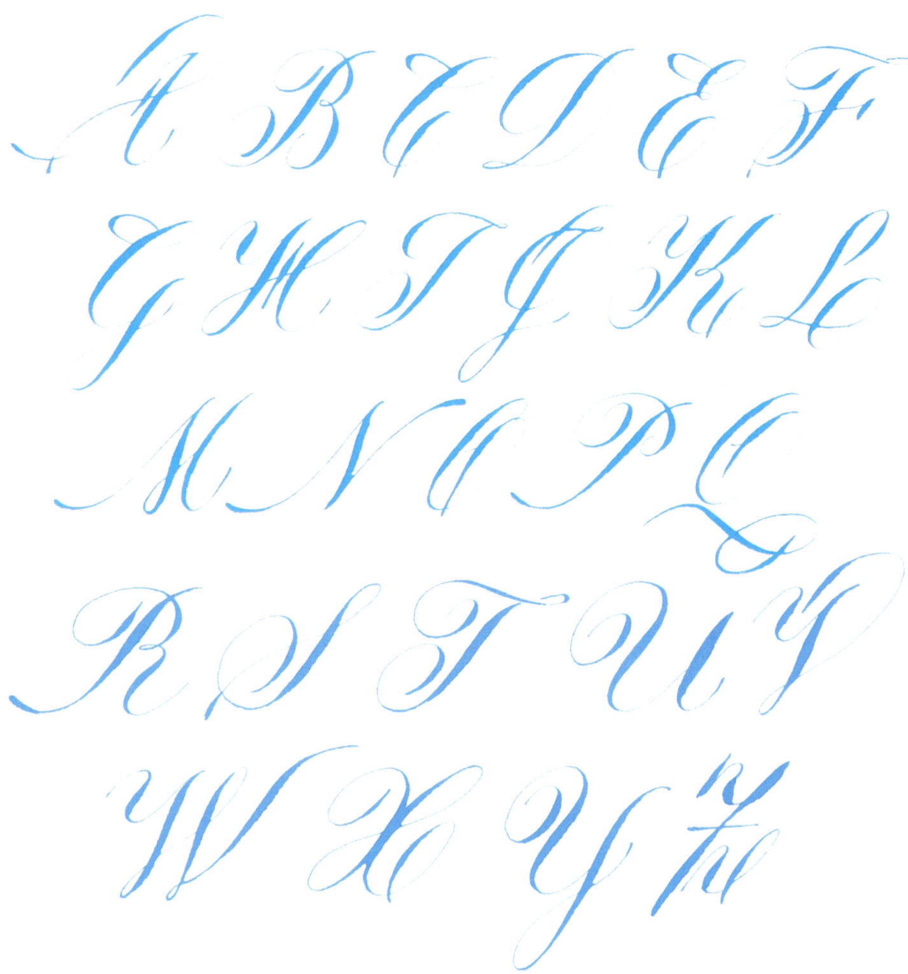

oval letters – a

The oval letters are based on the 'o'. The other letters are 'a', 'c' and 'e'.

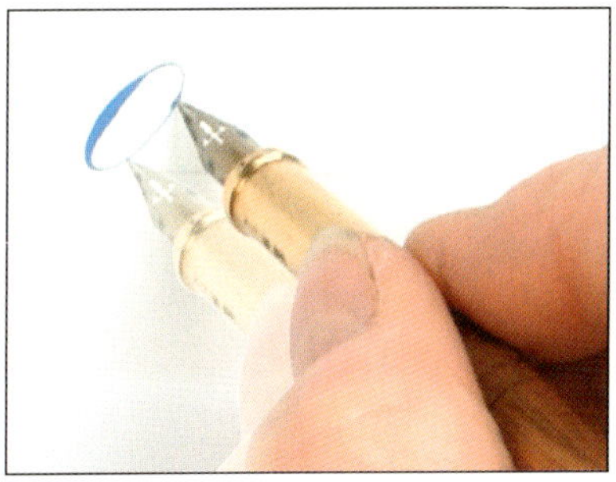

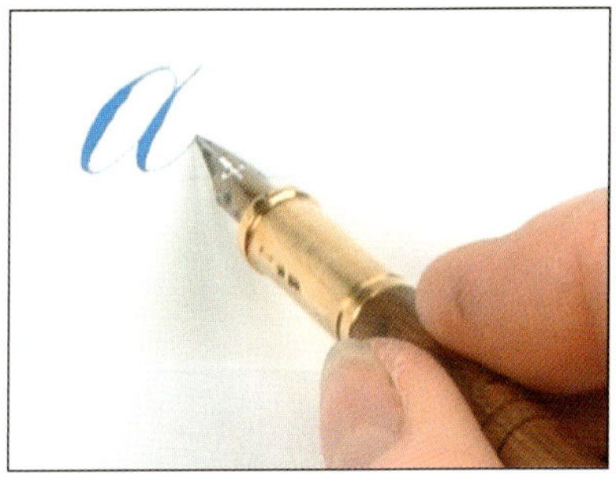

1 Working in an anti-clockwise direction, pull the pen down, increasing the pressure for the curve of the bowl. Decrease the pressure and loop upwards.

2 Starting at body height, pull the pen down, increasing the pressure. Loop upwards at the baseline.

Stroke reminder

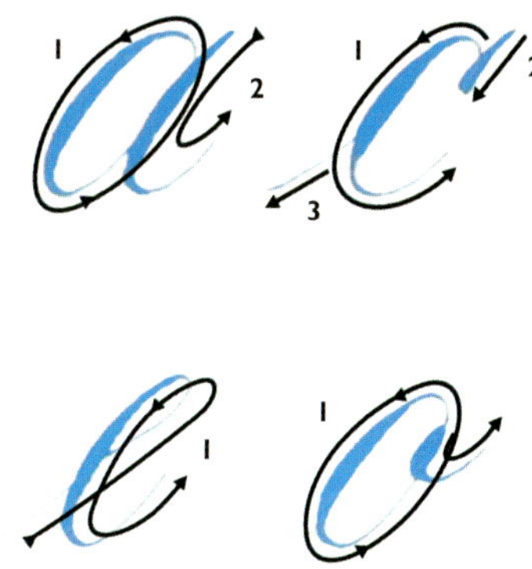

ovals followed by a straight stem – d

The three letters that make up this group are 'd', 'g' and 'q'.

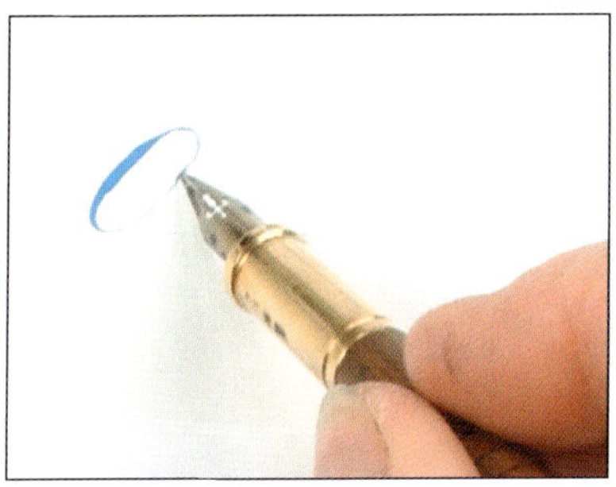

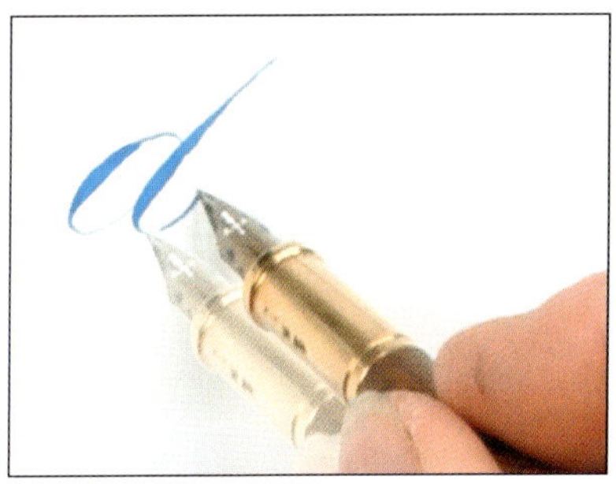

1 As for 'a' and 'o', start the letter in an anti-clockwise direction, then pull the pen down, increasing the pressure. Loop the stroke upwards, decreasing the pressure, to complete the bowl.

2 Keeping your stroke angle consistent, start the downstroke, increasing the pressure in the centre of the stroke. Decrease the pressure at the bottom then loop upward.

Stroke reminder

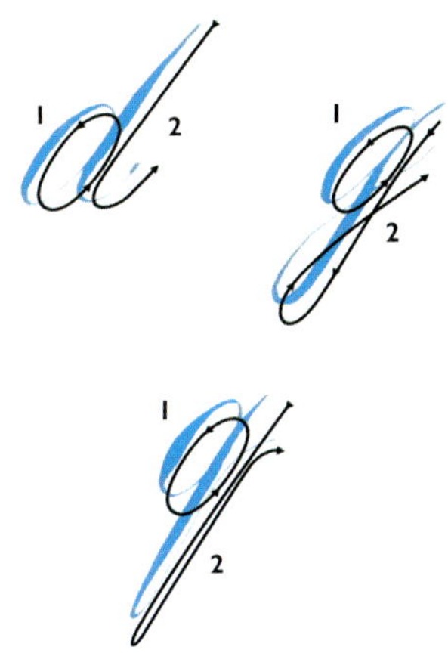

putting it all together

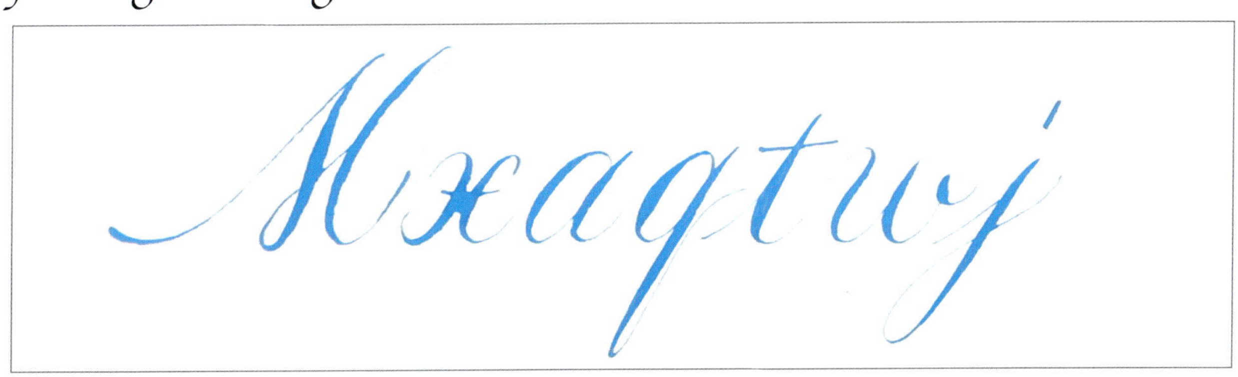

straight letters – f

The straight letters are 'f', 'i', 'j', 'l' and 't'.

Stroke reminder

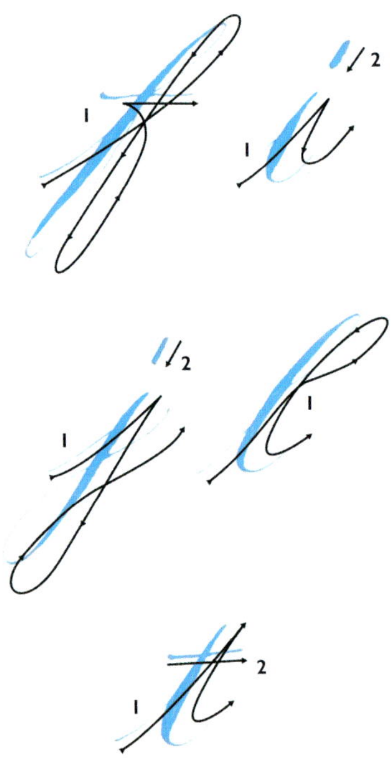

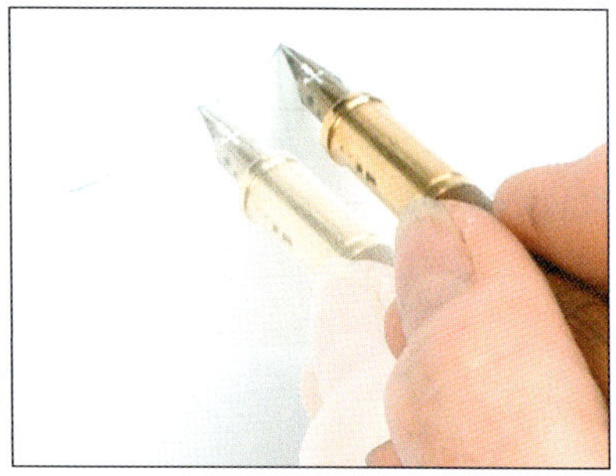

1 Start the letter with a lead-in stroke. Make another upward stroke above body height to form the loop.

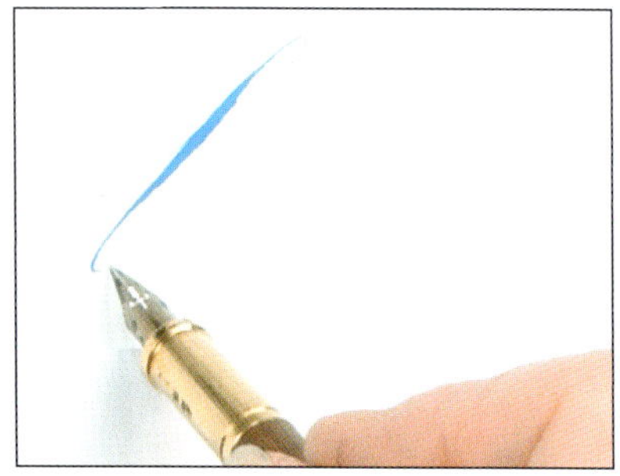

2 Loop around at the top, then increase the pressure on the downstroke, releasing it before the bottom.

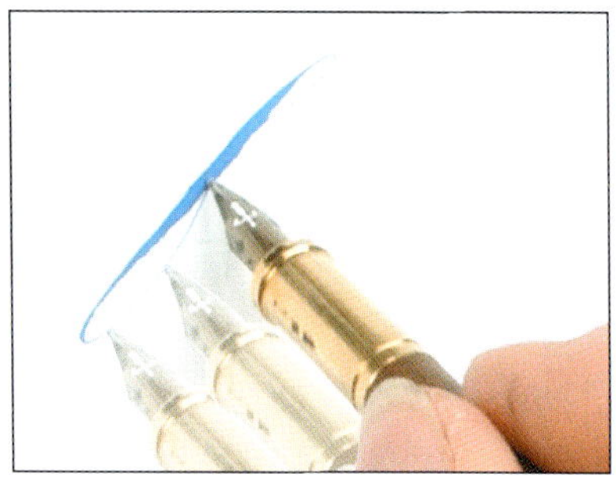

3 In one continuous smooth movement, loop the pen upwards to create a larger bottom bowl.

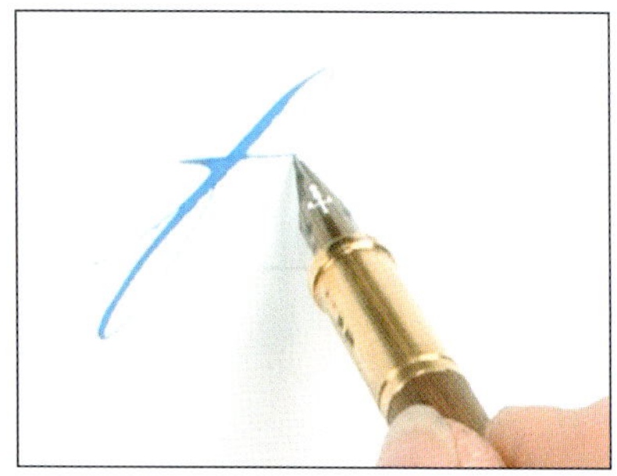

4 Continue the pen stroke to add the crossbar, above half way.

diagonals – w

The three diagonal letters are 'v', 'w' and 'z'.

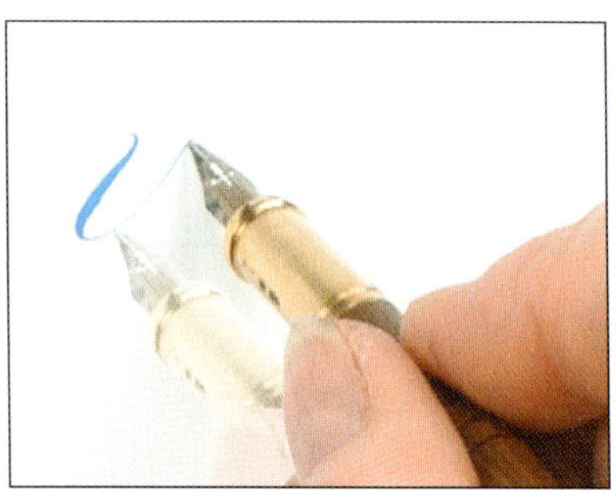

1 Start with a small upward loop then pull the pen down, increasing the pressure in the centre of the downstroke. Then loop upwards for the upstroke.

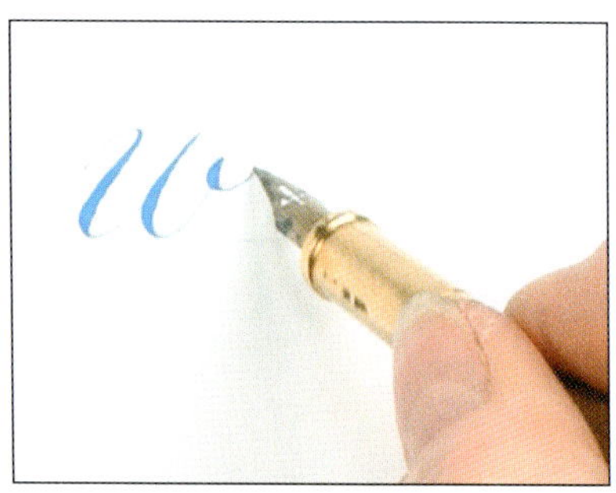

2 In a continuous movement, pull the pen down for the second downstroke. Finish the light upstroke with a circular loop below body height.

Stroke reminder

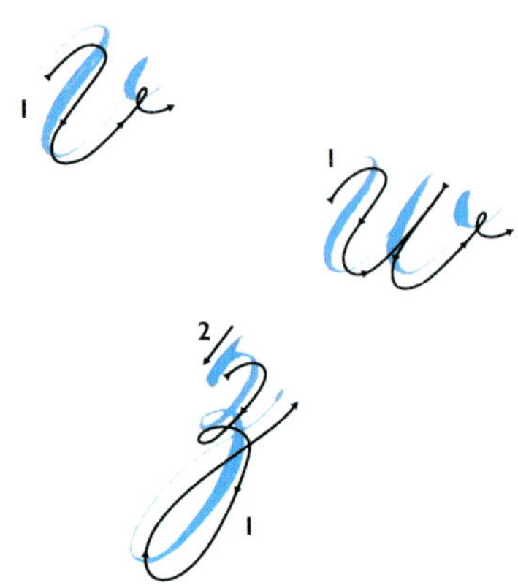

straight strokes with arches – m

This group is comprised of the letters 'b', 'h', 'k', 'm', 'n' and 'p'.

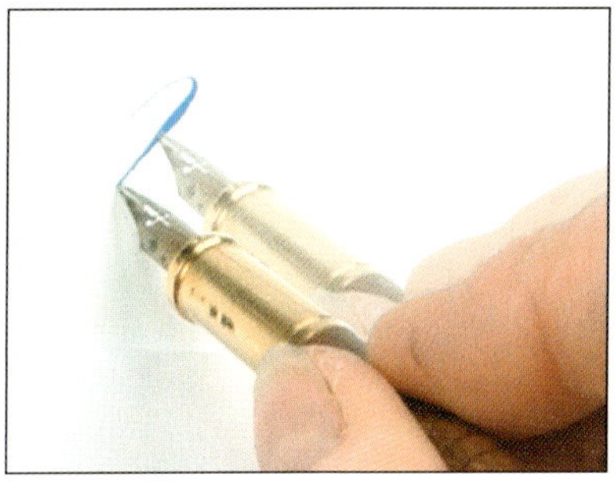

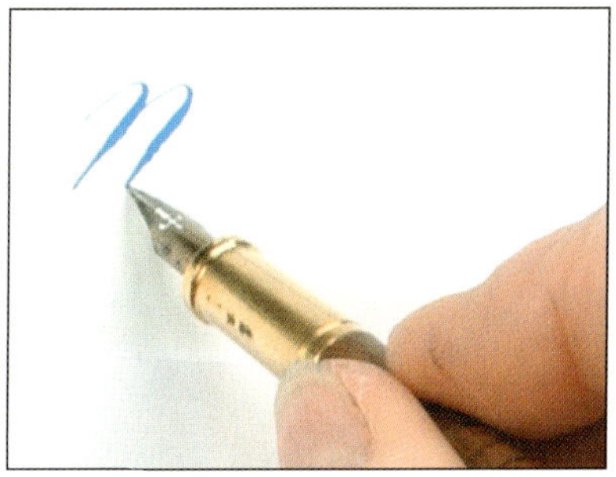

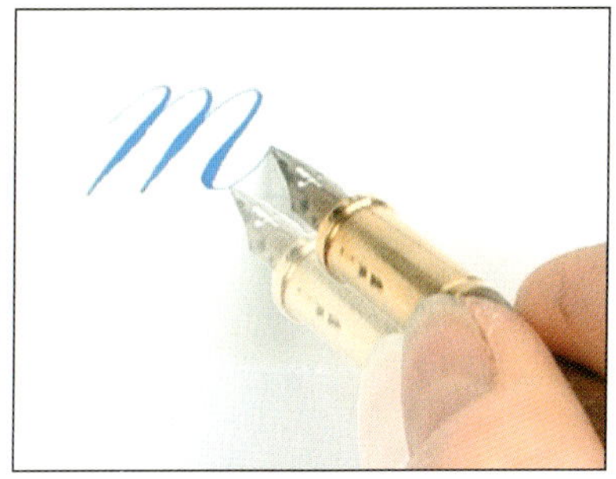

1 Loop upwards then pull the pen down to form a thick stroke, decreasing the pressure in the centre of the stroke.

2 In one movement, work upwards from the bottom of the stroke, then form an arch and downstroke.

3 Repeat the second arch and downstroke, keeping the spacing equal. Finish with a upward loop.

Stroke reminder

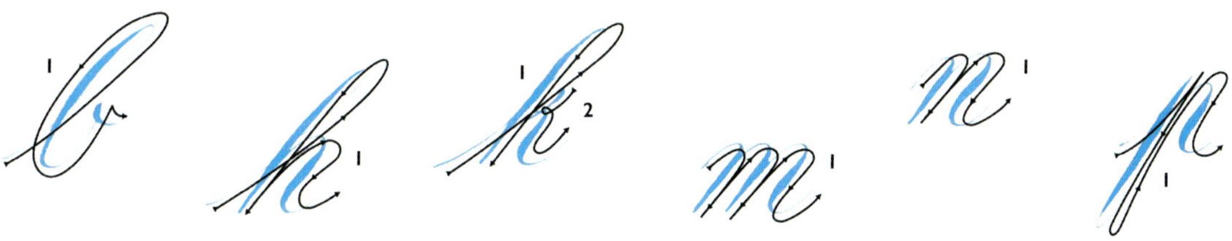

variants – s

The variants group is comprised of 'r', 's', 'u', 'x' and 'y'. There are two possible types of 'r'.

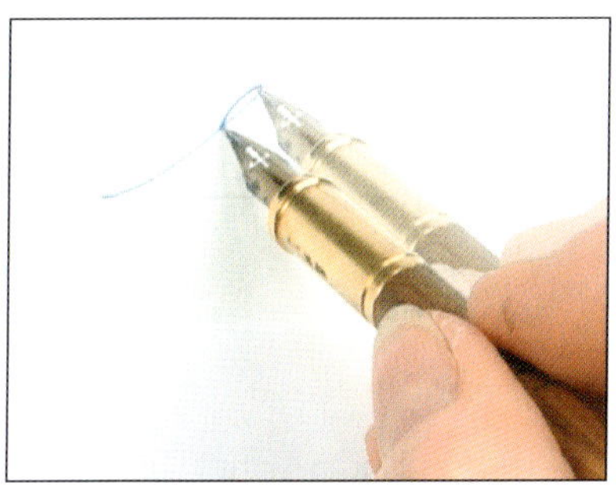

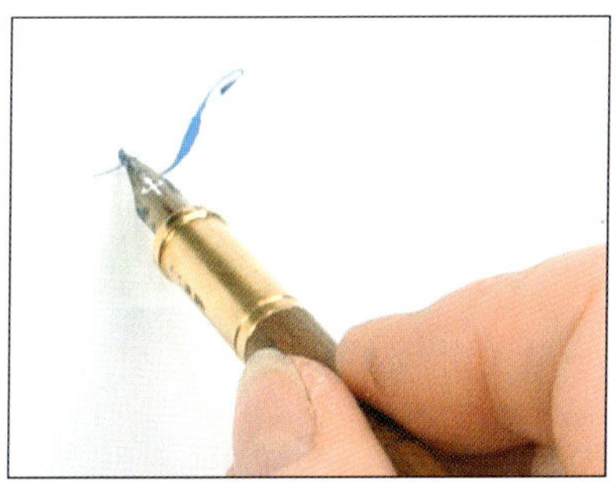

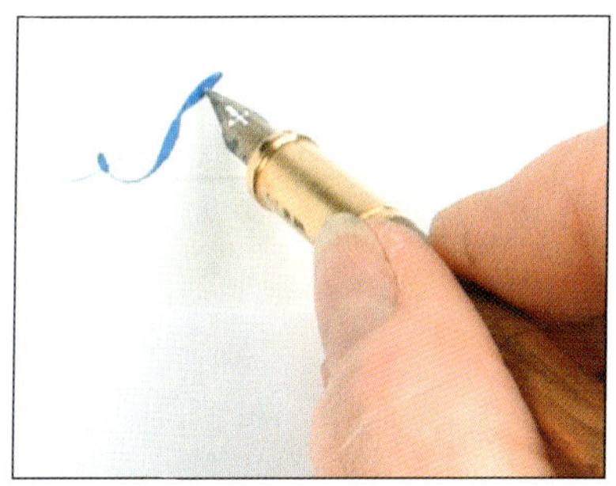

1 Start with a long, thin upward curve from the baseline to body height. Make a small loop above body height.

2 Increase the pressure on the nib on the downstroke. Finish off with a wide, smooth upward curve.

3 Carefully fill in the top loop to make it a solid colour.

Stroke reminder

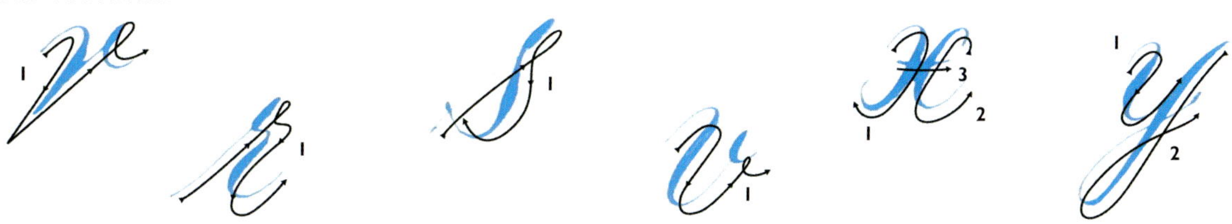

Copperplate capitals

letters starting with an upward movement (thin stroke) – N

'A', 'M' and 'N' are the letters in this group.

Stroke reminder

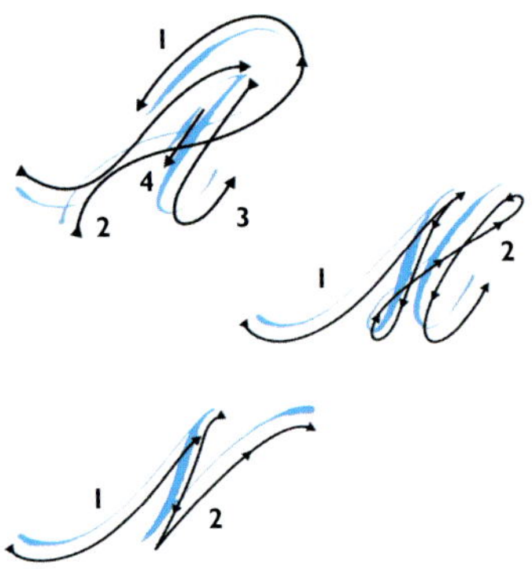

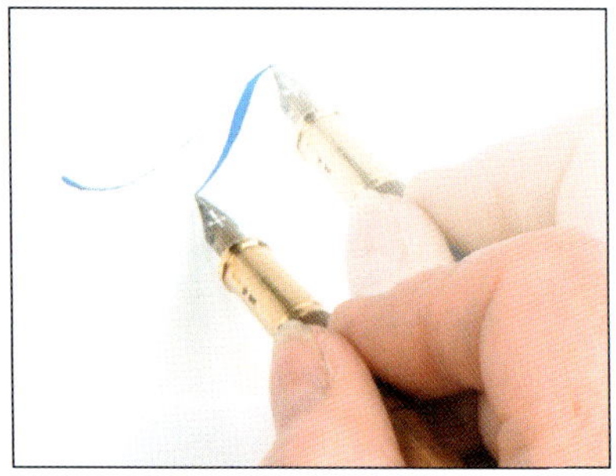

1 Start the letter with a long upward curve. Pull the pen down in a curve, with pressure in the centre of the stroke.

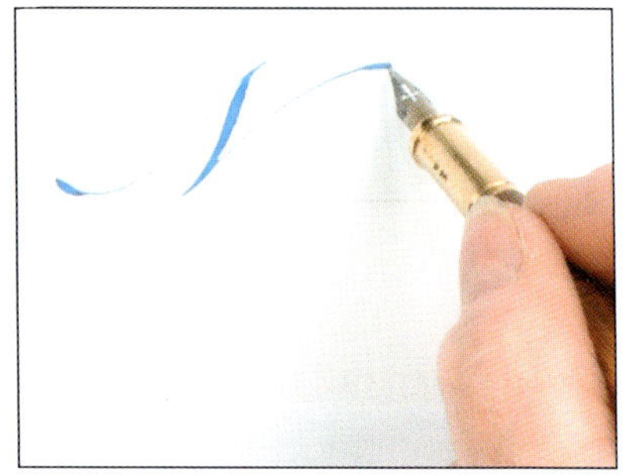

2 In a continuous movement, create another long upward sweep, extending slightly above body height.

letters starting with a downward movement (thick stroke) – F

Half the alphabet – 'B', 'D', 'F', 'H', 'I', 'J', 'K', 'L', 'O', 'P', 'Q', 'R' and 'T' – makes up this group.

Stroke reminder

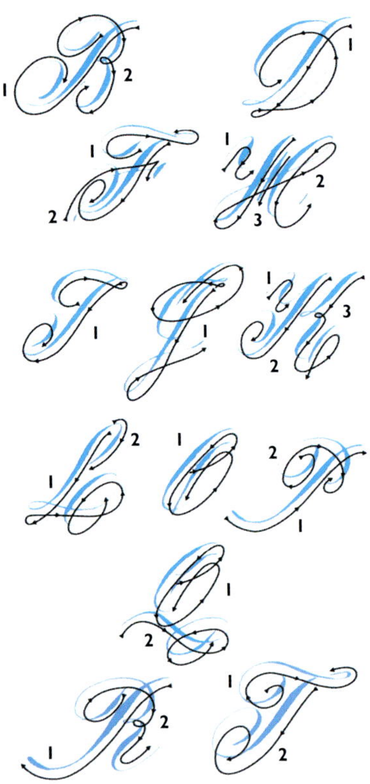

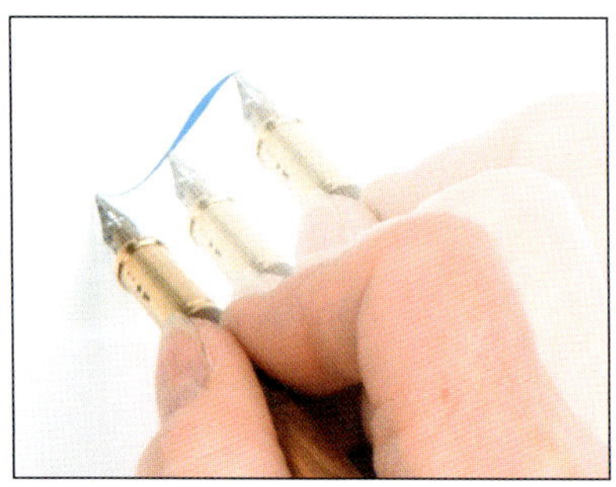

1 Starting from the top, pull the pen down in a flat curve, increasing the pressure in the centre of the stroke.

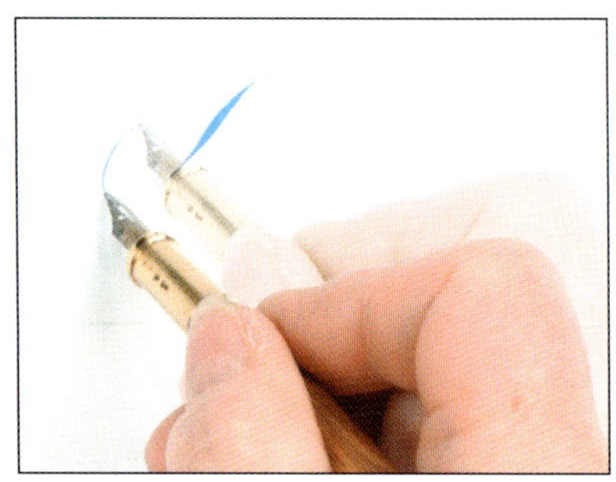

2 Loop the pen up and around to form a long tail.

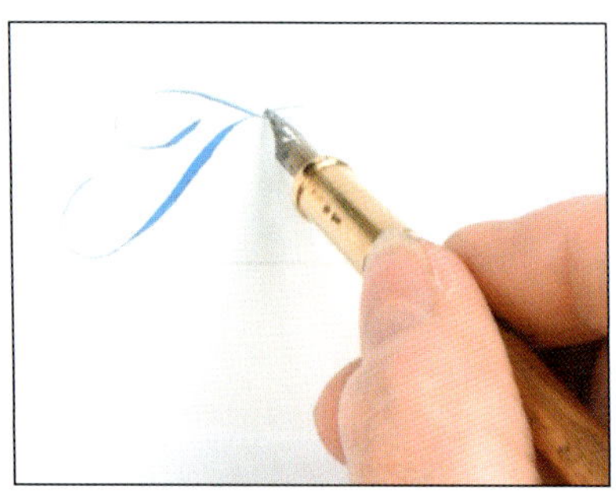

3 Working from the left, form a wide arc, finishing with a small loop.

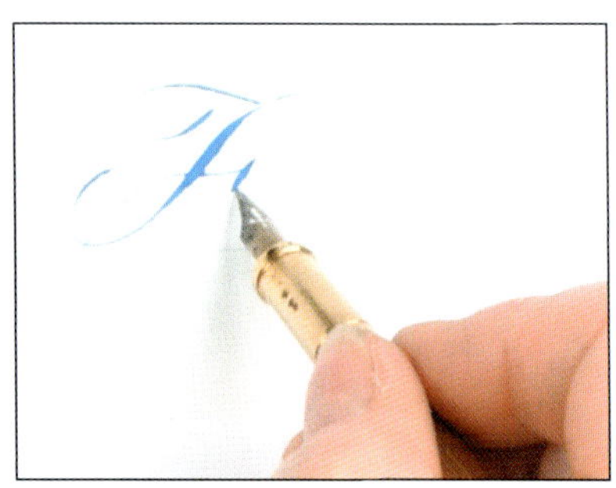

4 Add a decorative crossbar, starting from the tail.

letters starting with a flourish – W

'C', 'E', 'S', 'U', 'V', 'W', 'X' and 'Z' are the letters that make up this group.

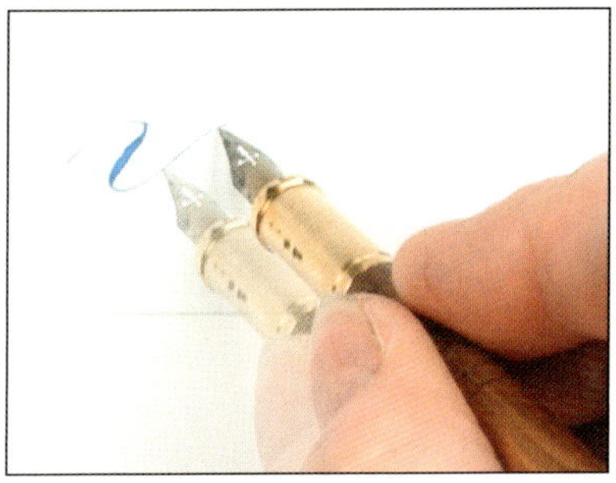

1 Begin with an upward stroke and oval loop. Form a thick downstroke and a second upward loop for the bowl.

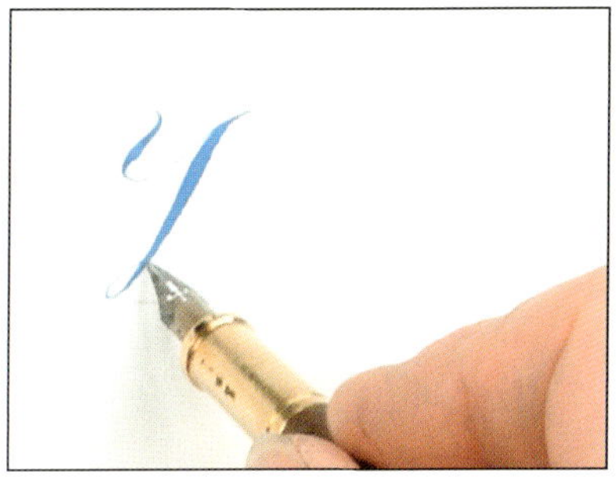

2 Increase pressure in the centre of the downstroke to create the tail of the letter, adding a small loop at the end.

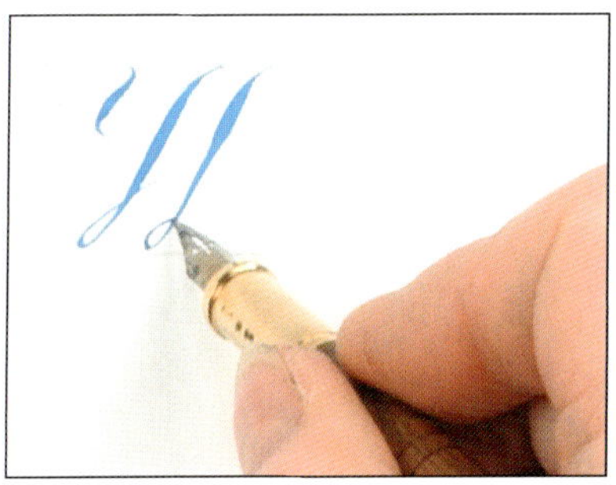

3 In the same movement, make an upward sweeping curve, loop over, and make a heavy downstroke, as before.

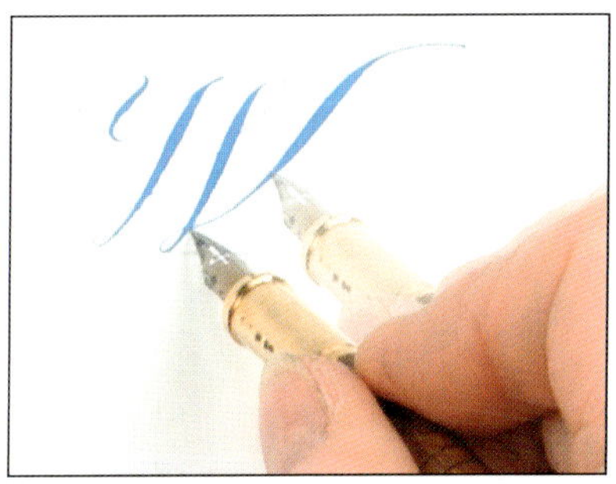

4 Starting above body height, pull the pen down in a thick, sweeping curve to join the bottom loop.

Stroke reminder

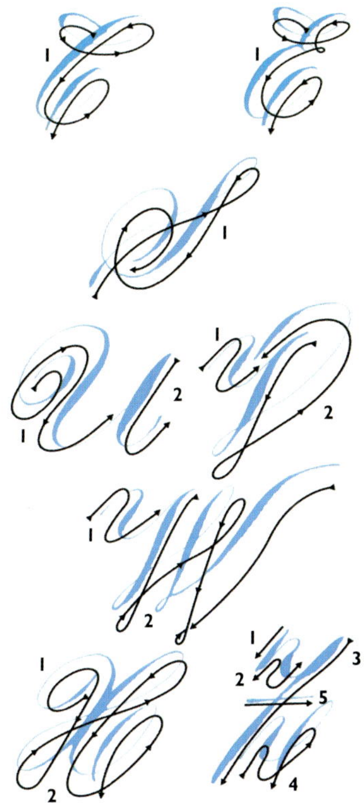

letters descending below the baseline – G

'G' and 'Y' are the only letters with descenders that go below the baseline.

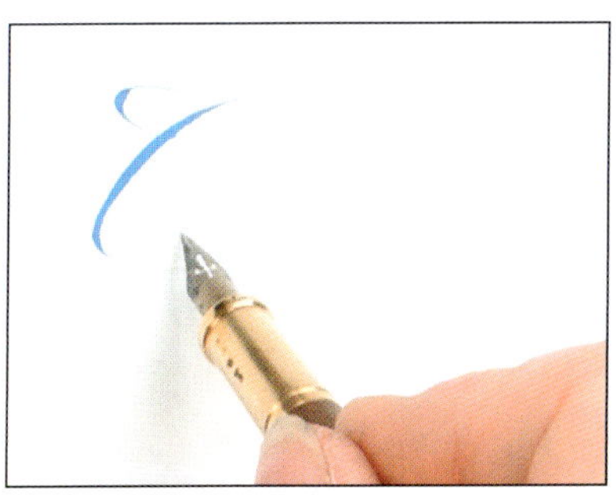

1 Start with an oval loop and continue in a downward curve for the body of the letter, placing pressure in the centre of the stroke and ending with an upward curve.

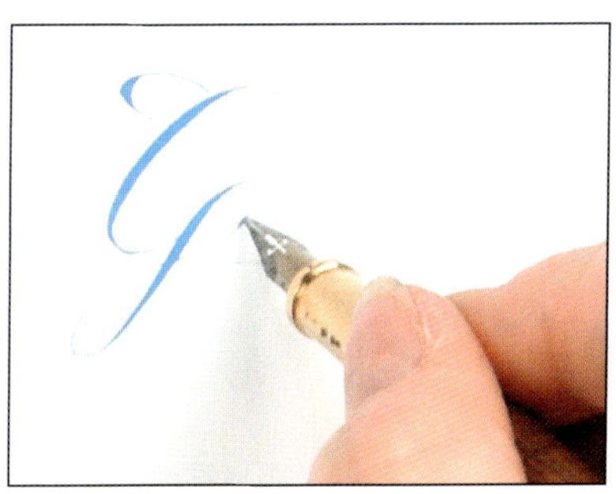

2 In the same movement, pull the pen down to form the thick stroke of the tail before finishing the tail with loop.

Stroke reminder

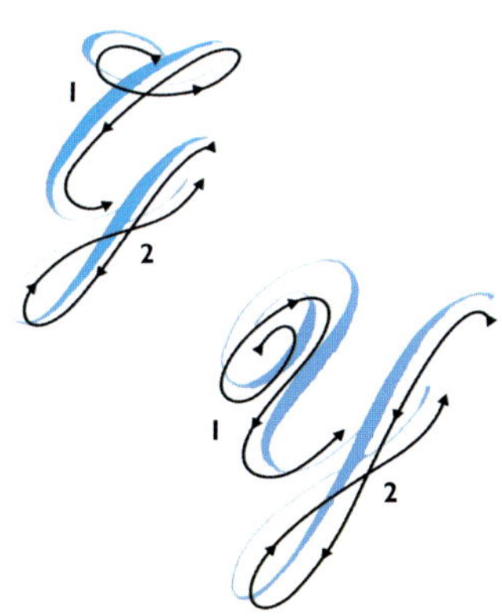

Gallery

Once you have mastered the basic hands, the possibilities for calligraphers are endless. These pages show a range of different hands, used for greetings cards, as artwork to hang on the wall and as books and keepsakes.

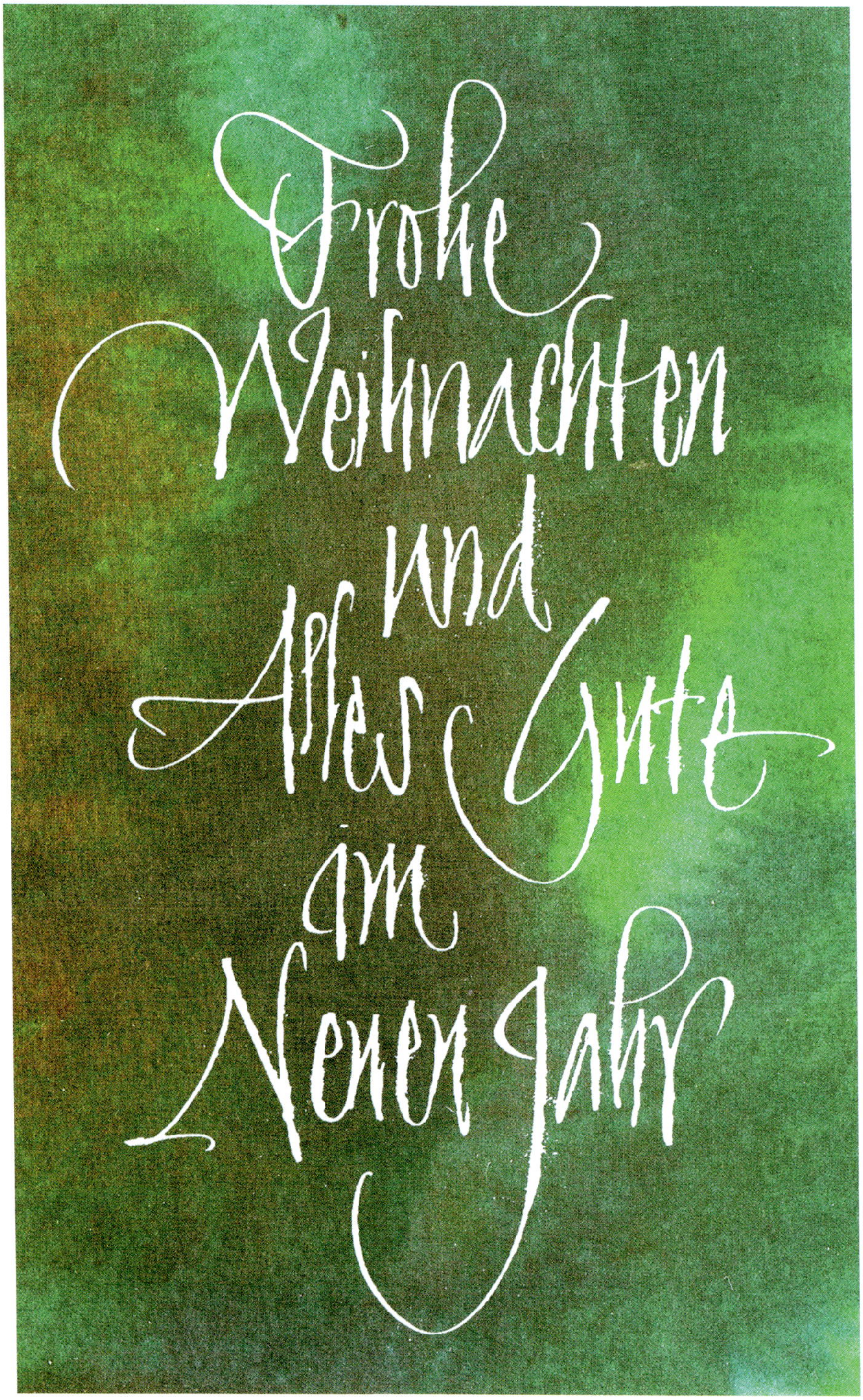

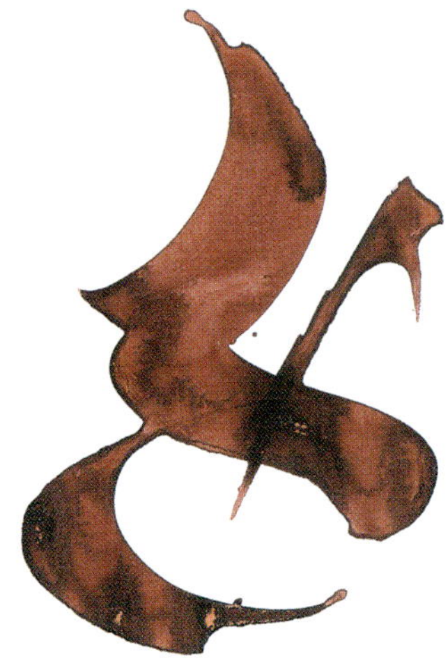

"Almost g"
Margaret Morgan
A small amount of gouache was poured onto the paper, then 'pushed' into shape using a chisel-edged colour shaper.

"Frohe Weihnachten und Alles Gute im Neuen Jahr"
Katharina Pieper
This is lettered in wood stain using a ruling pen. The calligraphy was reversed and matted to the watercolour background on computer.

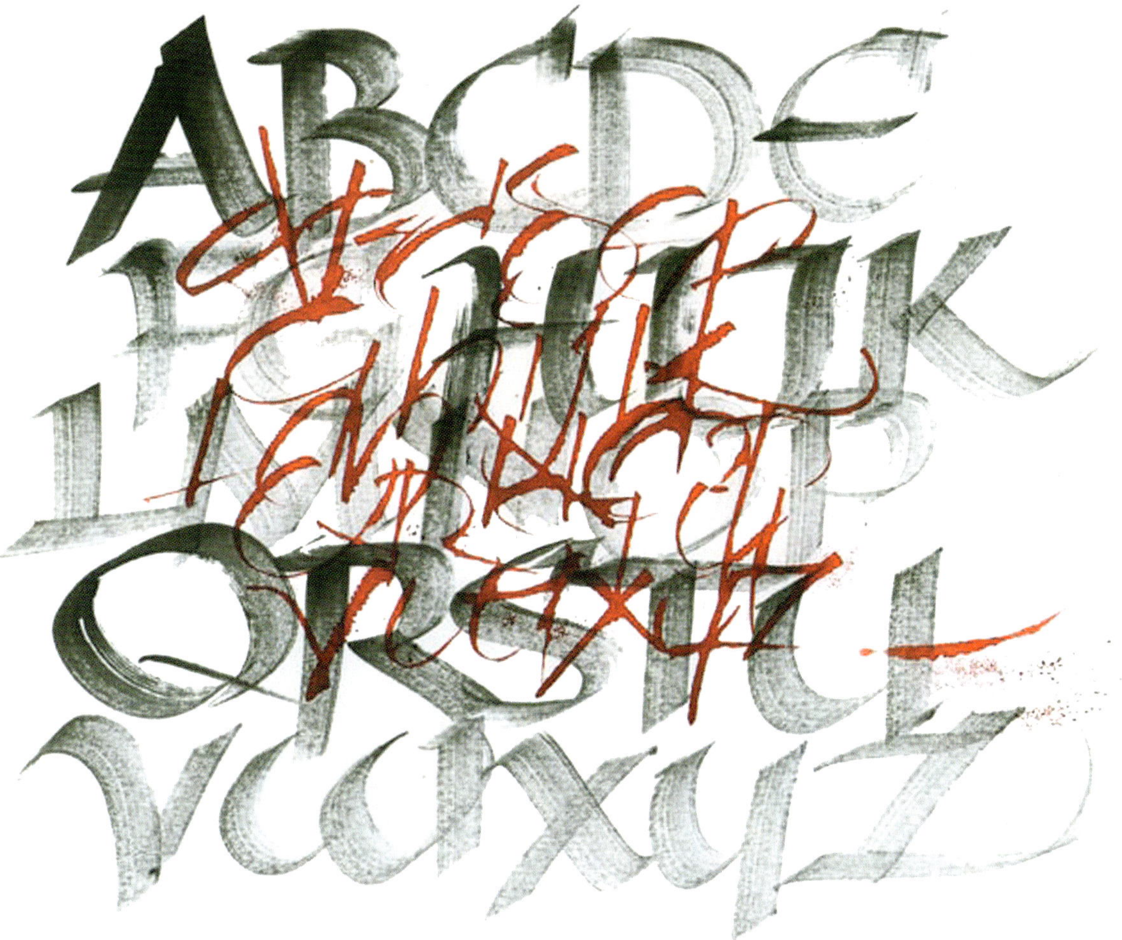

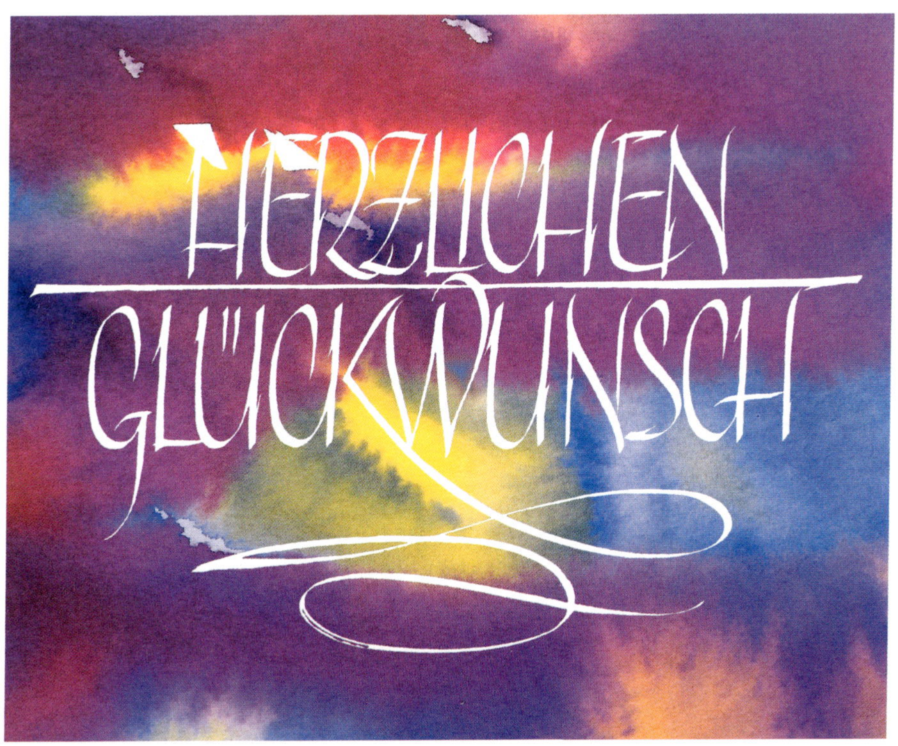

"Alphabets Overlaid"
Mary Noble
The main alphabet was written with a pen cut from balsa wood; its absorbency makes soft textural marks. The looser lettering on top was written with a ruling pen at speed, with frequent dipping to ensure plenty of ink and to contrast with the background alphabet.

"Herzlichen Glückwunsch"
Jean Larcher
Written using a Speedball nib and gouache, the calligraphy was then reversed out to white on a computer and added to the watercolour background on screen. The card, one of a series, was then offset printed.

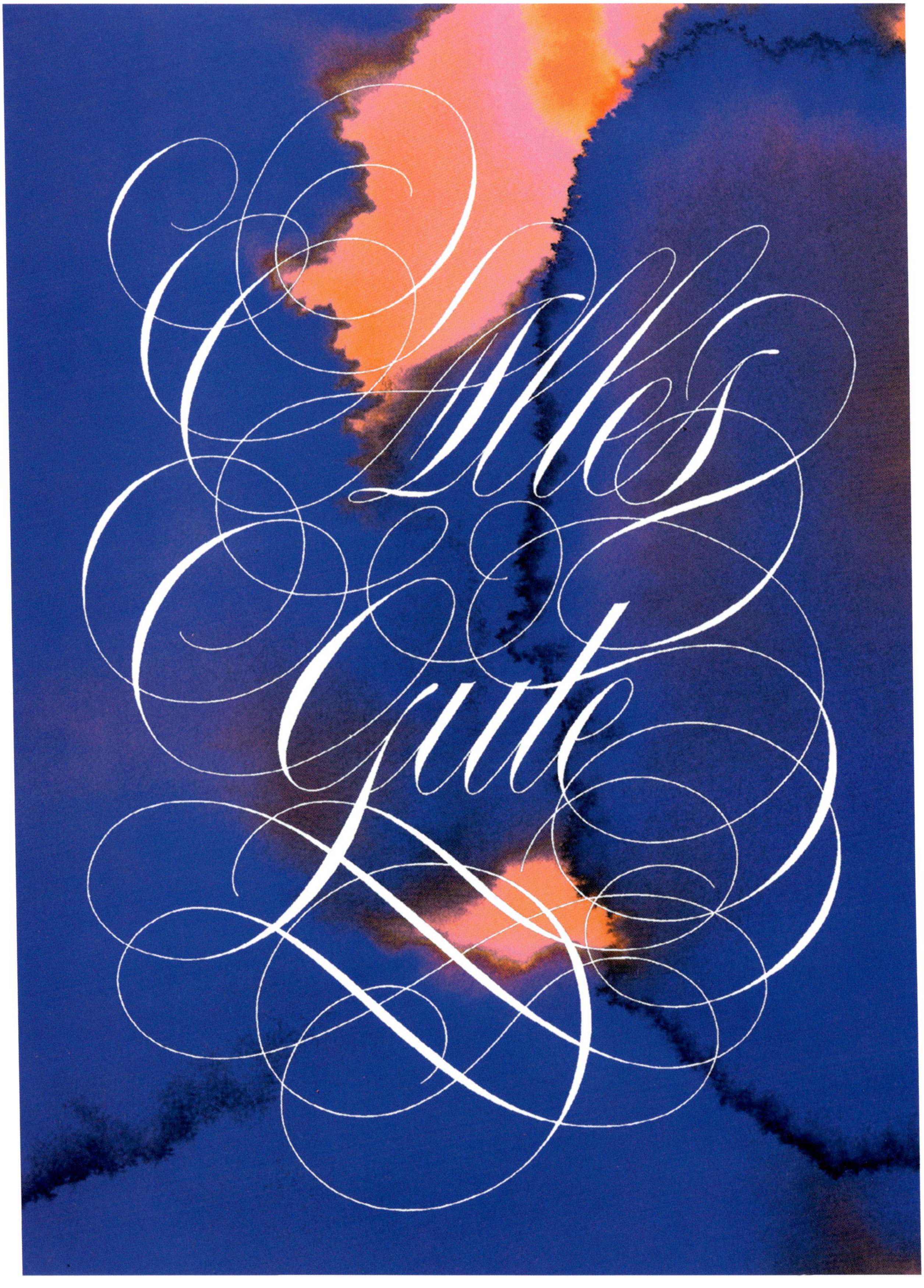
Alles
Gute

"Alles Gute"
Jean Larcher

The calligraphy for this card was created with a Gillot 303 nib using black gouache on a white background, then touched up. The text was reversed out to white on computer and added to the watercolour background.

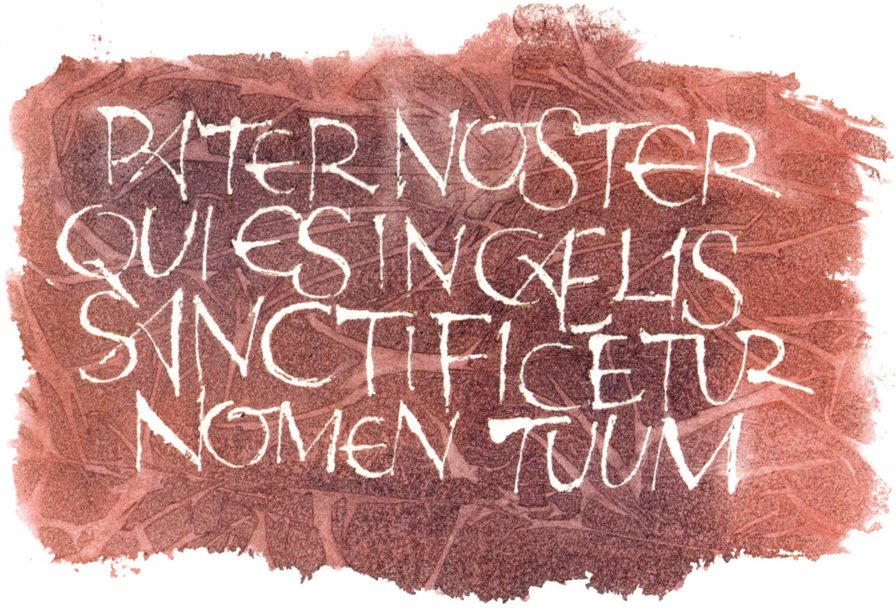

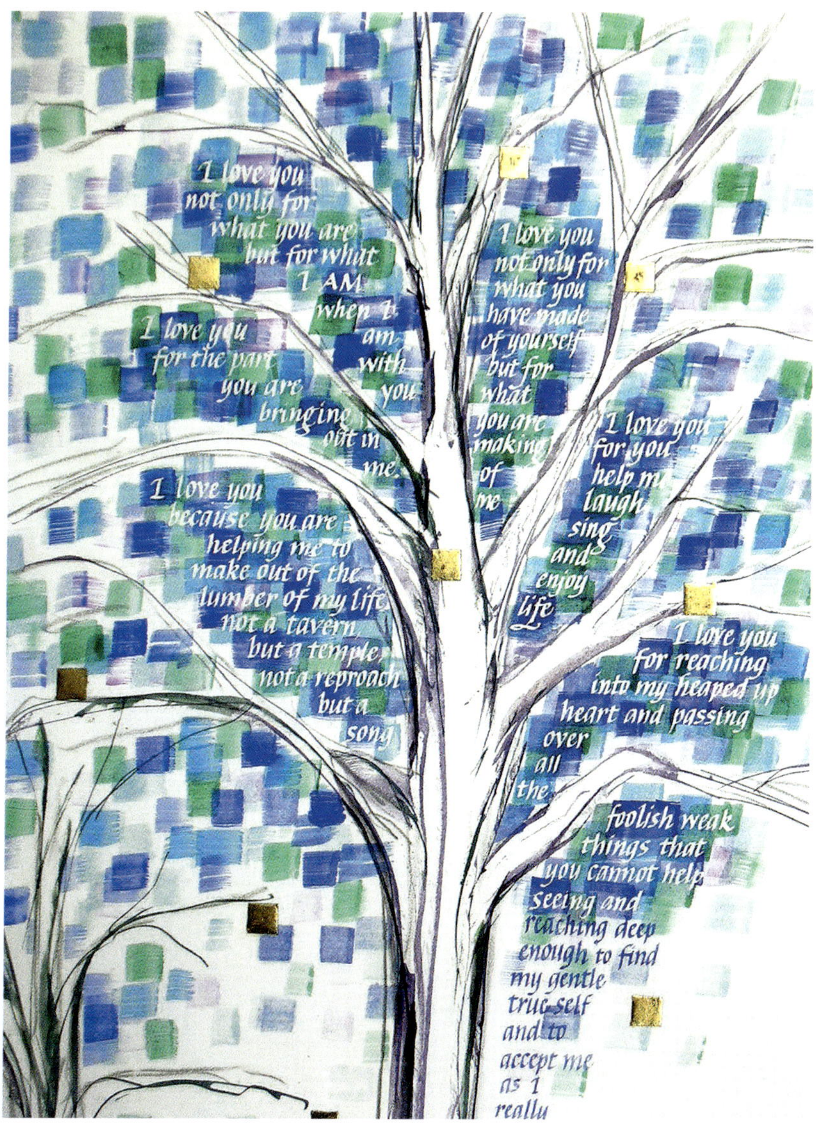

"Paternoster"
Margaret Morgan

The capitals were written with a pen, handmade from a cola can, and masking fluid on stretched rough-surface watercolour paper. When dry, a wash of alizarin crimson and purple lake gouache was flooded over the letters. Clingfilm was laid over the top and pinched into random patterns. The masking fluid was then removed using a cut piece of plastic eraser.

"Why Love?"
Nancy Ouchida-Howells

The text, the author's own words, was written using broad-edged pens in watercolours. Some areas were written with art masking fluid covered with a watercolour wash using a chisel brush and then removed to reveal the calligraphy. The gold squares are 23.5 carat gold leaf with a size base of gum ammoniac – the traditional way to apply gold leaf.

Index

acknowledgments

I would like to thank all those at Axis Publishing Limited who have made this book possible: Sean Keogh for his initial interest, Conor Kilgallon for his help and encouragement and photographer Mike Good for his patience.

Thanks to my family for their support. My thanks also to my former teachers, especially Gaynor Goffe, who have been so supportive and given of their knowledge so generously.